A Farewell to Glory

The Rise and Fall of an
Epic Football Rivalry

Boston College

vs.

Holy Cross

A Farewell to Glory

The Rise and Fall of an
Epic Football Rivalry

Boston College

vs.

Holy Cross

By Wally Carew

Ambassador Books, Inc.
Worcester • Massachusetts

The Publisher wishes to thank Boston College, Holy Cross and the *Worcester Telegram & Gazette* for permission to use the photographs in this book.

Library of Congress Cataloging-in-Publication Data

Carew, Wally.
  A farewell to glory : the rise and fall of an epic football rivalry :
Boston College vs. Holy Cross / by Wally Carew.
      p. cm.
Includes index.
  ISBN 1-929039-17-4 (hardcover)
  1. Boston College--Football--History. 2. College of the Holy Cross
(Worcester, Mass.)--Football--History. 3. Sports
rivalries--Massachusetts. I. Title.

  GV958.B66C37 2003
  796.332'63'097443--dc22
                                    2003018388

Published in the United States by Ambassador Books, Inc.
91 Prescott Street, Worcester, Massachusetts 01605
(800) 577-0909

Printed in Canada.
For current information about all titles from Ambassador Books, Inc.,
visit our website at: www.ambassadorbooks.com.

Dedication

In memory of
Father John J. Walsh, S.J.,
a dear friend and holy priest
who inspired many.

Table of Contents

Foreword

I THINK MY FASCINATION WITH THE BOSTON COLLEGE-HOLY CROSS football rivalry began on a rainy fall Saturday sometime during the 1950s.

The game was played at Fitton Field in Worcester, a cozy horse shoe-shaped stadium that looks like it was dropped by giant cranes fully constructed into the valley off I-290 without an inch to spare on any side. I was not at the game, and I don't remember which school won, Boston College or Holy Cross, on that long ago Saturday in November. But I do remember that the next morning when I opened the Sunday newspaper to the sports section, I was struck by the black and white photographs of the Crusaders in their purple uniforms. There was something compelling, something almost mythical about them.

When I was a boy I could tell you the nickname, colors and fight song of every major college football team in the country. In the fall, football was my passion. When I wasn't playing tackle football without pads, I was attending high school games, watching college and pro games on television, listening to games on the radio, reading about football, talking about the game and its heroes with my friends or dreaming about football.

I was fortunate enough to have an inside view of the game. My late dad, Walter, was a high school football coach. I often rode with him in

9

the car when he scouted future opponents. When he and I weren't singing college football fight songs, we often played a make believe game that involved road signs. When we passed a sign that listed the distances to various cities and towns, such as Marlboro 14 miles, Maynard 6 miles; or Medford 16, Arlington 12; or Boston 18, Cambridge 15; we would turn them into football scores.

If he spotted the sign first, he would say, "Gee, Marlboro beat Maynard, 14 to 6." If he beat me by spotting a sign along the road before I did, I would look extra hard for the next one. Then, as soon as I saw it, I would blurt out, "That must have been a good game, Medford beat Arlington, 16 to 12." It was fun, a father and son sharing their passion. The memories of those moments are still warm.

For me football was everywhere. Even at church. We belonged to Our Lady Help of Christians Parish in West Concord. There was a man there named Harold Baker, a large, barrel-chested individual who was a prison guard at MCI Concord. He was an intense Holy Cross football fan. During the fall, he talked about nothing but Holy Cross football. He never attended the college but he was as much a subway alumnus as any of the legions of Notre Dame loyalists who had never set foot on the South Bend, Indiana campus of the Fighting Irish.

Mr. Baker even wore a purple tie and socks as a tribute to the Crusaders. An avid listener, I was content to let him enthrall me with stories about Holy Cross football, past and present.

A friend of mine, Jim McMullen, skipped his senior year in high school and won an early admittance scholarship to attend Boston College. He was a mathematics major. He also played in the BC band. Occasionally, I would travel with him to the BC campus for band practice the night before an Eagles' home football game. The band would march back and forth playing "For Boston," the BC fight song, and I would march right along beside him as he played his trumpet. As the band played, my spine tingled with excitement.

It was during those visits to band practice that I first met Peter Siragusa, the Boston College band director. He was a stocky, cigar-smoking, much-liked warm-hearted man. Years later, when I worked in the public relations department for the New England Patriots, I ran into him again. He was the director of the half-time shows at Patriots' home games.

Over the years, I have attended many Boston College football games. One game stands out above all the rest. It was the opening game of the 1976 season. Boston College vs. Texas. Kelly Elias, who also went by the name of Mike, tackled speedster Johnny "Lam" Jones of Texas at the goal line, late in the fourth quarter, to preserve a thrilling 14-13 BC victory. It was a watershed win over a major college football power and it thrust the Eagles into the limelight and set the stage for the Doug Flutie era and all that followed.

I had watched and written about Elias when he played schoolboy football for Bedford High School. He was a most intense high school football player. His dream was to play in the NFL. He was not drafted by any NFL team, but he had a couple of tryouts. He had more than enough heart. He had ample size, too. But he lacked speed and quickness. After he was cut the final time, he told me that as he drove home, he pulled his car off the highway and sobbed like a baby, realizing that, for him, the dream was over. Soon after, the Hollywood handsome Elias turned to acting and male modeling and was very successful. But he wanted more out of life, and he found it by returning to football as a high school coach.

At all levels of the game, it is the great rivalry that gives football its soul. No matter if it is Medford vs. Malden, Winchester vs. Woburn, Wellesley vs. Needham, Army vs. Navy, Harvard vs. Yale, Ohio State vs. Michigan, the Philadelphia Eagles vs. the New York Giants or Boston College vs. Holy Cross.

When I was an adolescent, during the week of the Harvard-Yale and Boston College-Holy Cross games, the Boston newspapers would print photos of the starting lineups of the rival teams in the sports section. I would cut those photos out and stick them on the wall of my bedroom. Then, I would lie back on the bed with my head resting on my hands and become delightfully dizzy meshing and matching the maroon, gold, purple and white colors of Boston College and Holy Cross and the crimson, dull gold, blue and white colors of Harvard and Yale. For hours, I would just look at the photos of seven linemen kneeling on one knee with four backs standing behind them in the second row. A football was usually placed in front of each team's center who knelt in the middle of the first row. I became lost in a world I had created specifically for myself and I would just drift wherever my thoughts took me.

Regularly, my mother would come into my room and complain. "You have ruined my walls by putting all that 'stuff' on them. They are a real mess now." Thankfully, she never made me take anything down.

Those were great days, a marvelous era to be young and filled with dreams. It was during those years that I awaited the annual Boston College-Holy Cross football game with great anticipation. The fact that the game pitted proud Catholic, Jesuit colleges against each other elevated it to a special level for me, an altar boy who took his Catholic faith very seriously.

Each year, as the buildup to the game increased, I would wonder which team God was cheering for. Sometimes I would wonder who the saints were rooting for. "Maybe half the saints are on one side of heaven cheering for Boston College and the other half are on the opposite side of heaven rooting for Holy Cross."

Since the beginning of the series in 1896, when two games were played, including one in which the outcome is disputed to this very day, the BC-Holy Cross rivalry produced great games, players, coaches and stories. Countless men who played in the game went on to achieve even greater heroics in life—doctors, lawyers, priests, educators, business tycoons and war heroes, some of whom made the ultimate sacrifice by giving their lives for their country—men such as former Holy Cross star Eddie O'Melia. From 1945-1986, the Holy Cross Club of Boston awarded the Eddie O'Melia Memorial Trophy to the most valuable player of the annual Boston College-Holy Cross football game.

For me the BC-Holy Cross game celebrated "Faith of Our Fathers" to borrow the title of that great, old hymn. It is a story about sons of immigrants, many of whom were the first in their families to graduate from college. The game symbolized the courage of ancestors who risked all and fought with all their might to give their families a better life. It was about the arrival of Catholic men standing tall, carving out a niche for themselves and changing the fabric of American society. The game helped raise ceilings and break down barriers.

The game is also about the Jesuits and the excellence of a Jesuit-based education. I have always been awed by the Jesuits and their founder, the great soldier and scholarly saint, Ignatius of Loyola. Could there possibly be a more appropriate and hallowed name for a Catholic order of religious men: The Society of Jesus? I have known many Jesuits. The late

Father Charley Hancock, S.J. came from my hometown. He was a star halfback on the high school football team who spent much of his priesthood serving as a missionary in Japan.

I have even had the privilege of working with two Jesuits, the late Father John Walsh, S.J., who at one time taught German and Greek at Holy Cross, and Father Joseph Casey, S.J., a philosophy teacher at Boston College. Two brilliant and holy men, priests through and through.

As I look back on my lifetime as a fan, there are four events that I regret and would change if I could.

First, in 1951, Harvard Stadium was defaced by the elimination of the end zone section of seats nearest Storrow Drive. The seating capacity was reduced from 57,166 to 36,739 and the stadium was no longer a bowl, and a hallowed sports shrine was diminished.

Second, in 1953, the Boston Braves announced that they were moving to Milwaukee.

Third, Harry Agganis, ex-Boston University star quarterback and Red Sox first baseman died on June 27, 1955 at age 26 of a pulmonary embolism.

And fourth, after the 1986 game, it was announced that the Boston College-Holy Cross football rivalry would be discontinued.

I am powerless to change the whims of fate by preventing any of those four events from ever happening. However, may this book, in a meaningful way, help guarantee that the memories of the storied Boston College-Holy Cross football rivalry will endure the test of time.

The Early Years

1896: BC 6-2

1896: BC 8-6 (per BC);
Holy Cross 6-4 (per Holy Cross)

1897: Holy Cross 10-4; 2nd game BC 12-0

1898: 0-0; 2nd game BC 11-0

1899: BC 17-0

1901: Holy Cross 11-0

1902: Holy Cross 22-0

1910: Holy Cross 34-3

1911: Holy Cross 13-5

1913: Holy Cross 13-0

1914: Holy Cross 10-0

1915: Holy Cross 9-0

1916: BC 17-14

1917: BC 34-6

1919: BC 9-7

IN THE HOLY CROSS-BOSTON COLLEGE FOOTBALL SERIES THAT BEGAN in 1896, there was a rhythm—an ebb and flow, high tides, low tides, maulings, upsets and just plain surprises.

The series featured eighty-two games and spanned ninety-one years. When it began no one could have predicted its future importance, or for that matter, the role that football would play in the American consciousness.

This great series had its own evolution. It began before there was a T-Formation or a Split T, the pro set or even the forward pass. The scoring had not yet evolved to its present-day system.

Terms like wide receiver, split end, linebacker, safety, blitz, tight end, front four, fair catch and so many others were yet to be invented. But some things remain the same.

Football is more than a contact sport; it is a collision sport. The idea is to knock the other guy down, control the point of attack, move the chains and score touchdowns. It takes guts, athletic ability, mental toughness, commitment and stamina.

It attracts devoted fans, causes endless debates, great joy and terrible let downs; leaves the competitors totally drained, not to mention stiff and sore; and has become a spectacle like none other in sports.

———

The first two games of the Boston College-Holy Cross football series were played in 1896; nine years after Notre Dame made its intercollegiate football debut by losing to Michigan. In 1894, Texas and Texas A&M met for the first time. In 1899, Sewanee of Tennessee, also known as the University of the South, was a college football powerhouse. The nomadic team played all its games on the road and posted an unbeaten record. In 1899, Amos Alonzo Stagg, one of the all-time great coaches, led the University of Chicago to its first Big Ten Championship. Stagg, who played for the great Walter Camp at Yale while studying to become a Protestant minister, finally retired from coaching in 1960 at age ninety-eight. One of the great players of that era was Charley Brickley of Harvard, who coached BC (1916-17). Another great player and coach from that era was John Heisman, after whom the Heisman Trophy is named. He played for both Brown and the Quakers of Penn and coached at a string of colleges including Auburn, Georgia Tech, Pennsylvania and Washington and Jefferson. Later, he became athletic director at the Downtown Athletic Club in New York, where the Heisman Trophy is presented every December.

From 1896 to 1900, BC and Holy Cross met seven times. According to which side you were on, BC held the advantage over Holy Cross with a record of 5-1-1 or 4-2-1. But after beating Holy Cross in 1899, BC did not defeat the Crusaders again until 1916. In between, the Crusaders won seven straight over their Jesuit college rivals. The great Frank Cavanaugh coached Holy Cross from 1903-1905 and compiled a 16-10-2 record. In 1913, football was changed forever thanks to the forward pass. The first pass completion was thrown by Gus Dorias to Knute Rockne, helping Notre Dame stun mighty Army on the plains of West Point.

– 1897 –

Newspaper stories reported that the Boston College-Holy Cross rivalry began "in earnest" in 1897 when Holy Cross replaced Boston University on the BC schedule. BU withdrew from a scheduled game against BC on Thanksgiving Day. To fill the scheduling void, BC picked up a game against Holy Cross. BC won 12-0 on the holiday. A game played between the two teams earlier that fall was won by Holy Cross 10-4.

– 1899 –

In the final game of the century, James Hart's electrifying seventy-five-yard touchdown run applied the frosting to Boston College's 17-0 victory over Holy Cross.

By unleashing a pounding ground game, the Eagles controlled the game clock and kept the football away from the Holy Cross offense. Captain John Kelley and the great Joe Kenney, who starred on offense, defense and drop-kicked extra points, played standout games for BC.

For Holy Cross, Bill Toohig, Francis Monahan and Patrick O'Reilly were the top performers.

It was a banner season for Boston College, coached by John Dunlop. BC won eight games and shut out eight opponents. Brown not only beat BC, 18-0, but Brown was the only team to score a single point against Boston College in 1899.

– 1902 –

Coach Maurice Connor's Holy Cross eleven ended its season on a three-game winning streak by blanking Boston College, 22-0.

Ross Sullivan scored the opening touchdown for Holy Cross. With victories over the Pittsfield AC, Fordham and Boston College, Holy Cross ended the 1902 season with a 6-2-1 record.

Boston College, coached by Arthur White, did not win a game in 1902, going 0-8 and scoring only eleven points the entire season. Patrick Sullivan was the captain of the hard-luck and overmatched BC football team. Following the 1902 season, football was discontinued at BC and it was not reinstated until the 1908 season.

– 1916 –

Believe it or not, en route to a 17-14 victory in 1916, Coach Charley Brickley's Boston College eleven scored its first touchdown against Holy Cross since 1899.

John Lowney, who led the BC attack by rushing for 150 yards against the Crusaders, scored the first BC touchdown against Holy Cross in 17 years.

However, that statistic is deceiving. Since 1899 when the Eagles prevailed, 17-0, the rivals had met only seven times. Not only had Holy Cross won seven straight, but the Crusaders outscored BC 112-8 in those seven victories. In the years 1900, 1903 through 1909, and 1912, the rivals did not meet.

Entering the 1916 game, BC and Holy Cross had tangled on the gridiron fourteen times and the Crusaders held a 9-4-1 or a 8-5-1 advantage, taking into account the controversy involving the second of two games in 1896, a contest in which both schools claim victory.

In the three-point victory in 1916, freshman Jimmy Fitzpatrick kicked the winning field goal for the Eagles. Maurice Dullea, the BC captain, set up the winning field goal by blocking a Holy Cross punt. Fitzpatrick, a southpaw, passed to Ray Trowbridge for Boston College's second touchdown. BC led 14-0, but Holy Cross fought back and tied the game. The big play for the Crusaders was Gene Cummings' 69-yard interception and return for a touchdown.

– 1919 –

In Frank Cavanaugh's first season as head coach, Boston College outlasted Holy Cross 9-7 before 20,000 at Fenway Park.

Captain Jimmy Fitzpatrick was the game's number one star. He dropped-kicked a 25-yard field goal and then scored the deciding touchdown on a short plunge. Early in the game, Holy Cross struck first when Bill Daly gathered in a short pass and raced 20 yards for a touchdown.

The defense of both teams dominated the contest and the booming punts of Fitzpatrick and Daly forced the rivals to begin drives from deep in their own end.

BC might have won the game, but newspaper reports gave the cheering nod to the Holy Cross fans. "During the rest between halves, the Purple stands were rocked by the enthusiastic cheering and singing of the Holy Cross men, who easily out-pointed the Boston fans throughout the entire game."

A Rivalry Begins

IT WAS A SULLEN NOVEMBER DAY IN 1896.

Five hundred people had come out to a field in Worcester, Massachusetts. Snow was in the air and on the ground, and the field had become a quagmire.

Two groups of young men were lined up and ready to do battle. They were without helmets and wore unnumbered, lightly padded rugby-style jerseys. Their football pants were a drab brown, tending toward tan. Some were equipped with light hip pads that protruded at the waist. All the players wore high stockings, and instead of football cleats, they had ugly rectangular blocks of hard rubber that were fastened to the bottom of their athletic shoes for traction. A few of the players had tied bandannas around their heads. They looked more like aboriginal tribesmen than modern-day football players.

Unbeknownst to them, the young men who faced each other were about to initiate one of the great rivalries in football history. It would be a series that would begin and end in controversy. It would be a source of glory, pride and bitter contentiousness. It would produce great athletes, historic moments, elation, and gloom. The 91-year rivalry of the two Massachusetts Jesuit colleges, Boston College and Holy Cross, would prove to be, as they say, what sports is all about.

The country has changed greatly since that first game. Many of the onlookers that day remembered the Civil War, which had ended thirty-one years earlier, and some had fought in it. Four years after the war ended, Princeton and Rutgers met in the first intercollegiate football game on November 6, 1869, a game won by the Scarlet Knights, 6-4. In 1896, Grover Cleveland was serving as the 24th President of the United States. Automobiles were a novelty, and airplanes did not exist. The first Boston Marathon would be held the following spring, and athletes played for the joy of it and not for money. College football was not an end in itself. It was a student activity.

The first year of the series was in many ways symptomatic of the entire series. The rivals met twice that November. And the second game ended in controversy. In fact the outcome is in dispute even to this day.

The first game BC won, 6-2, and was a relatively tame contest. It was played in Worcester. Ed Shannahan tackled a BC back in the end zone to give the Crusaders a safety and a 2-0 lead. However, the Eagles rallied in the second half. A sustained drive led to the winning score. The drive was sparked by successful end runs and "double pass plays." Valiantly, Holy Cross stiffened, halted the BC drive and took over on its own one-yard line, under the shadow of the goal posts. Disaster with a capital "D" struck on the next play. Holy Cross fumbled, the football bounced into the end zone and White, a three-year starter, pounced on it for a touchdown. Bill Lyons kicked the "goal" to give Boston College a 6-2 win.

The second game was played in Boston. In the first half, Holy Cross' John Linnehan booted a "goal" through a "roaring wind" to give Holy Cross the lead, 4-0. A safety increased the lead to 6-0. But the Eagles fought back. Boston College running back Arthur White, who captained the 1897 BC team, turned in the game's most dazzling play—"a double crisscross." It must have been a double reverse, because just as he was about to be tackled, he handed the football off to Robert Crocker, who raced 60 yards to set up Boston College's first score, although BC still trailed 6-4. Reportedly, two ends, Bill Long and Bill Lyons, both played strong games for the Eagles.

With four minutes remaining, Boston College fullback Hugh McGrath, with his sights set on the end zone and scoring the winning points, tried to run wide, circling the end or flank of the Holy Cross defense. But he lacked the speed to get outside the defensive pursuit. Louis Francis Sockalexis, the Holy Cross star, a full-blooded Penobscot Indian from Old Town, Maine and a brilliant all-around athlete, cut

McGrath off at the pass. Sockalexis sped past a convoy of blockers and tackled the 130-pounder before he reached the end zone.

Almost immediately, a fight broke out with both sides throwing punches. The crew of officials rushed into the middle of the melee but it took them several minutes to break up the fight. In the meantime, while fists were still flying, McGrath, who was not sure if time had officially been called, casually picked up the football and raced into the end zone with what he thought was the winning touchdown.

Holy Cross screamed foul, and the officials upheld the protest. They said that BC had not lined up as required. The referee told Holy Cross Captain John Finn that BC "had refused to play" and he immediately declared Holy Cross a 6-4 winner. Holy Cross gave a cheer for BC and left the field.

Boston College Captain Joe Walsh protested vehemently, claiming that he and his teammates had not refused to play. Next, a delegation was sent to the Holy Cross locker room to retrieve the Crusaders. Holy Cross refused to return to the field, content with its 6-4 win. Reportedly, soon after the players left the field, the Holy Cross players traveled to downtown Boston and spent the night at a hotel. After Holy Cross refused to return to the field and resume the game, the officials ordered BC to run another play. Left halfback White took the snap from center and raced into the end zone giving the Eagles an 8-6 victory.

More than a century later, the dispute rages on and both schools claim victory in that second of two meetings during the inaugural 1896 season.

During the 91-year series, Boston College and Holy Cross played 82 games. The BC record books list a 48-31-3 advantage in the series, while official Holy Cross records reveal that the final series tally is 47-32-3 in favor of BC, giving the men of Mount St. James one additional victory.

It will forever be known as the game both Jesuit rivals won. The dispute will never be settled. Canon Law has no provisions for football.

It is generally agreed that the finest athlete on the field in 1896 was the Penobscot Indian of Holy Cross, Louis Sockalexis, "the Jim Thorpe of Mount St. James." One report gushed, "he was brilliant, all over the field."

At Holy Cross, Sockalexis ran track, was a triple-threat star in football and a sensational outfielder and hitter in baseball. At 5-feet-11 inches, 197 pounds, he had a body like a finely chiseled work of art.

In track, which exploded in popularity at the college level around the turn of the century, he was unbeatable in the dash. He was the star of the relay team and excelled in the hop, skip and jump, one of the most difficult events in track and field. Reportedly, no one ever beat him in the dash.

Sockalexis gained his greatest fame in baseball. Mike "Doc" Powers, an outstanding Holy Cross catcher from that era, spotted Sockalexis playing amateur baseball in Poland Springs, Maine during the summer and recruited him for Holy Cross. In his first college game against Brown at Providence, Sockalexis lined four hits, including a tape measure home run that shattered the top window on the distant Brown University Baptist chapel, and stole six bases.

In his first two varsity seasons, he hit .436 and .444 respectively. In the outfield, his natural grace and speed enabled him to catch fly balls others could not come close to reaching. He had a powerful and accurate arm. It is reported that he once threw a baseball a record 414 feet on the fly.

In a June 9, 1993 article that appeared in *Worcester Magazine*, Paul DellaValle chronicled the life of Louis Sockalexis. He was born on October 24, 1871 on Indian Island, a reservation near the Penobscot River. His grandfather was a Chief with a Penobscot tribe known as the "Bear Clan." He was a handsome man with mocha-colored skin, strong features, dark penetrating eyes and a shy, soft-spoken and unassuming manner. When he was recruited to play sports at Holy Cross (he actually was enrolled in the Prep School), his father, a respected Penobscot elder, objected, saying, "I don't want a son of mine playing white man's games." In one report, which seems far fetched, the story is told of his father seeking the assistance of President Grover Cleveland in attempt to stop his son from enrolling at Holy Cross. Legend has it that his father, traveling most of the way by canoe, went to Washington, D.C. in an effort to stop his renegade son from leaving home, fearful that he would never return.

Given the many injustices that Native Americans suffered, all the way back to the 17th century and the arrival of the Mayflower, Sockalexis' father had every reason to distrust the white man and to be leery of his ways.

Nevertheless, Sockalexis emerged as one of the greatest pure athletes ever to enroll at Holy Cross. In 1896, his second season of college baseball, he hit a robust .444, collected 56 hits in 26 games and was publicized as "baseball's heaviest hitter and the fastest base runner in the country."

Jesse Burkett, whose name graced the All-Star Little League team from Worcester that received national acclaim in 2002, was Sockalexis' college baseball coach at Holy Cross. Burkett was also a pro scout and he recommended that the Cleveland Spiders, then of the National League, sign Sockalexis. It was a case of an Indian attempting to break the race barrier fifty years before Jackie Robinson became the first African American to play in the big leagues.

Cleveland did sign Sockalexis to a $1,500 contract in 1897, making him the first Native American to play major league baseball. Immediately, many of his teammates became disgruntled. One player, Mike Delehanty, after he was benched to make room for an Indian, griped, "The league is all gone to hell now that they are letting those damned foreigners in."

Sockalexis was twenty-six years old when he made his major league debut against the New York Giants at the Polo Grounds. In his debut, he faced hard-throwing Amos Rusie, a Hall of Fame member who piled up 243 career wins and won 29 games in 1897. He immediately tested the proud Indian's toughness by knocking him down with high, hard stuff under the chin in his first at-bat as the Giants' fans ridiculed Sockalexis by making "Indian war whoops" in the stands.

Sockalexis got up, dusted himself off, dug into the batter's box and hit the next pitch more than 500 feet to dead center field, the deepest part of the park at the old Polo Grounds. By the time the Giants' outfielder had retrieved the carom off the wall, just underneath where the Chesterfield cigarettes sign was positioned years later, the rookie Sockalexis, using his blinding speed, had circled the bases with an inside-the-park home run.

He collected another hit in his big league debut and threw out three New York runners at the plate.

During the next three months Sockalexis went on a rampage. He hit .413, and only two players were ahead of him in the batting race. One was Honus Wagner, the Hall of Fame Pittsburgh Pirates shortstop who also was a rookie in 1897 and hit .344 that year en route to a career .328 batting average over 21 seasons.

Sockalexis' nickname was "The Deerfoot of the Diamond." Hughie Jennings, who later managed the Tigers and Ty Cobb, after watching Sockalexis play half a season, remarked, "He should have been the greatest player of all times."

The immortal John McGraw, skipper of the Giants, quickly recognized the Indian's overflowing ability. "No baseball player has ever crammed so many accomplishments into so short a period of time," said McGraw.

Years later, looking back at Sockalexis' brief stint in the big leagues, one old time pitcher said this about the Indian, "He had a gorgeous left-hand swing, he could hit a ball as far as Babe Ruth, and he was faster than Ty Cobb."

Sockalexis made such an impression during his only season playing in Cleveland that when the ball club switched leagues and joined the American League in 1915 the name of the team was changed from Spiders to "Indians" in honor of Sockalexis. The team that made Tris Speaker, Luke Easter, Larry Doby, Al Rosen, Bob Feller and Lou Boudreau household names to baseball fans, a franchise that last won a World Series in 1948 by toppling the Boston Braves in six games, is still named the Cleveland Indians.

Yet, as fast as Sockalexis rose to stardom in major league baseball, he tumbled to obscurity. In 1898, he played just 21 games for the Indians, hit only .224 and was released by his manager Patsy Tebeau. His decline started during the second half of the 1897 season when his performance slipped and his numbers began to fade drastically.

The problem was the fact that he fell victim to a disease: alcoholism. He had never drunk alcohol until he reached the big leagues and managed to have money in his pocket. He became a slave to hard liquor soon after he took his first drink and was regularly found sleeping on the sidewalks in front of saloons. In one newspaper report, he was described as "a slave to whiskey and a hopeless drunkard."

For a short time, he continued to play minor league baseball, but alcohol had eroded his natural skills and by the summer of 1900 he had become a homeless beggar. In 1901, he managed to sober up, and he returned to the Indian reservation in Maine. He played amateur baseball and landed a job as a woodcutter at a lumber camp that paid him $30 a month.

On Christmas Eve 1913, he did not show up for dinner at the lumber camp. That same night he was found dead in the woods. He was forty-two years old. The official cause of death was heart disease, although excessive drinking certainly contributed to his death. Did he break out and go on a binge at the time of his death? No one will ever know.

This once great athlete is buried on Indian Island not far from the streams and hills he loved; where he ran wild and as free as the wind long before he played organized athletics. His gravestone was paid for with contributions from the Cleveland Indians and Holy Cross. Many believe he was the greatest all-around athlete that ever set foot on the campus of the College of the Holy Cross.

No one knows if Sockalexis was a Christian when he arrived at Holy Cross. However, with a name like Louis Francis it is reasonable to suspect that he had been baptized. From the time they arrived in North America, they were missionaries. In fact, the Society of Jesus labored many years in Northern Maine, including Old Town, the home of the Penobscot tribe and Sockalexis' family. (Father John Bapst, S.J., the first president of Boston College, was considered a "national hero" because of his missionary zeal that nearly cost him his life.)

Anti-Catholicism was rampant in 1850 when he arrived in the area, and Father Bapst survived being tortured, tarred and feathered and left for dead. In 1859, "The History of Boston College" reports that the Jesuits withdrew from Maine and Father Bapst was assigned to the College of the Holy Cross as a spiritual father. Four years later, in 1863, he became the first president of Boston College. Holy Cross, the oldest Catholic College in New England, was founded by Bishop Benedict Joseph Fenwick 20 years earlier in 1843.

Who is to say that the effects of Father Bapst's near martyrdom and the heroic virtue of so many of his fellow Jesuits didn't somehow trickle down and touch the life of Sockalexis, who was born only eleven years after the Jesuits left Maine?

The Twenties

1920: BC 14-0

1921: Holy Cross 41-0

1922: BC 17-13

1923: BC 16-7

1924: Holy Cross 33-0

1925: BC 17-6

1926: 0-0

1927: BC 6-0

1928: BC 19-0

1929: BC 12-0

THE ROARING 1920S PRODUCED SOME OF THE GREATEST NAMES IN THE history of sports. Babe Ruth, Lou Gehrig, Bill Tilden, Jack Dempsey, Red Grange, and the Four Horsemen of Notre Dame.

Red Grange, who played for Bob Zuppke's Fighting Illini of the University of Illinois, was nicknamed the "Galloping Ghost." In October 1924, in the dedication game held at the new Illinois Memorial Stadium against Michigan, the first four times Grange touched the football he reeled off touchdown runs covering 95, 67, 56 and 45 yards. But after the fourth touchdown Grange told his coach, "I'm tired!" So Zuppke sat him down to rest. He returned in the fourth quarter and scored his fifth touchdown, a 19-yard run.

Frank Cavanaugh, "the Iron Major," coached BC from 1919 to 1926, compiling a 48-14-5 record. BC dominated the decade with a 7-2-1 record against Holy Cross, although Holy Cross blanked BC 33-0 in 1924.

– 1922 –

Before a crowd of almost 50,000 at Braves field, Boston College posted a 17-13 victory over favored Holy Cross and the Crusaders' brilliant superstar Bill Glennon.

The game was described as "fierce and merciless." Led by Captain Bill Kelleher, Chuck Darling and Grattan O'Connell, the Eagles held off a late Holy Cross rally to post the upset victory. Holy Cross had to play the game without its star end, Hilary Mahaney, who was considered one of the finest ends in Holy Cross history up to that time. He missed the game because of injury. Darling, the BC punter, got off two booming kicks, one that traveled seventy-three yards into a stiff wind and a second for sixty yards.

Ray Payton set up the first BC touchdown when he blocked Ken Simendinger's punt. O'Connell, wearing number 51, scooped up the blocked punt and raced forty-seven yards for the game's first touchdown.

The game was dominated by stout defense on both sides. Joe Kozlowski booted a field goal for BC and Harold Ward, on a tough inside run from inside the ten-yard line, scored the game-winning touchdown for the Eagles. The highly talented Glennon scored one Holy Cross touchdown and set up the Crusaders' second with nifty running and accurate passing. He scored on a 28-yard run and he passed to Al Butler to set up the second Holy Cross touchdown. Al "Hop" Riopel then scored on a two-yard plunge. Riopel became a coach and crack recruiter for the men of Mount St. James.

Late in the fourth quarter, Holy Cross threatened to score a go-ahead touchdown, but Ward intercepted a Holy Cross pass to preserve the victory for the Eagles.

– 1926 –

It was the final game that legendary Frank Cavanaugh coached at Boston College before he moved to Fordham. The annual battle between the Jesuit college rivals proved to be a disappointment for the Eagles after BC and Holy Cross fought to a 0-0 tie, the first scoreless tie in the series since 1898.

The game turned into a defensive struggle as the two teams slugged it out on a muddy field. Boston College was led by Joe McKenney, its brilliant captain and star back. McKenney later coached the Eagles (1928-1934) and had a prestigious alumni award named in his memory.

Despite the tie, Boston College ended the season unbeaten (6-0-2). Coach Cleo O'Donnell's scrappy Holy Cross team, led by star and

Captain Bill Wise, who later became a great high school coach at Springfield Cathedral in Massachusetts, lost only one game and completed the season with a 7-1-2 record.

In addition to McKenney, Bill Ohrenberger, who later became Superintendent of the Boston Public Schools, and John McNamara all played their final games for Boston College in Cavanaugh's swan song at BC.

Almost as soon as the game ended, plans took shape for a testimonial honoring Cavanaugh, who was nicknamed "the Iron Major" for his heroism during World War I.

– 1928 –

Led by Coach Joe McKenney and Captain Warren McGuirk, two great names from Boston College football past, the Eagles capped an unbeaten (9-0) season with a 19-0 victory over Holy Cross.

Patrick Creeden, a three-year starter and captain of the 1929 team, scored the Eagles' first touchdown on an acrobatic, tumbling catch in the end zone on a pass from Al Weston.

On offense, the highlight of the game was the nifty running of the shifty Weston, who ripped off runs of fifty, twenty-four and eighteen yards.

Trailing, Holy Cross fought back in the third quarter, but could not penetrate the BC goal line. Holy Cross outgained BC 125 yards to three in the third quarter, but could not score. For much of the game, the Boston College defense bent, but refused to break. Rugged Bernard Kilroy was one of the game's top stars for BC. For Holy Cross, Henry Shanahan, Stanley Weiss and Clarence "Blondy" Ryan starred for the Crusaders. Under Cleo O'Donnell, Holy Cross ended up 5-3-2 in 1928 and drilled Providence College 44-0 in its final game before facing Boston College.

Richard Phelan, one of the best all-around players in the East, was captain of the 1928 Holy Cross football team.

Frank Cavanaugh

The Iron Major

WHEN GEORGE M. COHAN WROTE, "OVER THERE—THE YANKS ARE Coming Over There"—his musical tribute to the fighting American Doughboys of World War I, he wrote about men such as Worcester's own Frank Cavanaugh.

Cavanaugh was born in Worcester, Massachusetts on August 28, 1876. He graduated from Worcester Classical High School and captained the 1898 Dartmouth College football team. He played end for the Big Green, but left college before he graduated to play pro football in Pittsburgh and to coach at the University of Cincinnati. Later, he went back to school and earned a law degree. He was a durable, solid football player, but he realized his greatest fame as a coach. A College Football Hall of Fame coach, Cavanaugh had head coaching stints at both Holy Cross and Boston College. He is one of the most famous athletic figures the City of Worcester has ever produced.

During World War I, Frank W. Cavanaugh, who was nicknamed "Cav," enlisted in the 102nd Field Artillery of Massachusetts' 26th Yankee Division. He was severely wounded at Chateau-Thierry after a battlefield explosion left shrapnel lodged in his head. In the book *'Til The Echoes Ring Again: A Pictorial History of Boston College Sports* by Jack Falla, published in 1982, Falla writes: "Armistice was less than three weeks away when Cavanaugh stepped from his dugout command post at the Battle of San Mihiel, France, to direct the fire of American field artillery against German positions. That step was almost his last. Cavanaugh disappeared in the smoke and shrapnel of a German 210 shell. When the medical corpsmen found him, most of the right side of his face had been blown away and he was holding his right eye, still barely connected to the socket, in his right hand.

"Medics thought he was mortally wounded and summoned a priest to administer last rights. The priest's services were not needed. After months of recuperation and reconstructive surgery, 'the Iron Major' returned to the United States to make national football powers of first Boston College and then Fordham."

Cavanaugh earned a Purple Heart and rose to the rank of major, which resulted in his colorful nickname, "the Iron Major." His story made it onto the silver screen. Pat O'Brien and James Cagney starred in the movie about Cavanaugh's life. Falla writes that Cavanaugh indicated that he was fussy about how people addressed him. "You can call me coach or you can call me Major," he said.

In *The Story of Football* by Robert Leckie, Cavanaugh is described as "one of the most beloved and colorful figures in football lore. The 'Iron Major' was a renowned professor of law, a superb trial lawyer, an eloquent orator and a delightful entertainer, as well as an outstanding coach."

Cavanaugh was the head coach at Holy Cross from 1903-1905. He guided the Crusaders to a 16-10-2 overall record. BC and Holy Cross did not meet during Cavanaugh's tenure at Holy Cross. His most significant victory as the head coach at Holy Cross might have been a 27-5 victory over Fordham in his final game at Mount St. James. It was at Fordham where he would later gain his greatest fame as a coach.

Cavanaugh was hired to coach football at BC by athletic director Frank Reynolds only ten months after he was wounded in battle.

Cavanaugh was the head football coach at Boston College from 1919 to 1926, compiling a 48-14-5 overall record, including unbeaten seasons in 1920 (8-0-0) and 1926 (6-0-2). Beginning in 1919, Cavanaugh's BC teams "astounded" the college football world, so wrote author Leckie, by beating powerful Yale two seasons in a row; edging Yale 5-3 in 1919 and whipping the Eli, 21-13 in 1920. In the 1919 game, BC's Jimmy Fitzpatrick kicked a field goal with two minutes remaining in the game for the win. A twenty-seven yard pass play from the versatile Fitzpatrick to pint-size Lou Urban set up the winning score. Before the Yale game, Cavanaugh told his underdog BC squad to forget about the odds. The essence of his message was: They might have more weapons, but like us, the Yale bulldogs can only play eleven at a time.

Cavanaugh's BC teams compiled a 5-2-1 record against Holy Cross, including a 0-0 tie in his final game as the Boston College head coach in 1926. That tie, along with a 21-21 tie against the Haskell Indians, were all that stood in the way of BC posting an unbeaten, untied season in 1926.

Cavanaugh's BC teams beat Holy Cross two years in a row, winning 9-7 in 1919 and blanking Holy Cross 14-0 in 1920. Before the 1920 game, The Major fired up a BC student pep rally with these words: "Men of Boston: Your team plays Holy Cross tomorrow. They've done their best to get ready. I've done my best. Will you be with them when they take the field tomorrow? When those maroon and gold warriors line up for the kickoff, to do or die for the school that is yours and theirs, will you be with them? Will you? When they offer their all, so that the whole world will know that up there on the Heights we still breed men, men who can fight, men who can win. Men of Boston, will you be with them? Will you? When that referee raises his arm and asks: 'Are you ready, Holy Cross? Are you ready, Boston?' Men of Boston, will you, indeed, be ready? Will you?"

Ready? You bet they were ready. The 14-0 victory the following day proved that the sly Cavanaugh knew a thing or two about perfect timing when it came to exhortation.

At BC, Cavanaugh managed to come up with one star after another. After Fitzpatrick graduated, the glamorous, triple-threat Chuck Darling took over as the go-to guy for the Eagles. In 1926, after BC refused to offer him more than a one-year contract, Cavanaugh left BC and accepted a three-year $15,000 contract to coach the Fordham Rams.

Cavanaugh was the head football coach at Fordham from 1927 to 1932, compiling a 34-14-4 record. In his final four seasons at Fordham, the Rams went 27-4-4, including 7-0-2 in 1929. At Fordham, he is best remembered for developing "The Seven Blocks of Granite," the most celebrated group of linemen in the history of college football. By name, the individual rocks who made up that collective block of hard-nosed and steel-willed linemen, a college football front wall made of granite, were Al Babartsky, John Druze, Ed Franco, Vince Lombardi, Leo Paquin, Nat Pierce and Alex Wojciechowicz. Correctly naming them is the answer to one of the great trivia questions relating to the storied history of college football. Lombardi, who coached at St. Cecilia's High School in New Jersey, Fordham, West Point, the New York Giants, the Green Bay Packers (winning the first two Super Bowls) and the Washington Redskins, was a remarkable coach, a highly principled man and one of the most fascinating figures in the history of the NFL. Today, the trophy presented to the annual winner of the Super Bowl is named after him.

When Fordham defeated Holy Cross 37-27 at Fitton Field on November 9, 2002, it was the second straight win for the Rams in the all-time series with Holy Cross and it kept the "Ram Crusader Trophy" in the Bronx.

First dedicated in 1951 in memory of Frank Cavanaugh, who coached at both schools, the trophy is the inspiration of William P. Walsh, who graduated from the College of the Holy Cross in 1952 and from Fordham University Law School in 1957. While in college, Walsh, a Fordham football fan since he was a boy, worked as a counselor at a summer camp headed by Ed Danowski, a former standout Fordham football player and coach. Walsh came up with the idea for the trophy when Danowski told him in August of 1951 that the rival schools—Fordham and Holy Cross—had signed a contract to play each other during the next four years and Danowski predicted that his Rams "would pin back the ears" of the Crusaders. Intrigued by thoughts of the Fordham-Holy Cross rivalry, inaugurated in 1902 with a 17-0 Holy Cross victory, Walsh suggested that a trophy should be instituted in honor of "the Iron Major," Frank Cavanaugh, whose last Fordham team was captained by Danowski. Walsh and a classmate, Joseph Breen, who also graduated from Fordham Law School, were appointed co-chairmen of the trophy committee.

In 1951, Holy Cross easily won the first "Ram Crusader Trophy" game, slaughtering Fordham, 54-20. That year, John Cavanaugh, one of the Major's nine children, made the trophy presentation to Holy Cross. The Fordham-Holy Cross college football series was interrupted after the 1954 season when Fordham dropped intercollegiate football, but it was resumed in 1990 when Fordham joined the Crusaders as members of the

Patriot League. The trophy is jointly sponsored by the Holy Cross College Clubs of New York and Long Island.

Over the years, the trophy has been fought for in exotic places including Limerick, Ireland and Hamilton, Bermuda. In 1991, Holy Cross defeated Fordham 24-19 in the Wild Geese Classic in Limerick, Ireland and in 1995 Fordham beat Holy Cross 17-10 in the Bermuda Bowl in Hamilton, Bermuda.

Frank Cavanaugh's career coaching record was 145-48-17, which included an amazing 105 shutouts in 210 games. During his career, he is credited with inventing the "hook pass." In 1929, his unbeaten Fordham team used the T-Formation with a back in motion eleven years before Clark Shaughnessy, the "grand daddy" of the T-Formation, introduced it at Stanford.

Toward the end of his life, Cavanaugh, who seldom missed a Fordham practice, became almost totally blind. Many believe that complications from his war wounds, pieces of shrapnel embedded in his head, ultimately contributed to his loss of sight. He died on August 29, 1933. He was fifty-seven.

The Thirties

1930: Holy Cross 7-0

1931: Holy Cross 7-6

1932: 0-0

1933: BC 13-9

1934: Holy Cross 7-2

1935: Holy Cross 20-6

1936: BC 13-12

1937: Holy Cross 20-0

1938: Holy Cross 29-7

1939: BC 14-0

DURING THE 1930S SOME OF THE BIGGEST NAMES IN COLLEGE FOOTBALL were Bryon "Whizzer" White at Colorado, Davey O'Brien at Texas Christian University, Bill Osmanski of Holy Cross, Bob MacLeod at Dartmouth, Fordham's "Seven Blocks of Granite" and Nile Kinnick at Iowa. Kinnick, a Heisman Trophy winner was killed fighting for his country in World War II. Dr. Eddie Anderson, who coached Holy Cross from 1933 through 1938, became the head coach at Iowa in 1939. He returned to Holy Cross in 1950 until 1964. Anderson made his debut as head coach at Holy Cross on September 30, 1933. On that date, the Crusaders crushed tiny St. Michael's College, 50-0. In 1936, Hall of Fame coach Gil Dobie took over at BC, going 16-6-5 between 1936 and 1938. A young Frank Leahy became the Eagles' head coach in 1939, although Holy Cross dominated the decade, posting a 6-3-1 record against BC.

– 1933 –

In a much ballyhooed match-up between the Jesuit college football rivals, Boston College outlasted Holy Cross 13-9 before a crowd of 25,000 in Boston.

The game was played for the mythical New England College Football Championship. Coach Joe McKenney's Boston College team entered the game with only one loss, a 32-6 defeat against Fordham. Dr. Eddie Anderson, in his first season as head coach at Holy Cross, also saw his Crusaders enter the showdown against Boston College with a single setback, a 24-0 loss to the University of Detroit.

The game featured many outstanding players. Two of the best were rival linemen—Buzz Harvey of Holy Cross and Flavio Tosi for Boston College.

BC's John Freitas, nicknamed the "Fairhaven Flash," was the game's number one star. His running, passing, faking, punting and tackling bedeviled the Crusaders. Boston College scored its first touchdown on an artfully executed "Statue of Liberty" play. Ed Furbush and Joe Killilea excelled for BC. Ed Britt, who scored Holy Cross' only touchdown, was the offensive star for the Crusaders. Rival linemen Peter Lingua of Holy Cross and Alphonse Ezmunt of Boston College were two of the game's unsung heroes.

Late in the game, Freitas, in a fete duplicated by Charlie O'Rourke years later against Georgetown, took a safety and then punted the Eagles out of trouble as the game clock wound down to preserve the hard-fought victory.

– 1937 –

Holy Cross capped an unbeaten season (8-0-2) with a resounding 20-0 victory over Boston College before a boisterous crowd of 35,000 at Fenway Park. The margin of victory was the largest in the fiercely contested series since 1924 when the Crusaders prevailed, 33-0.

The only imperfections on an otherwise perfect season for the Crusaders were a pair of 0-0 ties against Carnegie Tech. and Temple.

For the winners, the dandy duo of Bullet Bill Osmanski and Ronnie Cahill, two of the greatest backs in the history of Holy Cross football, led a pounding ground game that rushed for 205 yards. Osmanski scored two touchdowns and Cahill one.

Eddie O'Melia, a standout end, playing his final game split two blockers and made a key tackle behind the line of scrimmage to keep BC from getting into the end zone, thereby preserving the shutout. From 1945-

1986, the Holy Cross Club of Boston presented the O'Melia Memorial Trophy, in memory of the former end, Captain Eddie O'Melia, who gave his life fighting for his country during World War II, to the outstanding player in the annual BC-Holy Cross football game.

The nifty Cahill scored the first Holy Cross touchdown, "standing up from six yards out," on a "hidden ball" trick play, the same play that Columbia had employed to defeat Stanford 7-0 in the 1934 Rose Bowl. The Holy Cross coaching staff called the play "KF-79."

En route to the 20-0 whitewashing, Holy Cross double teamed Boston College's standout tackle John Janusas, the 185-pounder from Lexington, Massachusetts, at the point of attack. Following the loss, BC head coach Gil Dobie exonerated his star tackle. "Janusas is a great tackle," said the glib Dobie. "What more can you expect a tackle to do? The 'backers' didn't fill the hole quickly enough." Janusas went on to become a Hall of Fame schoolboy football coach at several Massachusetts schools including Saugus and Lexington High Schools.

Following the victory over BC, it was rumored that Holy Cross would be invited to play in a bowl game. But the invitation never came; perhaps because the southern bowl committees were prejudiced against Eastern teams.

– 1938 –

Holy Cross capped a superlative 8-1-0 season by crushing Boston College 29-7 at Fenway Park. The Crusaders only loss that season was a 7-6 heartbreaker against Carnegie Tech.

Immediately following the big win, Holy Cross coach Dr. Eddie Anderson sang the praises of his star fullback Bullet Bill Osmanski. "Bill Osmanski is the best back I have ever seen," he said. "He was the one who made the team go. It was Osmanski who was the standout back. He is the finest back in the country."

In the game, the Crusaders rushed for 217 yards while holding Boston College to only 41 yards on the ground. Osmanski, who battered the BC defense with his combination of speed and power, scored one touchdown and set up a second on a bolting run and lateral, pitching the football to a streaking Johnny Kelly, who caught the lateral and raced 46 yards for a touchdown.

Holy Cross' first touchdown came on a 14-yard pass from all-purpose star Ronnie Cahill to Henry Giardi.

Boston College's only touchdown came on a 14-yard pass play from Charlie O'Rourke, who was only a sophomore, to Alex Lukachik, a back-up left end. The starting left end for the Eagles was Bill Flynn, the captain of the team and one of the most important men in the history of Boston College athletics. From 1957-1991, during a period of unprecedented growth in athletics at BC, Flynn served as athletic director at his alma mater.

Henry Ouellette scored the second of Holy Cross' four touchdowns. For Boston College, Ed Cowhig, who later entered the seminary and was ordained a priest, was credited with several bone-rattling sticks on defense. Many of the players on the BC squad were the same bunch that in 1940, playing for Coach Frank Leahy, posted an unbeaten season and won the national championship.

– 1939 –

In the first of his two brilliant seasons at the Heights, Coach Frank Leahy's Boston College football team completed a 9-1-0 regular season with a 14-0 victory over Holy Cross before 40,432 at Fenway Park. On hand was the largest crowd to ever watch a sporting event at the House that Tom Yawkey rebuilt.

The convincing victory over Holy Cross, which came into the game with a 7-1 record, set the stage for the Eagles' first bowl appearance, a 6-3 loss to the Clemson Tigers in the 1940 Cotton Bowl.

After three quarters, the rock-'em, sock-'em game was scoreless. BC struck for two touchdowns within eight minutes of the final quarter to register the win. Pete Cignetti scored the first touchdown on a three-yard run and Captain Ernie Schwotzer blocked a Holy Cross punt and smothered it in the end zone for the Eagles' second touchdown.

For BC, linemen Gene Goodreault, Chet Gladchuk, Joe Manzo and big John Yauckoes, nicknamed "Super Granite," backboned the win with "heavy lifting in the trenches." It just so happened that Yauckoes, the 260-pound tackle wanted to celebrate his birthday and he had a birthday cake hidden away in the locker room. After the victory, he brought it out and shared the cake with his teammates. Coach Leahy, who was only thirty-one years old at the time, spotted the cake and barked, "Don't break training too badly, boys!"

For Holy Cross, two of the Crusaders' swiftest backs and top two punters were either out of the game or hobbled. Tommy Sullivan missed the game because of a bout with pneumonia and co-Captain Ronnie Cahill attempted to play with a gimpy knee, but his mobility was severely limited. BC's Henry Tocyzlowski's marvelous backfield fakes kept the Holy Cross defense off balance. When the Crusaders expected Vito Ananis to carry the football, Tocyzlowski faked to Ananis and handed the football off to Cignetti. Alex Nahigian and Jim Turner, the Holy Cross captain, were outstanding in defeat for the Crusaders.

Bob Jauron and Lou Montgomery, the first African American to play football at Boston College, sparked the Eagles on offense. Montgomery, who was from Brockton, was a slippery runner and a threat to go the distance any time he got his hands on the football. Jauron is the father of Dick Jauron, the former Swampscott High, Yale and Detroit Lions star. Currently, Dick Jauron, one of the most celebrated schoolboy football stars in the history of Massachusetts's football, became the head coach of the NFL Chicago Bears.

Frank Leahy

A Winner from Winner

THE MORNING AFTER THE NOTRE DAME-GEORGIA TECH GAME IN 1953, HIS FAILING health was front page news in Sunday newspapers all across the country.

At half-time during the game, legendary Notre Dame head football coach Frank Leahy collapsed on the field and was rushed to a South Bend, Indiana hospital. He had suffered an acute pancreatitis attack. He would retire from coaching after that season, in poor health and worn out. In thirteen seasons as a head coach, two at Boston College (1939 and 1940) and eleven at Notre Dame (1941-1943, 1946-1953) his record of 107-13-9 (.864 winning percentage) ranks second behind Knute Rockne for coaches with at least ten years of service.

After leaving coaching, he became an insurance executive, president of All-Star Sports Associates public relations firm and vice president of the Merritt, Chapman and Scott construction company. He also hosted a weekly college football highlight show that aired on Friday nights at 7:30 p.m. and was seen in all the major television markets across the country. I remember eagerly looking forward to watching the half-hour program with my father, a high school coach, every Friday night. It ran for one or two seasons at most during the mid-1950s.

Leahy hosted the show, dressed in a tweedy sports jacket and bow tie. In the world of college football, he was larger than life and he commanded complete attention just by his presence on the television screen. He came across as professorial with a dry sense of humor. He had the ability to fully engage the audience with a combination of intelligence, subdued Irish charm and professional pomposity. He was Frank Leahy, but you knew that even before he introduced himself. The show featured an animated bouncing football introducing the top games of the week, Navy vs. Virginia, Michigan vs. Illinois, UCLA vs. Oregon, Mississippi vs. LSU, etc. Back then, years before the advent of ESPN, there was a dearth of sports programming on television so the weekly college football highlight show was a bonus for diehard sports fans.

Francis William Leahy was born on August 27, 1908 in O'Neill, Nebraska, but grew up in (perhaps prophetically) Winner, South Dakota. He was the son of Frank and Mary Winnifred (Kane) Leahy. His father was an articulate owner of a freight and produce business and he was known for his shrewdness and toughness. As a youth, Leahy's father encouraged his son to box and young Frank became an amateur fighter of some note. He attended Winner grammar school and high school, where he played halfback on the high school football team. As a senior, because he lacked the necessary credits to be accepted at Notre Dame, he transferred to Omaha (Nebraska) Central High School, increased his academic load, graduated in 1927 and was accepted at Notre Dame, where he was president of the freshman class.

As a freshman, Rockne shifted him to center. At the start of his sophomore year, Rockne shifted him again, this time to tackle. He played in only three games as a sophomore, but he was a starter at tackle as a junior in 1929 when Notre Dame posted a 9-0-0 record and won the national championship.

In 1930, he suffered a knee injury prior to the season that sidelined him for his entire senior year of football. During his recovery, fate intervened. It just so happened that Rockne was struck down by a series of physical problems around the time that Leahy blew out his knee. Both men wound up at the Mayo Clinic and Rockne invited Leahy to share a room with him.

It was a rare opportunity to learn the game from the master and Leahy took advantage of his good luck by absorbing everything that Rockne was willing to teach him about the game of football. Leahy graduated from Notre Dame with a B.S. in Physical Education in 1931.

He began his college football coaching career as a line coach at Georgetown in 1931. From 1933-1938, he was Jim Crowley's line coach at Fordham. At Fordham, he helped develop the famous "Seven Blocks of Granite," the backbone of powerhouse Fordham teams that lost only two games in three years. Vince Lombardi, the great coach of the Green Bay Packers, was one of the Seven Blocks of Granite. He played guard.

In 1939, Leahy became the head coach at Boston College, replacing Gil Dobie who had guided the Eagles to a 6-1-2 record in 1938, but the loss (29-7) was to a superb 8-1 Holy Cross team, led by captain and all-time great Bill Osmanski.

In his first year, Leahy led Boston College to the pinnacle of success in college football. In two seasons at the Heights, his record was an astounding 20-2. The school played in its first two bowl games and, led by Charlie O'Rourke, Gene Goodreault and company, went undefeated in 1940, beat Tennessee 19-13 in the Sugar Bowl and won the national championship.

Several of the men who played for Leahy at Boston College were in agreement about what made him such a great football coach. "He had his own unique style of coaching," they said. "But the absolute bottom line was that he instilled confidence in his players and his teams believed they could beat any and all opponents."

Leahy coached seven undefeated and five national championship teams. Twenty-two of his players were named All-Americans. He coached four Heisman Trophy winners, five Walter Camp Award winners, three Maxwell Trophy winners and two Outland Trophy winners. He was voted both coach of the year (1941) and man of the year (1949). He coached the College All-Stars to a 16-0 victory over the Chicago Bears and he coached in a second College All-Star game, losing to the Chicago Cardinals, 28-0. He was elected to the College Football Hall of Fame in 1970.

As a coach, Leahy was a perfectionist and a workaholic, often sleeping in the office. Like Casey Stengel, the great manager of the Yankees, he manipulated and used the press to his own advantage. His stilted language infuriated rival coaches. He was basically an introvert, a shy, modest man who reinvented himself for the media. In 1953, the great Johnny Lattner, number 14 for the Fighting Irish, won the Heisman Trophy. Earlier in his college career, Lattner once fumbled five times in a game against Michigan State. After that game, Leahy said to the press, "Ooooh, Jonathan Lattner. Ooooh, you heretic, Jonathan Lattner. What am I to do with you!" Leahy was not afraid to criticize his players or his teams as a motivating tool. His approach worked, too. He understood, like all great coaches, that athletes are individuals. Some needed a pat on the back. Others needed a boot in the rear end. In the final analysis, Frank Leahy, the psychologist, got the most out of his athletes and his teams.

He was his own man, too. In 1942, he infuriated Notre Dame alumni by switching from the Rockne system to the T-Formation. His rational at the time was that "If Rockne were alive, he would have been the first to switch to the T-Formation."

During World War II, he served in the Pacific as a U.S. Navy lieutenant. He returned to Notre Dame in 1946. From 1946-1949, his Notre Dame teams posted a 36-0-2 record and won national championships in 1946, 1947 and 1949.

In 1936, he married Florence "Floss" Reilly of Brooklyn, New York. They had eight children, five boys and three girls. As a college football coach, he was one of a select group, an icon of the game.

In 1949, Pope Pius XXII appointed him to the Knights of Malta, a special honor for a Catholic layman and he cherished the award as much, if not more so, than all the football honors he received. Late in his life, he developed leukemia and he eventually died from heart failure on June 21, 1973 in Portland, Oregon. He was a little more than two months shy of his 65th birthday.

Dr. Eddie Anderson

A Special Presence

IN FEBRUARY OF 1950, MONTHS BEFORE PHILADELPHIA, THE CITY OF Brotherly Love, became abuzz over manager Eddie Sawyer's Phillies, nicknamed the "Whiz Kids," a spunky, surprising ball club that went on to capture the National League pennant, Dr. Eddie Anderson made a triumphant return to the City of Worcester and the College of the Holy Cross.

It was the beginning of his second tenure as head coach of the Crusaders. He first became head coach at Holy Cross in 1933 and, from 1933 to 1938, compiled a 47-7-4 record, which included unbeaten seasons in 1935 (9-0-1) and 1937 (8-0-2).

In 1939, he resigned his position as head football coach at Holy Cross to become the head coach of the University of Iowa Hawkeyes of the prestigious Big Ten Conference, where he coached from 1939 to 1942 and from 1946 to 1949. To take the Iowa job, he was released from a contract he had signed on November 26, 1938 to coach Holy Cross football that would have paid him $9,000 per season for five years. In 1939, he led Iowa to a 6-1-1 record and he was named Coach of the Year in the Big Ten. For his efforts, the University of Iowa Board of Trustees awarded him with a new six-year contract that paid him $12,000 annually and also gave him a $1,000 bonus.

During World War II, he served in the Army as a medical officer for four years and returned to Iowa as head coach in 1946. A dispute over tenure, which the University of Iowa denied him in 1949, made it easier for him to return to Holy Cross as head coach in 1950.

Never one to back down from challenges, Anderson returned to Mount St. James to rescue a football program that found itself in deep trouble. The previous two seasons, Holy Cross had won only six games and lost fourteen under Head Coach Bill Osmanski, one of the school's all-time greats. In Osmanski's final game as head coach, Boston College engineered the most lopsided win in the long history of the college football series, crushing Holy Cross, 76-0, which prompted the firing of Osmanski and the rehiring of Dr. Anderson.

In college football circles, Anderson's return to Mount St. James commanded the same type of attention—but on a smaller scale—that General Douglas MacArthur's homecoming received after President Harry Truman fired him and the great general returned to the United States from the Philippines. In both cases, the two men received welcomes that are reserved for heroes.

Dr. Anderson was rehired as head football coach by Holy Cross on February 8, 1950. In a February 9, 1950 story in the *Boston Herald* written by Arthur Sampson, it was noted that Anderson had changed little in the eleven years since he had departed the hills of Worcester for the corn fields of Iowa. "He hasn't put on any weight," wrote Sampson. "He hasn't acquired any gray hairs. He's the same quiet, affable character who talks frankly yet humbly about football topics."

He appeared to be unchanged with one exception. "Eddie now uses a long cigarette holder when he smokes," Sampson wrote, about a fact every college football fan in New England just clamored to know.

Sampson might have viewed Anderson as humble, but like all the great coaches, the true picture of the man was much more complex and mysterious. Like Frank Leahy, there was an aura about Dr. Eddie Anderson. He had a special presence. He was masterful in the uncanny way he could recognize ability and motivate his teams by getting the most out of his athletes. Yet, he was hardly one-dimensional.

At Iowa, he had been the first Big Ten coach to use the T-Formation. During his second tenure at Holy Cross, he would refine and tinker with it to capitalize on the multiple talents of a long list of superb quarterbacks.

Early in his coaching career, Anderson was known as an innovator among defensive coaches, but he was anything but naive when it came to running sophisticated offenses.

Wherever he coached, he stressed the importance of physical conditioning and he welcomed a return to the beautiful hills that surrounded Holy Cross. "At Iowa I didn't have the hills that I have at Holy Cross," he said. "Running those hills is a great way to get your teams into shape. We'll be running those hills again so my teams at Holy Cross will be in better shape than the squads I had at Iowa."

Anderson coached the Crusaders from 1950 to 1964, compiling an 82-60-4 record, including 8-2-0 marks in 1951 and 1952. His career record against Boston College, from 1933-1938 and from 1950-1964, was 11-10. His combined record at Holy Cross was 129-67-8 and he had just three losing seasons. In 39 years as a college head coach at four colleges, his career record was 201-128-15, which ranks tenth for most victories among Division 1-A college football coaches.

He won his 200th career game in 1964, his final season, with a 32-0 victory over Boston University. He had many memorable victories as well as his share of heartbreaking losses. Two of the most stinging losses were a 7-6 loss to Carnegie Tech in 1938, which spoiled a potential unbeaten season and denied Holy Cross a chance to play in the Sugar Bowl, and a bitterly hard-fought 10-8 loss to Boston College in 1964, his final game as a head coach.

From as far back as when he was a boy growing up in Iowa, he was filled with ambition, setting high standards for himself and having the courage to dream. At an early age, he was determined to become the first medical doctor in the Anderson family. When he graduated from Mason City High School, he appeared ready to enroll at the University of Minnesota and play football for the Golden Golphers. However, a high school teammate wound up at Notre Dame and Anderson soon followed him by enrolling at Notre Dame himself. When he first arrived at Notre Dame as a freshman, he was hardly brimming with confidence, and he questioned whether or not he had selected the right college. However, shortly after he arrived at Notre Dame, a Swedish-born chemistry professor and football coach entered his life and all doubts were swept away, as Anderson was caught up in the magnetism of Knute Rockne. In the history of college football, it is truly amazing how many of the game's greatest coaches were disciples of the dynamic Swede.

Almost immediately, Anderson became one of Rockne's favorites. Rockne, who had wanted to become a doctor himself, encouraged the freshman end to persist in his ambition to enter medical school. After graduating from Notre Dame, Anderson played pro football for the Chicago Cardinals, enrolled at Rush Medical School at the University of Chicago and it was in the Windy City where he met his future wife, Mary Broderick.

In the fall of 1918, Anderson's freshman year at Notre Dame and Rockne's first season as the head coach of the Fighting Irish, Notre Dame opened its football season with a road game against Case Institute of Technology in Cleveland. In a *Sunday Worcester Telegram* story written by Ed Scannell, former executive sports editor of the *Telegram & Gazette*, and published on April 23, 1950, Anderson relived the exhilaration he felt over making the Notre Dame traveling squad as a freshman.

"Making the traveling squad for the season opener was one of the big thrills of my life," Anderson told Scannell. "Rockne threw me a pair of well-worn football pants and he said, 'Here, try these. They are lucky pants.' "

A smart and opportunistic athlete, Anderson endeared himself to Rockne by quickly absorbing the great coach's system. He knew all the plays so he could play either left or right end. In those days, players were seldom shifted from one side of the line to the other, or from one position to another. In the game against Case Institute of Technology, he made his varsity debut, alternating between left and right end. It was a golden era for Notre Dame football. One of his teammates was the immortal George Gipp.

Throughout much of his college coaching career, from 1922 to 1964, Anderson remarkably balanced two careers, the demanding medical profession as well as coaching big-time college football. Any wonder that he often appeared to be preoccupied, distant or even aloof? His wife repeatedly remarked that the couple had almost no social life. In the evening, following football practice and meetings with his coaches, he regularly poured over medical journals and text books to remain abreast with the latest developments in medicine. If he and his wife went out, it was never planned, always a spur of the moment late-night dinner either alone or with another couple.

Part of his genius was the fact that, although he lived in the present moment, his mind busily calculated the future—the next play, the next series of downs, the next game, the x-rays he would examine later in the week or the rounds he would make at Rutland Veterans Hospital.

As a football coach, he wore many hats. To some, he was a father figure; to others, he was a stern disciplinarian; he patted a few players on the back; he could be cold and sarcastic to others; he was a keen judge of talent; but more than that, it was character that he looked for in his players. In some ways, he was a contradiction. He lorded over his sport, his athletes and his fellow coaches, yet he was not insistent about calling his own plays and he never ran up the score. In the final analysis, the sum of who Anderson was loomed larger than his parts.

He may have been the only coach in the history of college football who lined up a team of fellow physicians to assist him in recruiting talented high school student-athletes. Anderson, in whatever he did, seldom missed a trick, always sought an edge that would give him and his teams even a slight advantage.

The two best football players he ever coached, in the opinion of many, were Nile Kinnick at Iowa and Bill Osmanski at Holy Cross. Kinnick, who won the Heisman Trophy in 1939, was a Navy pilot during World War II and was killed on June 2, 1943 when the engine of his fighter plane went suddenly dead and the aircraft plunged into the Gulf of Paria in the Caribbean Sea.

When Anderson learned about Kinnick's death, reportedly he turned to his faith in God for both solace and strength. He was no flag-waving Christian, but quietly, without any fanfare, he was a daily communicant for years. He believed that actions, not mere words, were the mark of a man. In the final analysis, one of his players at Holy Cross, Bob Noble, who graduated in 1966, summed up the man best in another *Worcester Telegram* story about Dr. Anderson when he said, "He practiced virtue while most of my generation were still trying to define it."

Dr. Eddie Anderson died in Clearwater, Florida, on April 26, 1974.

Bill Osmanski

He Was the Greatest

IN SPORTS, SOME NUMBERS ARE INSTANTLY IDENTIFIED WITH THE athletes who wore them—Babe Ruth (3), Lou Gehrig (4), Ted Williams (9), Red Grange (77), Tom Harmon (98), Stan Musial (6), George Mikan (99) and Jackie Robinson (42)—just to name eight.

In the long history of Holy Cross football, the same is true of number 25. It was worn by "Bullet Bill" Osmanski (Holy Cross Class of 1939), by all accounts the greatest football player to wear the purple jersey of the Crusaders. As testimony to his greatness, Osmanski's number 25 is the only football jersey Holy Cross has ever retired.

Everybody, even former college presidents, admired Bill Osmanski, the athlete and the man. "Bill Osmanski is my all-time favorite Holy Cross football player," remarked Father John Brooks, S.J., president emeritus of the College of the Holy Cross. "He was a great player who had the ability to play in the pros. He was an outstanding student who later became a dentist, a great credit to Holy Cross, a good and decent man."

Osmanski was such an elite football player that even highly respected and normally unbiased sports writers, such as the *Boston Globe*'s Jerry Nason, jumped on the Osmanski band wagon. Following college, Osmanski played for the Chicago Bears (1939-1946). During that era, Osmanski and the Bears made a rare appearance in Boston and in a column, the estimable Nason revealed that Osmanski stood alone at the top of his list of football greats. "William has been our favorite football player for a long time," wrote Nason, "or since the afternoon in 1935 when Dr. Eddie Anderson paused on the campus at Holy Cross to hail a freshman with shoulders like the beam of a coal barge."

In the column, Nason told the story about how Osmanski, as a college freshman, began his climb to greatness. In a freshman football game against Boston College, Osmanski missed a tackle which allowed BC back Falla Gintoff to break free and race for a long touchdown.

After the game, Coach Anderson, sarcastically asked Osmanski, "Bill, are you going to let him [Gintoff] run away from you next year?"

"Mr. Anderson," responded the always polite but deadly serious freshman, "nobody is ever going to run away from me again."

"And nobody ever did!" wrote Nason.

After his freshman season, Dr. Anderson, who was a genius at recognizing talent and plugging it into the right position where an athlete could best maximize his talents, switched Osmanski from blocking back to fullback. "For the next three years a lot of people spent their Saturday afternoons chasing Bill," continued Nason. "He blossomed into one of the greatest fullbacks who ever split a defensive line in these or any other precincts."

Following his freshman season, many speculated that Dr. Anderson would switch Osmanski from blocking back to guard, but the great Holy Cross coach made Osmanski his starting fullback prior to the beginning of the 1936 season. From that moment on, Osmanski tucked the pigskin under an arm and ran right off the sports pages into history.

He came from Providence, Rhode Island and, according to Nason, hitchhiked to Worcester and arrived at the foot of Pakachoag Hill with only the clothes on his back and not a cent in his pocket. But he was rich in determination and the will to succeed. His exploits on the gridiron for Holy Cross are legendary. In three varsity seasons (1936-1938), Osmanski and Holy Cross lost only three games by a total of five points, posting a 23-3-3 record. In 1937, Holy Cross ended the season with an unbeaten 8-0-2 record, outscoring the opposition, 107-19.

In high school, he led Central High of Providence to the state title. In both high school and college, he reeled off long touchdown runs the first time he touched the football. In 1936, against Dartmouth, he intercepted a pass and returned it 76 yards for a touchdown. Holy Cross' 7-0 win, was the Crusaders first win over the Big Green in eleven games.

In a game against Colgate, Osmanski gained 250 yards rushing in three quarters before Coach Anderson sat him down for the entire fourth quarter. In another game, Bullet Bill scored three touchdowns against Brown in the first quarter and then sat out the rest of the game. Facing always tough Carnegie Tech of Pittsburgh, Osmanski gathered in the opening kick off, dodged one tackler after another, and sprinted 93 yards for a touchdown.

A fierce competitor, Osmanski practiced as hard as he played. He picked up his rigid work ethic at a young age, washing dishes on Friday nights and even on Saturday mornings before games. The second oldest of six children, he needed to work to help support his family after his father died. As a running back, he combined power and raw speed along with his natural instincts that allowed him to hesitate behind the line of scrimmage, setting up a block by allowing the play to develop. All the great backs have that ability.

In a story in the *Worcester Telegram & Gazette* the day after Osmanski's death in 1996, columnist John Gearan quoted Ray Monaco, Osmanski's former teammate in high school and college. "Bill was easy to block for," said the Providence, Rhode Island attorney and Holy Cross Hall of Fame lineman. "He would fade left, hesitate, and set up the block for a lineman. By the time you looked up, swoosh, Bill was gone."

He was a captain of the 1938 Holy Cross team and a first-team All-American. He made every All-American squad, even one that was hand picked by singer Kate Smith, whose powerful voice can still be heard on recordings belting out "God Bless America."

In his final college game, November 26, 1938, Osmanski shredded the defense while leading Holy Cross to a 29-7 victory over Boston College, the Crusaders second straight victory over the Eagles.

Following that game, amidst "salty tears of joy," according to one report in a Boston newspaper, Coach Anderson proclaimed, "Bill Osmanski is the best back I have ever seen. He is the one who made the team go today. It was Osmanski who was the standout back. He is the finest in the country."

Boston College coach Gil Dobie, after some prodding, concurred, saying, "I think Bill Osmanski is the best back I have ever seen in my life."

In the season-ending victory over BC, Osmanski scored one touchdown and pitched a lateral to Johnny Kelly, who bolted 45-yards for a second Holy Cross touchdown. Earlier in the game, triple-threat Ronnie Cahill pitched a 14-yard pass to Henry Giardi for the first Crusader touchdown. Henry Ouellette scored the fourth Holy Cross touchdown on a four-yard plunge.

In 1939, Osmanski was co-captain of the college All-Stars in the annual game against the NFL champions. The game was played at Soldier Field in Chicago before a crowd of 81,000. The New York Giants defeated the All-Stars, 9-0, but Osmanski was voted Most Valuable Player for the All-Stars.

As an NFL rookie in 1939, Osmanski led the league in rushing with 699 yards and averaged over five yards each time he carried the football. With the Bears, he won four NFL championships and he played a key role in the Bears' 73-0 victory over the Washington Redskins in the title game of 1940. It was played on December 8, 1940. On the game's first play, Osmanski took a hand off from quarterback Sid Luckman and galloped 68 yards for the game's first touchdown. The win avenged an earlier regular season 7-3 loss to the Redskins. After scoring their eleventh and final touchdown, the Bears were forced to run for the extra point, rather than kick it. Why? Because there was only one football left, and if it had been booted into the stands, the final minutes of the game, as meaningless as they were, could not have been played. Without a football, the officials would have had to stop the game. For winning the championship, each member of the Bears earned $873.

During World War II, Osmanski served as an officer and Navy dentist with the 2nd Marine Division in the Pacific and he saw combat duty at Guam and Guadalcanal. He once saved a medical officer's life by rescuing him from quicksand and he prevented an ambush by capturing a Japanese soldier who had been concealed in a cave. He disarmed the soldier of a grenade, a rifle and a knife. Osmanski spoke a little Japanese. Imagine the surprise on the face of the Japanese soldier when the burly American football star spoke to him in his native language.

In a bizarre story that took place near the end of the war, Osmanski also participated in a service football game, billed the "Atom Bowl," and held in a valley of the Urakami River in Japan just months after the bombing of Nagasaki. The date of the game was January 1, 1946. The contest pitted the Nagasaki Bears against the Isahaya Tigers, rival units of the United States Marines 2nd Division. Osmanski was captain of the

Tigers and Angelo Bertelli, the former Notre Dame quarterback and 1943 Heisman Trophy winner, was captain of the Bears. In the game, eerily played at "Atomic Athletic Field No. 2," Osmanski kicked the deciding extra point in a 14-13 Tigers win.

During the years he played for the Bears, Osmanski attended and graduated from Northwestern University Dental School and he set up a dental practice in the Chicago area. In 1948, he interrupted that practice to become the head football coach at Holy Cross. At the time of his appointment, he said, "I took the job because I wanted to give something back to Holy Cross." Despite the sacrifice of having to uproot his family, Osmanski did not succeed as a head coach. In two seasons under Osmanski, Holy Cross posted a 6-14-0 record. In his final game, Boston College annihilated Holy Cross 76-0. Following that game, Holy Cross bought out the final years of Osmanski's long-term contract and rehired Dr. Eddie Anderson to replace him in 1950.

William T. Osmanski died on Christmas day, December 25, 1996. He was 80 years old and during the final years of his life he had battled Alzheimer's disease.

The Forties

1940: BC 7-0

1941: BC 14-13

1942: Holy Cross 55-12

1943: no game

1944: Holy Cross 30-14

1945: Holy Cross 46-0

1946: Holy Cross 13-6

1947: Holy Cross 20-6

1948: BC 21-20

1949: BC 76-0

DURING THE 1940S, THE "WAR YEARS," THE BC-HOLY CROSS RIVALRY produced both chills and thrills. In 1940, Frank Leahy's unbeaten BC team won the Eagles only national championship in football. There was the huge 55-12 Holy Cross upset win in 1942 followed that night by the devastating Cocoanut Grove fire. The decade ended with BC's 76-0 slaughter of Holy Cross in 1949, which resulted in the firing of Coach Bill Osmanski. In 1946, Notre Dame and Army fought to a 0-0 tie at Yankee Stadium. By the middle of the decade, Leahy, who had taken over at Notre Dame in 1941, was well on his way to leading the Fighting Irish to four national championships. He retired after the 1953 season, a living legend who, by the time he quit, was totally burned out. During the 1940s, BC won four games and Holy Cross won five. On January 1, 1946, Holy Cross played in its only big-time bowl game, losing to Miami, 13-6, in the Orange Bowl. In its final game before the Orange Bowl, Holy Cross destroyed BC, 46-0.

– 1945 –

Tuning up for its only bowl appearance in the history of Holy Cross football, Coach John "Ox" DaGrosa's Crusaders blasted Boston College 46-0 before 32,457 at Fenway Park.

The forty-six-point margin of victory was the largest in the history of the series. It was eclipsed four years later when Boston College got revenge by destroying Holy Cross 76-0 in 1949.

Holy Cross led 20-0 at the half and 32-0 after three quarters. The Crusaders rolled up four hundred and fifty-seven yards on offense. Captain Stan Koslowski, Steve Conroy, Jimmy Dieckelman and Fran Bryson led the Purple. Coach DaGrosa cleared his bench in the fourth quarter and used forty players in the game. Gene "Flip" DeFilippo, who was only a freshman and was described as "cool and accurate" in the newspaper reports of the game, came off the bench and completed a string of passes. He is the father of Gene DeFilippo, the widely respected Boston College athletic director.

Holy Cross would go on to play the University of Miami Hurricanes in the 1946 Orange Bowl. Miami, which was coached by Jack Harding, the former Pittsburgh Panther star, ended its regular season with a 21-7 victory over Detroit.

In the Orange Bowl, Miami won a 13-6 thriller over Holy Cross, intercepting a pass and returning it 89 yards for the winning touchdown on the final play of the game. Koslowski passed sixteen yards to Walter Brennan for the only Holy Cross touchdown, which at the time tied the game 6-6 in the second quarter.

November 28, 1942

Day of Glory; Night of Sorrow

IT WAS AN UNEASY, FEARFUL TIME FOR THE COUNTRY, ALMOST ONE YEAR after Pearl Harbor. The war effort had intensified on two fronts. On the morning of the annual BC-Holy Cross football game, soldiers, sailors and marines stood out in the large crowd that packed Kenmore Square in Boston hours before the opening kickoff. What no one knew at the time was that the next 24 hours would not only turn the sports world, and college football in particular, upside down, but that the most horrific fire in the history of the country would paralyze the region and leave it numb with grief.

Entering its 1942 showdown against heavily favored, unbeaten and top-ranked Boston College, the Holy Cross football team was loose, confident and convinced it could upset the powerful Eagles. "We had good players on our team and we expected to win," said Andrew "Bubba" Natowich, the starting fullback who scored the Crusaders' final touchdown on a seven-yard plunge in the shocking 55-12 Holy Cross victory.

Entering the game, Holy Cross, with a 4-4-1 record, had only managed to play .500 football under new coach Anthony J. "Ank" Scanlon. Prior to the beginning of the season, Scanlon put in a new offensive system. He ditched the Split T, which had been run by former coach Joe Sheeketski, and went to a Single-Wing formation featuring an unbalanced line.

Both Natowich and Eddie Murphy, starting end and captain of the Crusaders, agreed that the team had a difficult time adjusting to the new system. "We didn't like it," both of them recalled. "As a team, all of the players preferred the Split T. The Single Wing had been around a long time. The Split T was more wide open, a better passing offense. It was the future of college football at the time."

That may explain, at least in part, why Holy Cross got off to such a sluggish start in 1942, losing three of its first four games. However, the turning point in the season was a game against North Carolina State. The Crusaders blasted the Wolfpack, 28-0, and entered the BC game on the heels of two straight victories, both shutouts, 13-0 over Temple and 28-0 over Manhattan. Holy Cross was on a roll playing its best football of the season.

At the end of November 1942, Boston College clearly was "The Beast from the East." In fact, many experts predicted that only an official coronation stood between Boston College and its second national championship in three years.

Tuning up for its annual battle with arch-rival Holy Cross, Coach Denny Myers' Eagles outscored their final four opponents, 168-6: beating Georgetown, 47-0; Temple, 28-0; Fordham, 56-6; and Boston University, 37-0. After the 56-6 rout of the Fordham Rams, BC was acclaimed the "top team in the nation." Locally, newspapermen started comparing the 1942 team to Coach Frank Leahy's unbeaten 1940 team, which beat Tennessee in the Sugar Bowl, 19-13, and went on to win the national championship.

The 1942 team, employing a different system under Myers than was used by Leahy, was bigger, averaging better than ten pounds per man. The 1940 team had more natural ability and skill, led by its triple-threat quarterback, Chuckin' Charlie O'Rourke. Eddie Doherty, who quarterbacked the 1942 team, was a heady, capable quarterback, but he was not as flashy as O'Rourke. While Leahy's team mixed finesse with strength and depth, the 1942 club bludgeoned opponents with old-fashioned brute power. In addition to O'Rourke, the 1940 team was loaded with individual stars. Captain Henry Tocyzlowski was a precision performer known for his deft faking and knack of hiding the football. He also was a terrific blocker. Frank Maznicki was nimble and quick on his feet, and Mike Holovak, a pile-driving fullback, was only a sophomore in 1940. In

1942, as a senior and co-captain, Holovak had matured into even a better player, a one-man wrecking crew both on offense and defense. Bob Mangene, Mickey Connolly, Johnny Kililea, Bill Commane, who later was ordained a priest, Carl Lucas and Willy Boyce shared backfield duties. In the line, guards Patsy Darone, Al Fiorentino and Rocco Canale were moose capable of running the herd over the opposition. George Kerr and Joe Zabilski, the guards on the '40 team, were a solid pair, but Zabilski was not big and he relied on toughness to get the job done.

In '40, John Yauckoes, Al Morro and Joe Manzo were physically dominant tackles, but as a group the 1942 trio of tackles, Gil Bouley, Angelo Sisti and Joe Repko, were every bit as devastating, possibly packing even more brute strength. On the '40 team, Henry Woronicz and the great Gene Goodreault, considered by some the best college end in the country, were a stylish pair, but the '42 tandem of ends, Don Currivan and Charley Furbush, were solid football players. Like Goodreault, Furbush was a nifty pass receiver. Chet Gladchuk, who anchored the '40 team's line at center, was a tremendous player and an All-American, but Frank Naumetz, co-captain and center on the '42 team, was an excellent football player and a scrappy competitor.

It is a difficult task to try and compare the two teams. As for the bottom line, both the '40 and '42 Boston College squads were powerhouses, although one Boston sports writer went out on a limb and picked the '42 squad as the better of the two great teams.

"I am sure in my own mind that this year's team ('42) is better," wrote Victor O. Jones in a *Boston Globe* column. "Maybe they haven't got the reserve strength Leahy had, but they haven't needed it yet."

Completing his endorsement of the '42 BC team over the national championship '40 club, Jones wrote, "In fact I don't think there are many college teams which belong on the same field with this Gold and Maroon powerhouse, and I'd be willing to back Holovak, Naumetz (the other co-captain) and Co. against at least a couple of the weaker National Pro League teams."

On a typically cold but sun-kissed late fall Saturday, November 28, 1942, 41,300 fans jammed Fenway Park to watch the Jesuit college rivals battle, fully expecting a ho-hum BC victory. What resulted was one of the greatest upsets in college football history and the most lopsided victory in a storied series up to that time.

On the first play from scrimmage, stocky Bobby Sullivan established the tone of the game by bolting nine yards, shredding the middle of the Boston College defense. Holy Cross, capitalizing on superior quickness and flawless execution, bolted into a 20-6 half-time lead. In the third period, the Crusaders turned the game into a rout by scoring 21 unanswered points and then added two more touchdowns in the final quarter. Left halfback Johnny Bezemes of Peabody scored three touchdowns (and passed for a fourth) to lead the Crusaders. Right halfback Johnny Grigas of Chelsea scored twice. The other Holy Cross touchdowns were scored by Sullivan, who was only a sophomore, Murphy and Natowich. Holy Cross ran for five touchdowns and passed for three more. Captain Murphy, who caught one of the touchdown passes, also converted seven of eight extra-point attempts. He finished the season connecting on 16 of his final 17 extra-point kicks. Following the game, Murphy was formally invited to play in the East-West Shrine All-Star game.

BC scored on a pair of passes; one from swing back Mickey Connolly, who was injured and had to leave the game, to end Don Currivan, which covered 22 yards. The second Boston College score came on a 46-yard pass and run from Carl Lucas to end Chet Lipka. It was a sweep option pass, a play that BC had used earlier in the season to score a touchdown in a 27-0 win over the Demon Deacons of Wake Forest. Heading into the game, BC had averaged 422 yards in total offense through its first eight games. Against Holy Cross, the Eagles moved the ball 147 yards rushing and 143 yards passing. However, eight fumbles and three interceptions proved costly. The Holy Cross defense bent, but hard hitting and opportunistic play frustrated heavily favored BC the entire game. As for Holy Cross, the Crusaders piled up 234 yards on the ground and 111 passing, connecting on 8 of 15 passes, good for three touchdowns. BC coach Myers expected his team to bounce back after falling behind. "I thought our offense would get rolling in the second half," he lamented after the stunning loss.

After more than sixty years, Holovak still could not explain what happened. "Not even a coach could explain it," he said. "All I know for sure is that everything went right for them and everything went wrong for us."

Holovak also added: "The shame of it all was that we had a very good football team, maybe the best in the country that year. The loss spoiled all that and many have forgotten how good we were."

Holovak coughed up one of the eight fumbles BC lost on that unforgettable, crushing afternoon for the Eagles. It negated a 75-yard BC drive. Holovak fumbled on the Holy Cross one-yard-line, just as he was about to pound into the end zone. "Were you hit especially hard?" he was asked.

"I sure hope I was!" Holovak remarked, a bruising back who ran with reckless abandon and seldom fumbled.

As for Gil Bouley, the 240-pound All-American tackle, he still blames the loss on Coach Myers. In fact, Bouley, to this day, has very little complimentary to say about his former coach. "He was a stupid ass of a coach," he said. "He was a fake, not a good leader at all. I have nothing but negatives to say about him. He was a nothing."

Bouley was recruited by Frank Leahy, who left BC after the 1940 season to coach Notre Dame. He loved Leahy and obviously never got over his leaving the Heights.

As a freshman, one of Bouley's biggest thrills was scrimmaging against the highly touted varsity. He more than held his own before Leahy had seen enough and sent him back to continue practicing with the freshman squad.

What infuriated Bouley most about the 1942 BC-Holy Cross game was that, according to him, BC never adjusted to any of the Holy Cross wrinkles. At half-time, as the teams were going off the field, Bouley said he shouted to Assistant Coach Carl Brumbaugh, who had played for George Halas' Chicago Bears, "Tell him [Myers] to get us out of this blankety blank seven-man line. It's killing us!"

Holy Cross took advantage of Bouley's natural strength and aggressiveness by trapping the All-American tackle all afternoon. By switching to a five-man defensive front, Bouley was convinced he would have had more room to operate. He wouldn't have had to penetrate so deep into the backfield and could have stood his ground better, fighting off blockers and getting to the ball carrier.

BC, however, never made the adjustment. Interestingly, Holy Cross also used a seven-man front on defense, ignored the backfield flow anytime BC put a back in motion, crowded the line of scrimmage and bottled up the normally high-powered BC offense.

Toward the end of the game, the Holy Cross fans, added insult to injury, by taunting BC and its All-American tackle with a sarcastic cheer.

The sounds of "Bouley made a tackle, Bouley made a tackle" wafted out of the stands and could be heard all over Fenway Park. Along with the eleven BC turnovers, the line play and the strategy employed in the trenches had a huge impact on the final outcome. To use modern football terms, Boston College stacked eight defenders (one linebacker—Holovak) in the box, so the fleet of Holy Cross backs had clear sailing once the Purple ball carriers burst through the point of attack. With a ground game chewing up yardage in chunks, it opened up the passing lanes and the well-balanced Holy Cross offense befuddled the Eagles with a polished, timely passing attack.

In the post-game locker room, the flash of light bulbs from cameras and Pepsodent white and wide smiles blinded the celebrants. Boston mayor Maurice Tobin made an appearance. There was plenty of rah rah noise, hugs and backslapping, but no singing reported Arthur Siegel, in the *Sunday Boston Herald* on November 29, 1942. "We'll do our singing at the dance tonight," roared big Jim Landrigan, the Crusaders' redheaded tackle from Wakefield.

Hugh Devore, the Holy Cross end coach, who later led Notre Dame and several other colleges and also coached in the NFL, was seen hugging his prize pupil, Captain Murphy. Lud Wray, another assistant coach, called the upset victory "the biggest thrill I have ever had in the game."

Holy Cross had many heroes. Linemen John DiGangi, Tom Alberghini, George Titus, who was a bear on defense at linebacker, and the great George Connor backboned the upset victory. Connor, after a hitch in the military during the war, transferred to Notre Dame and was a great college football player for Leahy and the Fighting Irish. Later, he became a pro football legend on Coach George Halas' Chicago Bears.

During the World War II era, many athletes had their college careers interrupted by military service, people like Bill Swiacki, who was a fine end on the 1942 Holy Cross team. After the war, he transferred to Columbia. The Lions were coached by the little professor, Lou Little. In 1947, Swiacki's diving catch helped set up the winning touchdown and sparked Columbia to a huge 21-20 upset victory over powerhouse Army, ending Coach Earl "Red" Blaik and the Cadets' 32-game winning streak.

Towards the end of the 1942 BC-Holy Cross game, two rival players got involved in extracurricular "pushing and shoving." Wally Boudreau, BC's back-up quarterback, played the role of peacemaker. Interestingly, his nickname was "Ma." Boudreau, who constantly looked out for the best interest of his teammates, was respected as a "mother hen" type character and guardian on the Boston College football squad.

As the game clock wound down and as the shadows lengthened and the temperatures dipped, skirmishes broke out in the stands and policemen were seen escorting rowdies out of Fenway Park.

Before the game, BC expected that a victory over Holy Cross would clinch an invitation to play in the Sugar Bowl in New Orleans. Travel plans were already being made. Sometime later that night, following the stunning loss, Boston College received word from Sugar Bowl officials that the Eagles would not be invited to play in the New Year's Day bowl game. Instead, BC wound up in the Orange Bowl, losing to Alabama, 37-21, despite three Holovak touchdowns, on runs of 2, 34 and 65 yards. The sting of the Holy Cross loss cost the Eagles a chance to play for the national championship. Playing in the Orange Bowl had to be anticlimactic.

Finally, large sums of money were bet on the game. For those who bet on heavily favored (the odds ranged from 4-1 to 14-1) BC, they went home with lighter wallets. The *Boston Herald* reported that hours after the game, a "huge fat" man, wrapped in a fur-lined trench coat, stood solemnly by the entrance to the subway in Kenmore Square. In between slugs out of a flask, he spoke to anyone who would listen about not one, but two losses. "Hoo, hoo, hoo," he droned. "I lost 10 bucks on the game and I lost my wife, too. What's a mere game when you lose your wife on the same day!" The sidebar in the *Boston Herald* did not report how the man lost his wife. Did she die somehow? Was she hit by a car? Did she have a heart attack? Or did she run off with another man, maybe with his best friend?

The pathos of the troubled man may have been a harbinger of the great tragedy to follow. Less than four hours after the end of the game, a deadly fire erupted in the Melody Lounge of the Cocoanut Grove nightclub located in the heart of downtown Boston. The nightclub was packed, overcrowded well beyond limits established by antiquated city fire department regulations. In fact, at the last minute extra tables were brought out to accommodate late arrivals. It is estimated that as many as 1,000 patrons were jammed into the popular nightclub on that fateful night. Music played, couples jockeyed for space on the crowded dance floors. In one of the ballrooms a band played a lively rumba just minutes before the first flames were spotted. It was a chance to forget the war for a few hours—it was party time in good old Beantown. Suddenly, someone was heard shouting, "Fire!" Within minutes flames were seen engulfing an imitation palm tree in the Melody Lounge. Crackling, spit-fire noises were heard as flames rippled across the overhead ceiling. Screams filled the lounge and a stampede began. Tables and chairs were knocked over as people frantically searched for exits—but the exits were few and far between.

Many patrons were trampled to death in the push to escape the flames. In the foyer, outside the main ballroom, people near the stairs that led to the downstairs lounge saw a terrifying sight and heard an ugly, menacing sound: a huge ball of black smoke billowed upwards and with it came the roar of a monster fire raging out of control. The fire quickly spread from the downstairs lounge to the second floor, picking up both speed and force as it was fed by oxygen. A mass of people rushed for the revolving doors, the only exit at the front of the main lobby. Some made it outside. But the crush of humanity caused the revolving doors to become stuck, trapping hundreds of people inside. All were burned alive, many beyond recognition. Within a half-hour, the entire nightclub was engulfed by flames, including the Cocoanut Grove lounge and bar on the Broadway Street side of the nightclub, a recent addition that had opened for the first time the previous week.

Too many people and too few exits contributed to one of the most deadly fires of the 20th century. A total of 492 people died, making it the most lethal domestic fire in terms of fatalities since the Iroquois Theater fire of 1903 in Chicago that took the lives of 602, including more than 200 children.

As the fire intensified, police had to cordon off much of the restaurant and entertainment district to control the crowds and to keep the roadways clear for fire department trucks, equipment and ambulances. The emergency response was swift. Fire department and rescue units from as far away as Worcester and surrounding states were rushed to the scene.

As temperatures plunged, the dead and injured were dragged out of the inferno and laid on the icy pavement. On Piedmont Street alone, the line of victims' bodies stretched more than 100 yards. It was a horrific scene. The stench of burning human flesh caused many rescuers and onlookers to vomit. In his book *Cocoanut Grove* author Edward Keyes wrote a spellbinding account of "The Most Famous Fire in American History." Every hospital within miles of the city was put on alert. A large percentage of the victims were taken to Boston City Hospital. It was later calculated, Keyes reported, that in the space of just over an hour one victim of the Cocoanut Grove fire arrived at Boston City Hospital every 11 seconds and that no hospital, even in London at the height of the Nazi blitz or air raids, ever had to treat as many patients during such a brief period of time.

Ambulances, cabs, post office trucks, newspaper delivery trucks—anything that had wheels and moved—were used to transport victims to hospitals and morgues. There were so many dead that a parking garage on Piedmont Street was made into a temporary mortuary. Hospital corridors were lined with rows of bodies covered by sheets with only a pair of shoes protruding. Occasionally, one or both shoes would twitch, which at times was the only sign that a harried attending doctor or nurse would have that a victim was still alive. As many priests as could be summoned were called to the hospitals and morgues. They administered last rights to victims, one at a time all through the night and into the next morning.

The Red Cross, according to Keyes account, organized airlifts of much needed blood from Washington, D.C., New York City and several New England cities. In the first 24 hours, more blood plasma was administered to Cocoanut Grove victims than had been used in Hawaii immediately following the attack on Pearl Harbor.

On Wednesday, December 2, the fifth day after the fire, Cocoanut Grove survivors became the first documented cases of patients being treated with dosages of penicillin. In the aftermath, the newspapers were packed with heartbreaking stories of the victims who perished in the fire. Newlyweds, like the couple who had been married at 7 p.m. on the day of the fire at Our Lady of Pity Church in Chelsea, were among the dead. Other couples, celebrating twenty-five, thirty-five and fifty years of marriage, died in the fire. Families and friends poured into the city. They searched hospitals and morgues desperate for even a tidbit of information about their loved ones and friends. Numerous servicemen and servicewomen died, some while exhibiting enormous heroism by going back into the burning nightclub to try to rescue others.

Many distinguished citizens died in the fire, people such as Dr. Gordon Bennett of Swampscott. A graduate of Harvard Medical School, who completed his internship at Boston City Hospital and was a resident gynecologist at the Free Hospital for Women in Brookline. As an undergraduate, he was a star two-sport athlete at Dartmouth, excelling in both football and hockey. Labeled "an indestructible tackle" in football, Bennett was co-captain of Dartmouth's 1936 Ivy League Championship football team, a club that lost to a stubborn 7-2-1 Holy Cross team that same fall, 7-0. Although a number of fans who attended the BC-Holy Cross game that day died in the fire, only one person connected with either team was among the fatalities. He was Larry Kenney, the athletic equipment manager at Boston College and a popular member of the athletic family. To him, the Boston College athletes were known as "his kids." Both he, his wife, and the couple they were with died in the fire.

Originally, Boston College had scheduled a victory party at the Cocoanut Grove, but after the humiliating loss the party was canceled. One can only guess how many BC fans had been spared their lives because of the loss to Holy Cross.

After the game, many of the players remained in and around the city but managed to stay away from the Cocoanut Grove. Eddie Murphy, the Holy Cross captain, ended up at a party at the Parker House Hotel, originally scheduled to be a Boston College victory celebration. The morning after the fire Murphy and Boston College co-Captain Fred Naumetz headed home, Murphy to Lowell and Naumetz to Newburyport, as quickly as possible so that their families would know they were safe. Other players did the same. Before either Murphy or Naumetz reached home, premature reports had already begun to spread that they had died and priests at their home parishes offered special prayers before morning Mass for the repose of their souls.

Andrew "Bubby" Natowich, one of the many Holy Cross stars, hustled out of the city as fast as he could because the next day, Sunday, he was scheduled to pick up $100 playing in a semipro football game for the Holyoke Golden Bears. Later, he made the jump to the National Football League and played briefly for the Washington Redskins.

In 1993, members of the 1942 Boston College football team, losers to Alabama 37-21 in the 1943 Orange Bowl, were honored, along with ex-Crimson Tide players, prior to the 1993 Orange Bowl between Nebraska and Florida State. In a *Miami Herald* story written about the 50th anniversary of the game, Robert "Red" Mangene, a member of the 1942 BC football team, was quoted as saying, "I still get shivers when I think about the fire. Such marvelous memories, such horrifying memories."

During that crushing loss to Holy Cross, Mangene was beaten on two Holy Cross touchdown passes, miscues or blown coverages which contributed to a stinging defeat and for which his son will be eternally grateful.

"Thank God," remarked Robert Mangene, Jr., in the *Miami Herald* story. "Boston College got massacred and I'm here today to talk about it."

Author Keyes wrote that in November of 1945, three years after the fire, researchers at Harvard Medical School pinpointed the source of the toxic fumes: a substance called acrolein, used in the making of tear gas, was used extensively in the Cocoanut Grove furnishings. Many of the victims were literally gassed to death.

"There is nothing in medical history that quite corresponds to this," Keyes quoted the medical examiner, Dr. Timothy Leary.

As a result of the horrific fire, sweeping changes were made in fire codes and regulations pertaining to all municipal offices and privately owned buildings. However many of the changes did not happen overnight. It took years before nightclubs were required by law to increase the number of exits and install automatic sprinklers, fire alarms and emergency lighting. As late as 1975, a fire at the Blue Angel nightclub in Manhattan killed seven people. The deaths were attributed to inadequate fire safety equipment and it wasn't until January 1, 1980 that New York City enacted new fire safety laws pertaining to nightclubs.

More recently, in February of 2003, one hundred people were killed and nearly 200 people were injured at The Station nightclub in West Warwick, Rhode Island.

The criminal and civil trials following the Cocoanut Grove fire became protracted proceedings. Ultimately, the owner of the Cocoanut Grove was convicted of negligence and sent to prison. It took two years for the civil cases to be resolved. In the end, after taxes, court fees and legal expenses, each claimant received a mere $160.

November 26, 1949

Slaughter at Braves Field

ON NOVEMBER 28, 1942, EVERYTHING SEEMED TOTALLY OUT OF whack. Surely, the stars had not been aligned properly. Holy Cross stunned the college football world that day by crushing top-ranked and heavily favored Boston College, 55-12. Later that same day, the Cocoanut Grove fire resulted in one of the worst tragedies in American history. As for the football game, on the cover of the program that was sold at Fenway Park were the photos of Boston College co-Captains Fred Naumetz and Mike Holovak, who wore the numbers 55 and 12 respectively. Before the game, no one took particular notice of the numbers worn by the BC co-captains. But after the huge upset, signs and symbols of the improbable seemed to be showing up everywhere.

In 1948, at Braves Field, BC won a 21-20 thriller over Holy Cross snapping a streak of five straight losses to the Crusaders. Prior to the win in 1948, BC had not beaten Holy Cross since the 1941 team triumphed 14-13. The Eagles entered the 1949 game with a 3-4-1 record. After dropping its opener to Coach Bud Wilkinson's powerful Oklahoma Sooners, 46-0, BC lost four of its first six games wrapped around a 13-7 victory over Wake Forest and a 25-25 tie with the Rebels of Ole Miss. However, after beating Clemson 40-27 and Fordham 20-12, the Eagles entered the Holy Cross game riding a modest two-game winning streak.

For Holy Cross, the 1949 season had been nothing short of disastrous. The Crusaders limped into the game with a 1-8 record. One had to go back to 1907 to find a Holy Cross football team that had lost as many as seven games. In addition, the Crusaders were riddled with injuries and their head coach, Dr. Bill Osmanski, a former Holy Cross great whose number 25 is the only jersey the school retired in more than 100 years playing intercollegiate football, was under siege. Many felt that even if Holy Cross upset Boston College Dr. Osmanski's job was in jeopardy.

On November 26, 1949, 38,771 packed Braves Field on a bitter cold day to watch the battle between the Jesuit college rivals. To put it simply, the game was a rout. BC annihilated Holy Cross, 76-0. It was the most lopsided defeat in the history of the series and the most humiliating Holy Cross loss since 1913 when Princeton blasted the Crusaders, 54-0.

Al Cannava, a shifty, fleet-footed back, was one of the many BC stars. In fact, he played major roles in both the 1948 and 1949 Boston College victories over Holy Cross. In the 1948 game, his fumble recovery of a deflected pass, intended for end Art Spinney, accounted for BC's final touchdown. Following that score, tackle Ernie Stautner, the future pro football great and Pittsburgh Steelers legend, kicked the deciding extra point in a thrilling 21-20 Boston College win. For his efforts in that game, Stautner earned the O'Melia Award as the game's most valuable player.

As a schoolboy, Cannava had been a great back at Medford High. In fact, Ralph Wheeler, Fred Foye and Jerry Nason, three well-known Boston sports writers at the time, had nicknamed him "Crazy Legs." Cannava ran wild that day in 1949 on the frozen tundra of Braves Field. "The ground was so hard that the rubber cleats we wore didn't help you at all," he recalled.

During the 76-0 rout, Cannava could have run barefoot and Holy Cross would not have been able to corral him. He scored four touchdowns, narrowly missed a fifth, and rushed for 229 yards. He ran for three scores, one on a 69-yard gallop, and also caught a touchdown pass from quarterback Butch Songin, one of three TD passes the Walpole native pitched that day. Cannava took off on what appeared to be another long touchdown run. However, after running 35 yards, he turned around on the ten-yard line and lateraled the football to fullback Ed Petela, who raced in for the touchdown, also his fourth of the day. By passing up a chance to score a fifth touchdown, Cannava could have set the all-time Boston College record for most touchdowns in a game. Instead, today he shares the record with a host of other former BC players.

"I still have a big, glossy photo of the play," reported Cannava. "I was all set to score until I heard Petela behind me calling for the football. At the time, I thought to myself, 'What the heck', so I just shoveled the football back to him and he actually scored the touchdown."

His 229 yards rushing are the third most recorded in a single game in the history of Boston College football, although Al claims that he gained 235 yards in a game against Sugar Bowl bound Mississippi during his junior year. "We carried the ball eight, nine or ten times a game at most," he recalled. "Today, the great backs carry the ball as many as twenty-five or thirty times. If I carried the ball that many times in a single game, I would have gained over 500 yards."

Fifty-three years later, Cannava remembers how cold it was that day, how BC scored almost at will—leading 48-0 at the half and 76-0 after three quarters—and how the lights had to be turned on in the second half. "I don't know why," he said, "but they always started those games at two o'clock in the afternoon. At that time of year, it would have made much more sense to start the games earlier." For Holy Cross, it surely hadn't mattered when the game started, but it certainly must have seemed as if the cold afternoon would never end.

After graduating from high school, Cannava headed to Notre Dame, but the war intervened and he ended up spending three years in the Navy. After the war, he decided to enroll at BC, rather than return to Notre Dame. It was at Notre Dame where he first met Art Donovan, the great BC and Baltimore Colts' lineman, who also had been recruited by the Fighting Irish. Donovan served in the Marines during the war and later also enrolled at BC.

In the Navy, Cannava served on the U.S.S. Harrigan, which was blown up off the coast of Okinawa by the Japanese. Over one hundred and sixty sailors lost their lives. Cannava somehow managed to survive. "To this day I have no idea what happened," he said. "We were never told what had hit us."

Following the 1949 season, Cannava, Donovan and Art Spinney, captain of the 1949 team, were also selected to play in the annual North-

South game, also known as the Senior Bowl. Spinney later became an all-pro offensive lineman with the Baltimore Colts. Herman Hickman of Yale was the coach of the North squad. The North won, snapping a string of South victories. The win delighted the rotund Mr. Hickman, who weighed over 300 pounds and was a college football legend as a player, as well as, a renowned poet. "Hickman had a lot of money," Cannava said, about a man who was known as "The Bard of the Great Smokies." "He was a wealthy man and he was so happy after the win that he gave each one of us on the squad $200."

Following the game, the Northern boys returned home in style. They drove nonstop, sharing the driving chores, in a new 1950 Buick "Roadmaster." BC teammate Dominic Papaleo had purchased the car. He was not selected to play in the game, but he made the trip anyway just to be with his friends.

During the era when Cannava played, Northern boys had the added burden of facing prejudice and bigotry when they played against teams from the South. "You had to keep your helmet on when you played against teams from the South, particularly in their own backyards," said Cannava. "They played dirty football. Many of them hated Northerners, especially blacks and Catholics."

At BC Cannava played for Coach Denny Myers, about whom he said: "He could coach you during the week, but on game day he got confused." Cannava admitted that he had spats with coaches from time to time. In fact, he said in one instance, he told one of the Boston College assistant coaches to "go home . . . just let us play and we'll do fine."

At Boston College, Cannava started out as a business major. However, he switched to liberal arts, he said, because "two-hour afternoon accounting classes made it hard for me to make it to football practice on time."

To this day, Cannava remains respectful of the education he received at Boston College. "The Jesuits are the greatest teachers in the world," he said. "They can teach anything."

Al is the son of Salvatore and Rita Cannava. He is the fourth born in a family of four boys and two girls. His father worked as a candy maker and also for General Electric in Lynn. He and two of his brothers, Sonny and Sal, played football at Medford High. In all probability, he inherited his speed from his father. "My father was pretty agile," he said, "especially when he chased me and my brothers around."

During the era that Cannava played high school football, hundreds tried out for the team. Many fine athletes never made the squad. Tryouts, in fact, were held in street clothes. You were not issued a uniform until you had made the squad. After the first tryout, Cannava said that he returned home with his good pants ripped in several spots. He said that his mother took one look at him and immediately drew a line in the sand. "That is it," she screamed at him. "You are never to play football again. I forbid it!"

Fortunately, for Medford High and Boston College football teams, shifty Al managed to get around his mother's disapproval.

Like Cannava, Tom Kelleher, a terrific end for Holy Cross, was at the center of the action in both the 1948 and 1949 Holy Cross-BC games. In fact, Kelleher and Jim Deffley, were co-captains of the 1949 Crusaders. As a senior, Kelleher tore ligaments in a thumb and played in pain most of the year. Reflecting back on the embarrassing 76-0 defeat against BC in 1949, it is Kelleher's opinion that the defeat was simply the final straw in what turned out to be a dismal season for the Crusaders. "The 1949 season had gotten away from us a long time before the Boston College game," he said, speaking from his home in Miami, Florida. "We only won one. That was against Colgate (35-27)."

Although Osmanski was a great player at Holy Cross, he was a bust as a coach at his alma mater, going 6-14-0 in 1948 and 1949.

"Where did he ever coach before?" asked Kelleher. "He just was not a communicator. What I remember most about playing for him was that nobody knew what was going on—the backs, the linemen and even the assistant coaches. We were a team that was not on the same page."

Yet, despite the losses, 14 in two years, Kelleher is particularly proud of the fact that he and his teammates never quit and never turned on each other, which often happens on losing teams.

"Sure we were embarrassed," he recalled. "The loss to BC was a crushing defeat, but I learned more lessons while losing than I ever would have if we had won. Our suffering brought us closer together as a team and helped us prepare for the rest of our lives. No one on any Holy Cross team I played for ever quit."

Kelleher made his way to Mount St. James via Philadelphia. As a schoolboy, he was an outstanding athlete at Northeast Catholic High School in South Philly, a school run by the Oblates of St. Francis. In addition to football, he ran track and played second base on the school's baseball team. When it came time for him to head to college, he was ready to head to the University of Pennsylvania until one day he got a telephone call from his father, who instructed him "to come home immediately."

As soon as he arrived home, he found his father, the pastor of his home parish and John "Ox" DaGrosa, the Holy Cross football coach, sitting in his living room. "Sit down," ordered his father, "and listen to what he has to say about the value of a Catholic college education."

Kelleher, who was totally caught off guard by Holy Cross' interest in him as a student-athlete, said that he listened and soon became spellbound by the words that came out of DaGrosa's mouth. "He was a golden orator," recalled Kelleher, laughing to himself as he thought about the memory. "He could have two hands full of turds and after he was through talking, you would be bidding for it."

Interestingly, the silver-tongued Holy Cross football coach was not even a Catholic. He was a card-carrying Mason. "Oh, could he extol the merits of attending a Catholic college and Holy Cross in particular," said Kelleher. "The Pope couldn't have done it better!" Kelleher's father was sold. The UPenn Quakers didn't have a chance. Young Tom was headed to Worcester and Holy Cross almost before his backside had a chance to get warm sitting on a chair in the family living room.

"Now that I know that non-Catholics as well as Catholics get to heaven," said Kelleher, displaying his wit, "I'm gratified to think that all of us, including Coach DaGrosa, will all be together in heaven."

DaGrosa, who had a law degree from Georgetown, was a line coach for the Hoyas. He also coached at Temple, where he was a professor, and in the NFL for the Philadelphia Eagles. In three seasons at Holy Cross (1945-1947) he guided the Crusaders to a 17-10-2 record, including an 8-2-0 mark in 1945 when Holy Cross made its only appearance in a major bowl, losing to Miami on January 1, 1946 in the Orange Bowl, 13-6.

As for a career, Tom Kelleher was a division sales manager for Wilson Sporting Goods and he also was a back judge in the National Football League for 28 years. He officiated or worked five Super Bowls, which is a record for back judges. Although he is retired from the field, he still works for the NFL as an observer and evaluator. For most of his career, he was paid $2,000-$2,500 per game and $5,000 for each Super Bowl assignment.

His son, Tom, Jr. is also a graduate of the College of the Holy Cross. Another son, Dennis, played on two University of Miami national championship football teams (1987 and 1989). He was a tight end for Coach Jimmy Johnson's Hurricanes.

Like many from his generation, Kelleher, who was a corporal with the 2nd Marine Division in the Pacific during the war, served in the military before heading to college. His brother, George, who briefly played college football before an injury ended his career, attended Holy Cross at the same time he did.

Today, Kelleher stays in touch with ex-teammates Walter Sheridan, Walter Brennan, Jack Reader, who also was an official in the National Football League, and others. He has many fond memories of his college years, which includes the football players eating out at Worcester establishments such as "The Blue Goose," "The French Club," "Benny's" and "Cosgrove's Steak House."

Enjoying retirement amidst the warmth and sun of southern Florida, Kelleher counts his blessings. "I have had a great life and I have much to be thankful for"—including the trip he made over 50 years ago from South Philly to Mount St. James and the College of the Holy Cross.

George Kerr

Lineman, Boxer, Monsignor

EIGHTY-EIGHT-YEAR OLD PETER KERR, BC CLASS OF 1939, IS MIGHTY proud of his little (as in younger) brother, the late Monsignor George Kerr, BC Class of 1941, a legendary football player, scholar and a beloved priest of the Archdiocese of Boston.

The elder Kerr, who also is a graduate of BC Law School, is a retired Coast Guard Commander and the former chief attorney for the telephone company. Among his classmates in the Class of '39 were such outstanding men as Blue Chips athletic fund raising founder Dr. Alfred Branca, BC sociology professor John Donovan, F.B.I. agent Paul Keane and former BC athletic director Bill Flynn, who also was an F.B.I. agent, and many other prominent men.

Although he was not a football player, Peter Kerr was very close to the BC football family during the fabulous Frank Leahy era of Boston College football (1939-1940). He even got to know the great coach when Leahy first arrived at Boston College from Fordham, where he had been assistant coach.

At the time, Leahy was getting settled in the area. He had just bought a home in West Newton and he had not yet sent for his wife and children. "I got to know Leahy just after he arrived at BC," he recalled. "He needed help, so after classes I would help him get his new house ready. I helped him set up the furniture, hang curtains and put new screens in the windows, things like that."

After the chores were done, Peter Kerr said he had the opportunity to sit down at the kitchen table and share a bite of supper with the great coach. "Frank Leahy was a very personable man," he said. "Everyone liked him and he made friends easily."

Peter, who has served on the board of directors of the Alumni Association and Varsity Club at BC, closely followed his younger brother's athletic career from high school through college, climaxed by Coach Leahy's great unbeaten 1940 team winning the national championship.

Msgr. George Kerr was a three-sport star at St. Mary's High School in Brookline. Fr. Mike Durant, a former BC football player (1924-1927), was a priest assigned to St. Mary's. Fr. Durant tried unsuccessfully to get George Kerr an athletic scholarship to BC. At the time, he was told, "We have too many top prep school guards on scholarship already. There are no scholarships left for any more." So, George Kerr was a football walk-on at BC.

Peter Kerr keenly remembers the first game his younger brother played on the varsity for Coach Leahy. "It was against Temple in Philadelphia," he recalled. "A couple of linemen were getting pushed around and Leahy sent my brother into the game. He played well, started every game after that and BC eventually gave him an athletic scholarship."

George Kerr was a brilliant student. He graduated magna cum laude and he was valedictorian of his class (1941) at BC. He also was one of the stars of the college debating team. "His BC debating team went across the ocean to England and licked the All-Oxford University team in a head-to-head debate," said Peter.

In college, George Kerr stood 6-foot-1 and weighed 215 pounds. He had good size, but he also was quick and obviously tough. "Gil Dobie (the BC coach before Leahy) liked big, dumb and slow linemen," said Peter Kerr. "Leahy was different. To play for him, you had to be quick and smart. Just being big wasn't good enough."

Following his senior year, George Kerr played in a college all-star game against the Chicago Bears. "My brother was the Bears' number one draft choice," said Peter Kerr. In that game, George Kerr tangled with Danny Fortmann, the Bears' great guard and a personal favorite of Papa Bear George Halas. "After that game Fortmann made the comment that my brother was the best football player he had ever faced," he said.

On November 29, 1940, 39,000 fans packed Fenway Park to watch BC and Holy Cross battle, a game the heavily favored Eagles won 7-0 to complete an unbeaten regular season and set up a date with Tennessee in the Sugar Bowl for the national championship.

Holy Cross, which entered the game with a 4-4-1 record, totally outplayed BC throughout the game and came within a whisker of overturning the BC apple cart that overflowed with national championship aspirations. The game was scoreless after three quarters. Adolph "Dolph" Kissell, a reserve fullback, scored the game's only touchdown. It was a frustrating afternoon for the embattled Crusaders. Numerous pass plays, including one in the end zone from Andrew "Bubba" Natowich to back Ed Murphy, just missed connections, slipping through the outstretched finger tips of the sure-handed Murphy. Late in the game, George Kerr, moving from a down lineman to a pass defender on passing situations, deflected a Natowich pass to Frank Saba, an aerial that, if caught, would have put Holy Cross in a position to score the tying touchdown.

The game was a fierce defensive battle. Paul Dorrington, a future Hall of Fame high school football coach in Massachusetts, blocked a Charlie O'Rourke punt and led the charge for the fired up Holy Cross defense. A fumble recovery set up the game's only touchdown. For Boston College, the number one star was Chet Gladchuk, the Eagles 6-foot-5, 250-pound All-America center. In one newspaper account of the game, these words were written about Gladchuk's performance: "He roved all over the field making tackles. Gladchuk played like an All-American against Holy Cross. He tackled Osmanski [Joe, Bill Osmanski's younger brother] and [Johnny] Grigas when it looked like that they were just one block away from racing for a touchdown. He did yeoman work for BC."

Following the game, the Holy Cross players were shaken and newspaper stories of the game reported that many wept openly in the post-game locker room. The athletes who competed in the game for their particular college were as close as blood brothers, and a shared family feeling that united the members of each squad was an extension of the same bond that many athletes from that era experienced at home.

Felix and Ann Kerr raised three children—Peter, Mary, who was a graduate of Regis College, and George. The family eventually settled in Brookline. Felix was a traveling salesman. Peter and Mary were born in Philadelphia and George was born in Rochester, New York. Peter was a sickly child. When he was five, he was sent back to Northern Ireland to live on the cattle ranch of his maternal grandfather. The clean, fresh air of County Down in Northern Ireland helped Peter regain his health and he returned to the family in America when he was around ten or eleven. "I attended the Cathedral School," he recalled. "I had a thick brogue, which made me different. At first I was not accepted by the other boys; I wasn't one of them. I must have had a hundred fights. I was a foreigner to my fellow students, even the Irish lads whose parents had come from the old sod."

What many might not know is that Peter Kerr's younger brother, George, was a heck of an amateur boxer, who flattened a string of opponents en route to winning the Northern New England Heavyweight Championship. "Leahy heard about my brother's boxing and he was wild," said Peter. "He put a stop to it immediately, telling my brother, 'You're a football player. There is no time for any of this boxing baloney.' "

Peter Kerr said that no one in the family knew that his younger brother intended to study for the priesthood. "I can't say I was surprised, though," he said. "He was always very devout about the Catholic faith, attending Mass and receiving the sacraments—that kind of thing. But there was no talking about it. You kept those feelings to yourself."

George Kerr was ordained a priest on June 9, 1945 and he died, after a six-month battle with cancer, on January 23, 1983. Even after he was ordained a priest, he maintained his passion for boxing. Regularly, he sparred with Paul Pender, the Brookline fire fighter and ex-middleweight boxing champion. "He also was very friendly with Rocky Marciano," said Peter. "If he had continued boxing, he could have faced Rocky in the ring in an amateur bout held in a remote place somewhere in New England."

As a youth, George learned to box at a gym in Brookline and he sometimes trained for fights in Bar Harbor, Maine, where the family had a summer home. It is a long way from scenic Maine to New Orleans and the Sugar Bowl where the Eagles completed their quest for the national championship in 1940 by beating Tennessee, 19-13.

One important Eagle did not play in that game. His name was Lou Montgomery, the first African American to play varsity football at Boston College. Because of his color, he was barred from competing. In those days, southern colleges refused to compete with or against black athletes. Seven years before Jackie Robinson broke the color barrier in major league baseball, the rule shamefully was not challenged. You played by the antiquated rules, the segregated law of life in the South, or you did not play.

Montgomery, known for his slight build and blinding speed, traveled with the team to New Orleans, but did not dress for the game. Instead, he played in an All-Black College All-Star game that was being played in the area around the same time. The Sugar Bowl might have slighted him, but he had the last laugh: while the Sugar Bowl rivals played for pride, he was paid in cold, hard cash—as much as $1,000, according to Peter Kerr, to play in the Black College All-Star game.

On the way home to Boston, Montgomery was the only player with a wallet filled with bills and change in his pocket. "On the train on the way home, Lou was the only one who had any money," recalled Peter, who traveled with the BC team to the game. "He was a generous guy. I remember him smiling and buying drinks for everyone."

Montgomery, who came from Brockton, Massachusetts, never realized his vast potential as a college football player at BC. Some, including Peter Kerr, have theorized that his considerable talents could have been better utilized if Leahy had switched to the more wide open T-Formation, rather than sticking with the old Notre Dame box, which he learned playing for Knute Rockne in college. While he attended BC, Montgomery was a regular at the Kerr home. "My brother often brought Lou home for dinner," said Peter. "He liked my mother's simple Irish cooking. Old fashioned meat and potatoes. There was no dessert. Sweets were bad for you. They rotted your teeth. No one ate sweets in our house."

Who needed sweets? Not Peter or George Kerr. They were too busy compiling a lifetime of sweet memories from a truly golden era in American history, a large chunk of which includes the storied past of big-time college football and the spirited BC vs. Holy Cross rivalry.

A Special Breed

Holovak, Bouley, Murphy, and Natowich

Mike Holovak, Gil Bouley, Eddie Murphy and Andrew "Bubba" Natowich were superb athletes. Holovak and Bouley played for Boston College, Murphy and Natowich for Holy Cross. All four are veterans of the classic 1942 game, the shocking 55-12 Holy Cross upset win.

They helped make the Boston College-Holy Cross series one of the greatest rivalries in the history of college football. There is, of course, another great series involving New England teams—"The Game," Harvard vs. Yale. For the Brahmins it is known simply as "The Game."

But the BC-Holy Cross rivalry certainly did not play second fiddle to that or any other football rivalry in the hearts of BC and Holy Cross fans. Certainly, in the beginning of the series there was a difference in affluence, backgrounds and bloodlines.

Most of the players from the Jesuit schools were the sons of immigrants, the first generation in their families to attend college. Many came from poor but proud families who got by on a combination of towering faith in God, the unbreakable strength of the extended family unit and a heroic work ethic. Holovak, Bouley, Murphy and Natowich played college football during a golden era. There were no offensive or defensive specialists. Players played both offense and defense for pretty much the whole game. Equipment was crude compared to today's technologically-advanced helmets, plastic pads and sleek, lightweight jerseys. Recruiting was unsophisticated. There were no agents, scouting combines or huge pro salaries to cast stars in their eyes.

They played the game for two reasons: the love of football and to help secure a good education. Without a scholarship, some could not have afforded to go to college.

Holovak was the head coach at Boston College from 1951-1959. He compiled a 49-29-3 record, including a 6-3 mark against Holy Cross. He has been involved in football for more than 60 years as a player, coach, scout, personnel director and general manager. He played in the NFL for the Chicago Bears and "Papa Bear" George Halas, coached the old Boston Patriots in the AFL, and later served as general manager of the Houston Oilers. He is a member of the Boston College Hall of Fame and a football legend. More important, Holovak is a gentleman, a ferocious competitor on the field, but a classy, low key, quietly spiritual man off field. A devout Catholic, Holovak has been a daily communicant for years.

Art Graham, captain of Coach Jim Miller's 8-2 1962 Boston College team, played for Holovak on the Patriots. He was a gifted receiver who could go deep. During the 1960s, the Patriots were a homeless team short on cash. The team practiced in East Boston on a gravel pit amidst the noise of jetliners taking off and landing at Logan Airport. Players seldom enjoyed the luxury of hot water for showers after practice. They stayed at bargain basement hotels on the road and pooled their meal money, stretching it as far as possible.

Graham recalled that he always knew where he stood with Holovak. "He always gave it to you straight from the shoulder," said Graham. When the Patriots were on the road, Graham remembered that Holovak would take dinner orders on Fridays. (The AFL played on Friday nights.) "When it came to the pre-game meal, Coach Holovak knew who the Catholic players were and who the non-Catholic players were. Automatically, as if counting in his head, he would order fish for the Catholic players and beef for the non-Catholic players."

Billy Sullivan, former public relations man of the old National League Boston Braves and president of an oil company, was the Patriots owner. He had paid only $25,000 of his own money for one of the original AFL franchises in 1959. He was a BC graduate, and a public relations natural. Known for his broad smile, wit and obsession with being in the limelight, he could produce flowery press releases and thank you letters in his sleep. Sullivan honed his natural skills in public relations during a stint at Notre Dame trumpeting Coach Leahy and his legendary football teams. He deserves credit for bringing pro football back to Boston in 1960. Without him, there would be no Patriots, no New England Patriots and no World Champion New England Patriots. When the Patriots won the Super Bowl in 2001, Sullivan did not get the credit he deserved. Nevertheless, he was a lace curtain Irishman—just the opposite of Holovak, who has neither pretense nor guile, and is a modest, straight shooter.

Mike Holovak comes from Czechoslovakian blood. He grew up in Lansford, Pennsylvania, a town of about 8,000. His father, Peter, a coal miner, died when Mike was young. He and his wife, Helen, had six children, five boys and a girl. Mike was the youngest. Two older brothers also went to college. Charles Holovak graduated from the United Sates Naval Academy and was a career Navy officer. Brother Peter Holovak went to Fordham and was an outstanding running back for the Rams. Mike attended Seton Hall Prep School and it was there where he met Frank Leahy, who at the time was a line coach at Fordham. Leahy was the architect of the Seven Blocks of Granite, one of whom was the great Green Bay Packers' coach, Vince Lombardi.

Leahy recruited Holovak for Fordham. In fact, Mike expected to attend Fordham—that is until Leahy got the head coaching job at Boston College. Shortly after that, Leahy approached Holovak and offered this news to Holovak: "Everything is the same," he told a wide-eyed Holovak. "Nothing has changed. You have a football scholarship. But you won't be attending Fordham. You are going to Boston College instead!"

Leahy, let it be said, transformed the act of kissing the blarney stone into an art form. As a sophomore at BC, Holovak, helped lead the Eagles to the 1940 national championship, culminating with a 19-13 victory over Tennessee in the Sugar Bowl.

As a boy from a small Pennsylvania town, Mike might have listened to two or three bowl games on the radio. So, playing in the Sugar Bowl before 73,181 people for the national championship was about as good as it gets. "That was a big thrill," Mike remembered, "the kind of thing that would make you want to pinch yourself. Prior to that, the closest I ever got to a game like that was reading about it in a newspaper."

Today, Holovak has seen the years roll by. "It happened so long ago that nobody talks about it anymore," Holovak said, with a hint of acceptance mixed with sadness in his voice.

Asked to compare coaches, teams and eras, Holovak is cautious not wanting to offend anyone. He did say this about Leahy: "He was a great coach. With the record that he compiled, it would be difficult for anyone to follow someone like that." Holovak admired and respected Leahy. As a coach he said that Leahy instilled tremendous confidence in his players and his teams. Unlike Holovak, he was loaded with charisma, which was part of his legend and the aura that surrounded him.

Holovak was a player's player. All business on the football field, the kind of competitor who laced up the shoulder pads, put on the helmet and went to work on the gridiron. "You tried to do your job as best you could," he said. "What I remember most is that we had good teams back then. We went into games thinking we could beat anybody."

During the war, Holovak was a physical fitness instructor in the military. Throughout his life, he has kept himself in impeccable physical condition, maintaining his weight at or below the 195 pounds he carried as a player. He was a habitual jogger, running laps around a circular track after practice as the sun set. Dr. Tom O'Connor, celebrated author of many books, including *Boston Catholics*, and University Historian at Boston College, ran into him during boot camp. "He could run the troops right into the sand," Dr. O'Connor said, remembering PT training along the shores of New Jersey beaches.

During the 1930s and 1940s, the lives of the best athletes were often intertwined. The athletes on rival college football teams, more often than not, knew each other and were friends off the field. Holovak and Murphy, the great Holy Cross end, are a case in point. Both attended Seton Hall Prep. "Mike is a great guy," said Murphy. "We lived on the same floor in the dormitory at Seton Hall Prep and we hung around together."

With Holovak's older brother Peter, a star running back for Fordham, Murphy recounted how he and Holovak would get free tickets to watch the maroon-clad Fordham Rams play their home games at the Polo Grounds in New York City.

Leahy, in fact, tried to recruit Murphy for Boston College. "By that time, I had already committed to attend Holy Cross," recalled Murphy. "Leahy got to me too late."

Murphy comes from Lowell, which has turned out many great athletes over the years. In fact, during that era, the Greater Lowell and Greater Lawrence area produced many star athletes, including a long list of Holy Cross and BC greats. At the heart of the area's legendary sports past was the storied high school football rivalry pitting Lowell against Lawrence, an annual battle that attracted standing room only Thanksgiving Day crowds as large as 15,000 or more.

Murphy was a superb all-around athlete at Lowell High who was highly recruited by many of the top name college football powerhouses. When he graduated from high school, he could have gone to the college of his choice. He wound up at Holy Cross, where he played big-time college football and received a first-class education studying the classics.

At Mount St. James, Murphy, who wore number 35, became an All-American back and a member of the Holy Cross Hall of Fame. A few hours after Holy Cross' stunning victory over Boston College in 1942, Murphy received notification that he had been selected to play in the prestigious East-West Shrine Game in California. That alone was a big thrill for the only son (he had a sister) of Joseph D. Murphy, a women's wear designer for a Lowell textile company. By the time Murphy graduated from college, World War II was raging and he was already an officer in the Marine Corps. In fact, the U.S. Marine Corps brass had his orders switched so he could play in the East-West game. As a result, Eddie, who was a captain and a combat veteran who fought at Okinawa and participated in other key battles in the Pacific, served with many Marines from the West Coast. Numbered among the men he served with were big-name Hollywood stars such as Tyrone Power, who was a Marine pilot, and Sterling Hayden. In fact, he said that at one time his bunk mate was a man named Will Price, who at the time was the husband of actress and Irish-born beauty Maureen O'Hara. Price was one of the directors of the movie classic *Gone With the Wind*. "He was a dialogue director if I remember correctly," said Murphy. "He was a good guy."

After the war, Murphy briefly played pro football for the Pittsburgh Steelers, but he quit after one exhibition game. "You didn't make any money playing pro football in those days," he commented. "I had just gotten married and when I had a chance to get a job I took it." That job was as a teacher-coach at Dracut High School. Murphy, a member of the state football coaches Hall of Fame, was the head football coach at

Dracut High for 48 years. I will always remember his induction because he and my father, Walter, who coached at Concord High and St. Bernard's in Fitchburg, were enshrined in the state football coaches Hall of Fame on the same day. The induction ceremony, in fact, was held at Boston College. During a coaching career that spanned almost five decades, Murphy led the Dracut High Middies, a school that outfitted its athletic teams in the same pale blue color worn by UCLA, Columbia and the University of Rhode Island, to 248 wins.

Eddie and his wife Dorothy, a former nurse, were married on July 20, 1946. The couple had four boys. October 2002 was a particularly painful time for the Murphys. I had the privilege of speaking with Eddie just a few days after the funeral of his son Brian, who had cancer and left a wife and three sons behind. Like the Murphys, Mike Holovak also lost a child. His daughter, Terri, was killed in a tragic automobile accident on the night she graduated from high school.

During happier times, Murphy experienced the thrill of seeing two of his sons, Dennis and David, follow him to Holy Cross and play football for the Crusaders. Dennis, a versatile player who could do almost anything on the football field, played for the Crusaders during the era of the Hepatitis outbreak in 1969. During that ill-fated season, all but two (a 13-0 loss to Harvard and a 38-6 loss to Dartmouth) of Coach Bill Whitton's squad's games were cancelled. That season could have totally wiped out (and almost did) Holy Cross football. The fact that it did not is a tremendous credit to the college and the resiliency of its administrators, coaches and athletes.

David Murphy, a second son, was a nifty and cerebral option quarterback for the Crusaders during the early 1980s. A third son, Danny, also was an excellent college football player. He played for the Northeastern University Huskies.

Murphy's teammate, Natowich, comes from a Ukrainian background. Way back, his family immigrated to this country one person at a time. "One person came over first, one sister and then another," he explained. "Each got a job, saved money and then sent for someone else."

As a child, he was known around the family home as "Little Bub." Natowich was born on December 11, 1918, and by the time he started walking, his family began referring to him as "Bubba." After that, his nickname stuck. Of course, in school, his teachers called him by his baptized name, Andrew. To tease him, his buddies used to say, "Hi, A-n-d-r-e-w" and then giggle and point fingers at him. Regularly, he said he would complain to his mother by saying, "They are calling me names at school; they are calling me Andrew and I don't like it."

Natowich hails from Ansonia, Connecticut. His father, Philip, died in the flu epidemic of 1918, just a few days before he was born. His mother, Elizabeth, a true heroine like so many of her generation, quickly wiped the tears away, pulled her apron tightly around her waist and did whatever it took to raise her large family. Looking back, Natowich remembers the strict discipline that was enforced at Holy Cross. "You got up and went to 7 o'clock Mass every morning," he said. "If you wanted to eat any meals, you had to wear a shirt, tie and a sports jacket into the dining hall. You also had to write a letter home to your mother at least once each week."

Even before the 1942 season began, Natowich remembered that the Holy Cross football team got a head start on the bonding process, the all-important task of building team chemistry. First-year coach Anthony "Ank" Scanlon was a wealthy businessman. He owned a factory that produced the fireproof material asbestos. "He'd think nothing of handing Captain Eddie Murphy $400 in cash and tell him to buy whatever was needed for a big team party," recalled Natowich. That might not pass muster with the NCAA today.

Prior to the beginning of the season, the Crusaders ate thick juicy steaks and held a team party after renting a cabin on the shores of one of the many beautiful lakes and picturesque wooded areas not far from the Holy Cross campus. In addition, it was not uncommon for the team to hold its pre- and post-game meals at a Worcester eatery known as "Cosgrove's Chop House."

Speaking of violations, Natowich said that at least a few teammates were tempted to take the $400 given to them by Coach Scanlon and wager the money at a race track in hopes of making some easy money. However, he said that rational thinking won out and the money was spent on the team party. Imagine what would have happened if the economics majors on the team had prevailed on their teammates to wager the $400 on the horses? Natowich said that the players were given free tickets for home games. Sometimes, he said, the varsity players would sell their tickets for $2.50 each to pick up extra pocket money.

Although he served in the Army during the war, Natowich had "bad ears" which prevented him from going overseas and seeing any combat duty. He ended up serving in special services and was stationed in Buffalo, New York. He was a corporal and he remembered that Buffalo was the country's fifth largest producer of munitions for the war effort. After the war, Natowich settled in Brattleboro, Vermont where he was a teacher-coach at the local high school, retiring in 1974. Today, the football field at the public high school in Brattleboro is named after him. He has carved a good life for himself and his family in southern Vermont. When he was contacted, the first words out of his mouth were, "We have plumbing and newspapers up here, too, you know. I don't live in any Hickville! Vermont is a great place to live."

He taught social studies, coached football, basketball and baseball for twenty years. A self-taught landscape expert, he retired to work on the football field named after him. When he first started coaching, the local high school athletic teams did not have a nickname. Three nicknames were proposed to the student council: the Whiz Kids, the Organ Grinders and the personally very flattering Natowichmen. The nickname selected was Organ Grinders, a tribute to the area's landmark industry, Estey pipe organs, which were produced by the Estey Organ Company.

Pound for pound, Boston College's behemoth tackle, Gil Bouley, may have been the best as well as the most feared football player on the field when BC and Holy Cross squared off in 1942. "Bouley almost ended up at Holy Cross," said Natowich. "He was a big star in high school and all the top name colleges were after him."

Incidentally, Bouley's brother Larry, a speedy back who once was clocked at 9.8 seconds in the 100 yard dash, was also on that 1942 BC squad. Later, he transferred to the University of Georgia, earned a master's degree and became a high school principal in New London, Connecticut.

Murphy, after all these years, still remembers the respect that Gil Bouley commanded on the football field. "He was aggressive, a real force," Murphy said. "To beat BC, we had to neutralize his effectiveness along the line of scrimmage."

Consequently, the Crusaders played a cat and mouse game with Bouley. Holy Cross allowed Bouley to penetrate and then trap blocked and double teamed him before he reached the point of attack.

Bouley, who comes from a French-Canadian background, grew up in Connecticut. His father, who was a barber in Jewett City, was a superb semipro baseball player, an outfielder who could fly. In those days, the Blackstone Valley region was a huge manufacturing area. Practically every company fielded a baseball team and many of the players on those teams, with a little luck, could have played in the big leagues. Leagues and teams thrived and baseball was truly the national pastime. During the first 50 years of the 20th century, the most popular American sports were baseball, college football, boxing and horse racing. Bouley's father belonged to that storied legion of great semipro baseball players.

Like many of his fellow college athletes, Bouley served in the military during the war. He took flight training with the Army Air Corps. He was just one training flight away from receiving his wings when the war ended. "At the time, I remember how disappointed I was," he said. After the war, Bouley played six seasons of pro football with the Rams, first in Cleveland and later in Los Angeles. Later, he was Holovak's line coach at BC. With the Rams, he played with a string of great players such as Bob Waterfield, Tom Fears and Elroy "Crazy Legs" Hirsch. He and Hirsch were roommates. Waterfield, who was married to buxom actress and pinup girl Jane Russell, was one of the first postwar glamour boy quarterbacks in the NFL.

In that epic 1942 BC-Holy Cross football game at Fenway Park, Bouley admitted that George Connor, the former Holy Cross and later Notre Dame star, got the better of him. However, a few years later, when the two squared off in the pros, Connor playing for the Bears and Bouley for the Rams, Bouley got a measure of revenge. "I did a great job on him in one game against the Bears," said Bouley, speaking more out of pride than conceit.

Bouley, like many of the pro football players back then, played both offense and defense. There were no specialists during the cradle years of pro football. Bouley said that the most money he ever made in a single season in the NFL was $14,500. He also said that Waterfield and Hirsch, two superstars, never made more than $22,000 and $17,500 respectively.

Today, Bouley detests the holding that college and NFL lineman are allowed to get away with. "It's not the game," he said. "That's wrestling not football." Bouley also experienced the thrill of seeing his son, Bob, follow him to Boston College and play football for the Eagles. The Baltimore Colts drafted the younger Bouley, who was an offensive tackle, but an injury ended his career. As a collegian, he was awarded the prestigious Thomas F. Scanlan Memorial Trophy, which the BC Varsity Club awards to the senior football player who best combines scholarship with leadership and athletic accomplishment. Today, Robert Bouley is a well known and highly respected attorney.

In 1942, the Boston College-Holy Cross series produced one of the most unforgettable upsets in the history of college football. The game today is a distant memory, but the stories surrounding the athletes, the coaches and the rival Jesuit colleges they represented abound, a natural consequence of a classic college football rivalry.

There was no official game film taken of the 1942 BC-Holy Cross football game. However, Murphy and others have gotten their hands on copies of the grainy black and white newsreel clip of the game, the one that was shown in movie theaters across the country after the game. It was found hidden in the archives at the University of Southern California.

For this writer, the worst catastrophe in Boston sports lore was not the trading of George Herman "Babe" Ruth to the Yankees. It was either the Boston Braves moving to Milwaukee in 1953, or the official ending of the Boston College-Holy Cross football series, one of the greatest college football rivalries ever—take your pick.

Bill Swiacki

The Catch

AT MARINO'S BARBER SHOP IN SOUTHBRIDGE, MASSACHUSETTS, A sleepy little town about twenty minutes by car from Worcester, everyone knows about "the Catch."

The same is true at the Polish-American Club and even at Applebee's Restaurant in nearby Sturbridge, where the athlete who made "the Catch" is featured, in photos and newspaper articles, on a wall of the restaurant reserved for "hometown heroes."

"He was a great athlete, starting when he was in high school and then at Holy Cross," said Jim Marino, who has been the proprietor of Marino's Barber Shop, located at 50 Elm Street, for the past thirty-nine years. "But it was 'the Catch' that really made him famous when he played for Columbia."

At Marino's Barber Shop, you can sit back, relax, get your ears trimmed and marvel at a black and white photograph of "the Catch" hanging on a wall.

"The Catch" was actually made in October of 1947, in New York City, twenty-one days after another unforgettable athlete, Al Gionfriddo, of the Brooklyn Dodgers, produced his own "great grab" when he robbed the "Yankee Clipper," Joe DiMaggio, of the New York Yankees, of a home run with a miraculous catch in the sixth inning of the sixth game of the 1947 World Series at Yankee Stadium. Gionfriddo's circus catch of DiMaggio's 415-foot blast with two runners on base preserved an 8-6 Brooklyn win and set up a winner-take-all game seven, which the Yankees won, 5-2.

"The Catch" was made, not in a baseball game, and certainly not in a World Series. It was made in a college football game—not just any college football game, but in one of the most memorable college football games ever played.

The date was October 25, 1947. Army vs. Columbia. Coach Earl "Red" Blaik's West Point Cadets, unbeaten in thirty-two straight games—since the Navy game which was played in November of 1943—marched smartly and confidently into New York to battle Coach Lou Little's Lions. With a record of 2-2, Columbia was a huge underdog.

As expected, Army led 20-14 in the fourth quarter. However, as the game clock wound down and darkness began to settle over the city, the Lions let out a roar by mounting a game-winning drive, highlighted by "the Catch."

On the game's biggest play, Columbia quarterback Gene Rossides passed to Bill Swiacki, the pride of Southbridge and a former Holy Cross football player. Swiacki, fully stretched out after leaving his feet, made a diving, fingertip grab of Rossides' pass. His tumbling reception, forever known as "the Catch" in college football lore, gave the Lions a first down on the Army one-yard line. Columbia scored on the next play, kicked the deciding extra point and shortly thereafter one of the most dramatic upsets in college football history, Columbia's shocking 21-20 win, went into the books. It triggered a wild celebration with thousands of fans storming the field, while waving baby blue and white Columbia banners.

William Adam Swiacki was a graduate of Mary E. Wells High School in Southbridge, graduating in the Class of 1941. Today, the trophy case at the high school, renamed Southbridge High School, honors him as one of the school's greatest athletes.

He was a three-sport standout. In baseball, the 6-foot-2, 195-pound Swiacki was a catcher with big league baseball potential. In fact, the Red Sox wanted to sign him, but he opted to play pro football after graduating from Columbia.

In Southbridge sports history, Swiacki, John Fitzgerald and Gene Desautels are three of the town's most famous athletes. Fitzgerald played football at Boston College and then for the Dallas Cowboys. He played in the NFL for thirteen seasons. Desautels was a catcher for thirteen seasons in the big leagues. He hit .291 for the Boston Red Sox in 108 games in 1938. He also played for the Tigers, Indians and A's during his big league career.

Swiacki entered the College of the Holy Cross in the fall of 1941. He played two seasons of football for the Crusaders. As a sophomore, he was a left end on the upstart Holy Cross football team that shocked Boston College 55-12 in 1942.

In March of 1943, Swiacki entered the military. He was a second lieutenant in the Army Air Corps during World War II and served six months as a navigator in the European theatre of the war. He played on the 3rd Army Air Force football team in 1945 and he was discharged from the military in 1946.

In the fall of '46, he entered Columbia. Swiacki was one of three football greats to transfer from Holy Cross to other colleges after the war. The other two were George Connor, who transferred to Notre Dame, and Fritz Barzilauskas, who transferred to Yale.

In the huge upset over Army, Swiacki caught ten passes in the game. In a *New York Times* story, written by Red Smith, and published after Swiacki's untimely death on July 6, 1976, Smith quoted another writer, Bill Heinz of the *New York Sun*, who wrote after the big win, "Columbia had a man named Swiacki who catches passes the way the rest of us catch the common cold."

In 1947, Swiacki was a first team All-American for Columbia and he finished eighth in the Heisman Trophy balloting. He was so popular in the Greater Worcester area that legions of fans from the area where he grew up hit the road and traveled to places like New Haven, Connecticut, to watch their hometown hero play for Columbia against Yale.

Swiacki, Rossides, Lou Kusserow, and, of course, Coach Lou Little are all part of a golden era in the history of Columbia football. Little, a College Football Hall of Fame coach, played college football for the University of Pennsylvania Quakers. In appearance, Little looked more like a stuffy banker than a football coach. Short and stout, he wore rimless glasses and he was known for his elaborate wardrobe of expensive, exquisitely tailored suits. The Leominster, Massachusetts-born coach also was a big-time celebrity. He often was seen at Toots Shore's in New York and he rubbed elbows with starlets, politicians and sports celebrities. At Yankee Stadium, he often was seen chatting with Joe McCarthy, the manager of the Bronx Bombers. As a coach, he was known as a brilliant strategist who treated his players as if they were family.

In 1934, it was Little who engineered Columbia's shocking 7-0 victory over Stanford in the Rose Bowl.

Following the 1947 season, in numerous reports, Little called Swiacki, "not only the best receiver in the country, but the best receiver I have ever seen or coached."

Swiacki, a business administration major, graduated early from Columbia, completing enough credits to graduate in February of 1948. He played for the New York Giants (1948-'50) and the Detroit Lions (1951-'52). He, along with Doak Walker, Bobby Layne and Leon Hart, were all members of the Lions 1952 NFL Championship team. During his NFL career, he caught 139 passes, good for 1,883 and 18 touchdowns. Later, he worked as a scout for the Lions and as an assistant coach for the Giants and the Los Angeles Rams. He also was the head coach of the Toronto Argonauts of the Canadian Football League in 1955 and 1956.

Swiacki, who was married and the father of two boys, returned to Southbridge after he left football. At one time, he owned and operated a combination real estate and insurance business on Main Street. Dorothy Aucoin worked for him in the real estate business. She has fond memories of the man. "He was a wonderful man," she said. "I can't say enough good things about Bill. He was kind and everyone respected him."

Mrs. Aucoin, during the three years she worked for him, remembered that Swiacki was a detail-oriented perfectionist who approached business matters with the same intensity he exhibited on the football field.

"I can see why he was such a great athlete because he drove himself in business just as hard as people said he pushed himself to be the best in sports," she said.

For Swiacki, that inner drive proved to be a double-edged sword. It propelled him to greatness in athletics and it also mysteriously led to his demise. On July 6, 1976, the college football great took his own life with a self-inflicted gunshot to the abdomen. He was fifty-three.

Swiacki, the boy from Southbridge, one of six children born into the family of a factory worker, is a legend in his hometown area. A model citizen who served as chairman of the school committee, president of the local chamber of commerce and director of a national association of realtors, people remember and still talk about him today. He will forever be the star athlete and hall of famer who entered Holy Cross, left school to serve in the military, and then after the war gained even greater fame playing end for the Columbia University Lions.

In the Greater Worcester area, when you mention, "the Catch," people are not talking about Dwight Clark's leaping catch of a Joe Montana pass in the 1981 NFL playoffs that gave the San Francisco 49ers a thrilling 28-27 victory over the Dallas Cowboys in the NFC championship game. No indeed.

"The Catch" they still talk about is native son Bill Swiacki's clutch pass reception against mighty Army on the day Columbia staged one of the biggest upsets in the long and storied history of college football.

Art Donovan

Weight Was Not a Problem

HE IS THE MOST FAMOUS AND MOST LOVED "FATSO" IN THE HISTORY of football. At birth, some have said, he was so big that when the doctor gave him the standard whack on the butt, he looked the attending physician straight in the eye and slapped him back.

Arthur J. Donovan, Jr. was born on June 5, 1925 at home in the Bronx, New York, all sixteen pounds of him. He was a big boy then and he's a big boy now, almost 80 years later. He was a great football player, and he is a natural comedian. Without even trying, the man is flat out funny. If you want to laugh, just read his book, *Fatso: Football When Men Were Really Men*, which he co-authored with Bob Drury. It is hilarious.

Commenting on his fondness for beer, baloney, kosher salami and all the cold cuts he can get his big mitts on, Donovan brags, "I'm a light eater. When it gets light, I start eating."

Donovan played football at Boston College from 1946 to 1949. In the pros, he played with the New York Yanks, the Dallas Texans, briefly with the Cleveland Browns and with the Baltimore Colts from 1953 to 1961. He was All-Pro four straight years from 1954 to 1957 and he played in five NFL Pro-Bowls. On August 8, 1968 he was inducted into the Pro Football Hall of Fame in Canton, Ohio.

A defensive tackle, he played on the Colts' 1958 and 1959 NFL Championship teams, two of the finest pro teams ever assembled. He also

103

was part of a defensive front four, along with Gino Marchetti, Gene "Big Daddy" Lipscomb and Don Joyce, considered among the best defensive line units ever.

The Colts' share for winning their first championship in 1958 was $4,500. During his NFL career, Donovan never made more than $17,500 in a single season. He calls today's NFL players "overpaid and spoiled." He also blames the television announcers for fabricating myths about today's players and not telling the truth. "When I played," he said, "if you broke a leg and a bone broke the skin, they taped it up and you went back into the game. The players I played with and against were tough."

After graduating from Mount St. Michael's High School in 1942, Donovan headed to Notre Dame on a football scholarship, although he would just as soon forget the experience. The city kid from New York, "Da boy from da Bronx" who wanted to attend Fordham and follow in the footsteps of his college football hero Alex Wojciechowicz, did not fit in at Notre Dame. During the war, he left school and served in the Marines. He fought with a machine gun squad in battles on Okinawa and Guam.

Even on the front lines, his prodigious appetite for food nearly landed him in the brink. While unloading a Navy ship, big Art swiped thirty pounds of Spam and got caught. Fortunately, the adjunct, Marine Major Joseph McFadden, a former college quarterback at Georgetown, went easy on the big Irish lug from Manhattan. McFadden was from nearby New Jersey and he ordered Donovan, as punishment, to eat the entire case of Spam, which Art gleefully devoured in six days. In the book, Donovan recounted the incident. "The cooks put the Spam in batter and I ate all of it. I was eating Spam all day long. To this day I still have a sweet spot in my heart for Spam."

Following the war, Donovan turned to a wealthy businessmen who had connections to help him select a college because he had no intention of returning to Notre Dame. He considered Brown University in Providence, Rhode Island, but ended up at Boston College after BC Coach Denny Myers offered him a scholarship. He was the first recruit from the Bronx to play football at Boston College. At the time, his focus was crystal clear. "Most people go to college to study and get a good education," he said, speaking as a street-smart philosopher. "I went to college to play football."

Despite his lack of interest in academics, he majored in Education and passed his courses. In the book, he recalled what one Jesuit history professor told him. "Arthur," said the priest, "I'm going to tell you one thing you have to do to get by here. Don't cut my classes. You cut my class, I will flunk you. As long as you come to my class, you are going to learn something, at least through osmosis."

For four years, although he popped many more beer cans than he opened books, he faithfully attended classes and eventually graduated. He lived with other returning veterans in double-decker type Army barracks that BC constructed on campus. He played football and off the field he enjoyed the time of his life. "I loved everything about Boston and I hated to leave," he said.

In football, he played both offensive guard and tackle as well as several spots along the defensive line. He said that teammate Butch Songin was the best all-around athlete he ever played with. "He could do anything and everything," Donovan said, about an athlete who was a gifted quarterback as well as an All-American college hockey player. Songin, who hailed from Walpole, Massachusetts, was a star in the Canadian Football League. Later, when he was over forty, he quarterbacked the Boston Patriots during the early days of the old AFL.

Unlike others, Donovan said he got along fine with Coach Myers. "I was grateful that he gave me a chance to play," said Art, one of only seven former BC football players to have their jerseys retired. The others are Lou Urban, Charlie O'Rourke, Mike Holovak, Tony Thurman, Bill Flynn, and Gene Goodreault. Doug Flutie (22) and Mike Ruth (68) are the only former BC greats to have their numbers retired.

During his two seasons as a starter (1948 and 1949) he played on BC teams that posted 5-2-2 and 4-4-1 records. The Eagles nipped Holy Cross 21-20 in 1948 and then crushed the Crusaders 76-0 in 1949. In the '49 game, Ed Petela led the rout by scoring 34 points, a BC record for the most points in a single game that still stands. Al Cannava shared the spotlight against Holy Cross in '49. He rushed for 229 yards and scored four touchdowns. Donovan and Cannava devised their own way of communicating once the Eagles broke the huddle. Donovan would grunt into a three-point stance along the line, eye the defense and then signal by pointing with a finger behind his ample rump which way he would drive block the defender lined up opposite him, either left or right. Cannava would take the handoff, follow the cue, look for an opening and burst through the hole in the defense created by Donovan's wide-body block at the point of attack. Donovan had this to say about the 76-0 rout over Holy Cross: "We beat them that badly and we didn't even score a point in the fourth quarter." Despite the lopsided score in the one game, he said the Holy Cross players were "tough guys." He singled out one Crusader in particular, Tom Kelleher, an end who later became an NFL official. "I distinctly remember that Kelleher was a good football player, a real solid end."

During the winter, Donovan remembers a trip to Worcester to watch a BC-Holy Cross basketball game, which the nationally ranked Crusaders, who won the NCAA title in 1946-1947, dominated. "We could never compete with them in basketball," said Donovan. As for the game in Worcester that Donovan attended, he recalled that he and several of his friends squirmed quietly in their seats as Holy Cross rolled up the score. Seated behind them was a row filled with Jesuit faculty members from Holy Cross, cheering wildly. Finally, one of Donovan's buddies, a fellow Boston College football lineman wearing a maroon BC sweater, couldn't take it anymore. "How could I ever forget it?" said big Art, laughing as he spoke. "One of the guys I was with turned around and in a loud voice told the priests, 'That's enough. Why don't you loud mouths sit down and shut up!' " Art denies that he was the culprit who attempted to silence the Jesuits from Holy Cross as they cheered on their college basketball team.

Interestingly, Donovan recalled that two of the toughest scrimmages from his college football days were against Harvard. "We scrimmaged them two weeks in a row one year," he remembered. "Both were brutal, real tough. All that proves is that a football player is a football player regardless of where or for what team he plays."

Donovan grew up a long way, geographically and culturally, from Harvard. The family dwelling was located about forty blocks from Yankee Stadium. His father, Arthur J. Donovan, Sr., like his father before him, was the boxing instructor at the New York Athletic Club. Art Sr. was seldom home, except on Sundays, but when he was home, he was king of his own castle. He was a patriarchal Irishman who seldom showed emotion but dutifully wore a shirt and tie when he took out the garbage. Art's mother Mary was responsible for raising both Art and his sister Joan. Donovan expresses great love for both his parents. When his mother was dying, one of her final requests was to have a lobster dinner and Donovan, then a star for the Colts, rushed home from Baltimore and arranged for his mother to have twin lobsters delivered to her hospital room.

The elder Donovan, a member of the Boxing Hall of Fame, was the top boxing referee of his era. He was the third man in the ring for nineteen of Joe Louis' heavyweight title bouts, including both fights against the hard-hitting German, Max Schmeling. In the first bout, June 19, 1936, Schmeling, the Nazi hero and Adolph Hitler favorite, knocked out Louis in the twelfth round, handing him his first defeat. Two years later, on June 22, 1938, in the rematch Louis destroyed Schmeling, knocking him out in less than a round. At the end of the fight, Schmeling was helpless, and if Donovan hadn't gotten between the two fighters, Louis might have killed him.

The elder Donovan discouraged his only son from getting into boxing, which was perfectly fine with big Art, who said, "I never liked getting rapped in the face anyway." When Art was about to leave home for the first time, his father gave him two pieces of advice. "Pick your friends wisely, and if you get a tattoo, get it on the bottom of your feet so no one will be able to see it."

Art probably would have made a heck of a heavyweight fighter, an Irish version of "Two Ton" Tony Galento. Although he weighed anywhere between 275 and 310 pounds, he had quick feet, excellent hand-eye coordination (he could hit a baseball a country mile) and he was plenty tough. His "tub of jello" physique was deceiving. Donovan was the first of the Baltimore Colts from the fabulous Johnny Unitas era to make it into the pro football Hall of Fame. Like Unitas, he is one of the most cherished figures in the history of Baltimore sports.

Donovan credits Weeb Ewbank, his coach with the Colts, for helping to make him a Hall of Famer. The two shared a love-hate relationship, particularly when it came to big Art's propensity for packing on the pounds. When Ewbank died, Donovan and many of the former Colts attended his funeral in Ohio.

Donovan paid his old coach the ultimate compliment after the funeral by doing what he does best. "We paid our own tribute to a great coach by sitting around together, drinking beer and telling Weeb stories," said Donovan, old number 70 in Baltimore Colts' blue, silver and white. Arthur J. Donovan, Jr. is an American original.

Ed King

The Governor Was a Tackle

EVEN THE POLITICAL CRONIES AND PUNDITS, JUST BY LOOKING AT HIS strong, square jaw, knew that he had been a football player. Edward J. King, Governor of the Commonwealth of Massachusetts from 1979 to 1983, was indeed an outstanding football player, both in college and in the pros.

King graduated from Boston College High School and went on to Boston College. He played two seasons of varsity football for the Eagles (1946-1947) and three years in the pros, two with the Buffalo Bills of the old All-American Conference (1948 and 1949) and one with the Baltimore Colts of the National Football League (1950).

In college, he played for Coach Denny Myers, who coached the Eagles in 1941 and 1942 and from 1946 to 1950. King said Myers was a coach who "was good for the players. He stuck up for the guys." Myers' career record at BC was 35-27-4. King was a tough, rawboned tackle. In his playing days, the six-foot King weighed 222 pounds.

At BC, he played with some great names from the past, players such as Art Donovan, Art Spinney, Will DeRosa, Joe Diminick, Jack Farrell (whose brother Bob played for Holy Cross at the same time), Mario (Yoyo) Gianelli, Ernie Stautner, Don Panciera, Robert "Red" Mangene and Al "Crazy Legs" Cannava. King played left tackle and Spinney played left end. "Art Spinney was a tremendous two-way football player. Art was known for his guts. He was one heck of a pass catcher, too," the former governor said.

Despite playing a murderous schedule, Boston College racked up a string of impressive victories in 1946 and 1947, beating Michigan State, 34-20; Villanova, 14-12; Alabama, 13-7; Clemson, 32-22; and Kansas State, 49-13. There was only one problem: the Eagles could not defeat their Jesuit arch-rivals, Holy Cross; losing 13-6 in 1946 and 20-6 in 1947. "My sophomore year, we beat an Alabama team that had played in the Rose Bowl the previous season," the former governor said. "But we couldn't beat Holy Cross, although we played a much tougher schedule. It was like they were hiding in the bushes, just waiting for us. Gunning for us. Wham! Bang!"

Boston College finished 6-3-0 in 1946 and 5-4-0 in 1947. Holy Cross, playing primarily an Eastern schedule against colleges such as Brown, Colgate, Dartmouth, Harvard and Columbia, wound up 5-4-0 in 1946 and 4-4-2 in 1947, although the Crusaders tuned up for the 1947 game against BC by demolishing the Fordham Rams, 48-0.

Former Governor King was a two-sport standout at Boston College. In baseball, he was a catcher. Just as he never experienced a football victory over Holy Cross, the baseball teams on which he played at BC came up empty or struck out against the Crusaders. "We used to play a three-game series against Holy Cross every spring," he explained. "I don't think we beat them one time. Not once. It was constant futility. What stands out most in my memory is that Holy Cross had a pair of dominant left-handers, two pitchers who could really throw hard."

During his first two seasons in the pros, King and his Buffalo Bills made it to the championship game of the All-American Conference. They lost both title games to the powerhouse Cleveland Browns, a club that dominated the old league before joining the NFL. Two of the offensive stars for the Buffalo Bills were George Ratterman, a former Notre Dame quarterback who later backed up Otto Graham on the Browns, and Chet Mutryn, a former college star at Xavier. Mutryn's nephew, Scott Mutryn, played college football for BC from 1994 to 1998.

King said that he was paid a $500 bonus to sign with the Buffalo Bills. "That was big money in those days," he remarked. He also said that the most he ever made playing pro football was $6,600, a substantial yearly salary in 1950, but mere pocket money for today's millionaire professional athletes.

During his only season with the Colts, he played along the defensive line with two of his former Boston College teammates—Donovan and Spinney. King played nose tackle, Donovan lined up at defensive tackle, and Spinney was positioned at defensive end. The Colts later switched Spinney to offensive guard and he went on to become a perennial All-Pro offensive lineman. Both Donovan and Spinney were fixtures for the Colts in 1958 during the team's championship run, culminated by a sudden death 23-17 victory over the New York Giants in the championship game at Yankee Stadium. That game, considered the greatest pro game of all-time, ushered in the modern era of pro football and the National Football League as we know it today.

Edward J. King grew up in East Boston. His father was a "starter" for the MBTA. When he was a teenager his family moved from East Boston to Newton, "directly across the street from Boston College in Chestnut Hill," he pointed out. At Boston College, he majored in mathematics. After his football career was over, he studied accounting and finance at Bentley College in Waltham, Massachusetts. "I guess that means I can count, that I can add," he said, poking fun at himself.

King and his late wife, Jody, were married for 43 years and the couple had two children. One of his sons, Timothy Douglas, was named after one of his heroes, General Douglas MacArthur.

Reflecting on his undergraduate years at Boston College, he said he has always marveled at the overall excellence of his own Jesuit college educational experience. For him, he said that it was the presence of the Jesuits themselves that made his college journey extra special and elevated it to a higher level. "The Jesuit Fathers were always around. Back then, there were so many of them. You would see them in groups of three or four or five walking on the campus reading their breviary. They were so available. They really cared about you and they always made time for you. It was a great atmosphere for a young person to go to college."

King said that his Jesuit education was the foundation that helped define his values and sharpened his outlook on the world. At an early age, he said that a call to service motivated many of his career decisions. Before entering the political arena, he spent sixteen years working for the Massachusetts Port Authority and became its chief executive officer.

In the 1978 Democratic gubernatorial primary, he defeated Michael Dukakis and he went on to defeat Republican Frank Hatch to win the corner office at the State House. "In the long history of the Commonwealth of Massachusetts, I became the sixty-sixth governor," he said. "The sixty-six include a number who served more than one term. For example, John Volpe served three terms. So, when you think about it, that's not many people, a very select group . . . Serving as governor is genuinely a special honor and privilege that I enjoyed immensely and for which I thank God."

The Fifties

1950: Holy Cross 32-14

1951: BC 19-14

1952: Holy Cross 21-7

1953: BC 6-0

1954: BC 31-13

1955: BC 26-7

1956: Holy Cross 7-0

1957: Holy Cross 14-0

1958: BC 26-8

1959: BC 14-0

DURING THE 1950S, EVERYONE WAS SHOUTING "OKLAHOMA" ACROSS the football plains. Coach Bud Wilkinson's powerful Sooners mounted a record 47-game winning streak. Notre Dame, on Dick Lynch's end run, ended the streak in 1957, 7-0. Dick Kazmaier of Princeton won the Heisman Trophy in 1951. Coaches Clarence "Biggie" Munn and Hugh Duffy Daugherty turned Michigan State into a college football monster. On December 2, 1950, trailing BC, 14-0, lightning fast Johnny Turco, a Holy Cross all-time great, broke a kick off return 97 yards for a touchdown sparking the Crusaders to a thrilling 32-14 comeback victory over their arch-rivals. In 1950 Dr. Eddie Anderson returned to Holy Cross as head football coach. In 1951, Mike Holovak, an all-time BC great, became the head coach at his alma mater, compiling a 49-29-3 record during nine seasons. BC's Alumni Stadium opened in September, 1957. However, Navy sprayed water on the dedication game, trouncing the Eagles, 46-6. During the decade of the 1950s, BC held a 6-4-0 advantage over Holy Cross.

– 1953 –

A blocked punt set up the game's only touchdown, powering Boston College to a 6-0 victory over Holy Cross at Fenway Park.

In the second quarter, with Holy Cross backed up under the shadow of its own goal post, Boston College linemen Frank Marr and Al St. Pierre collaborated to block Henry Lemire's punt in the end zone. BC took over inside the one-yard line. Holy Cross stiffened on defense and stacked up the first two rushes for no gain, but on the third try Dick Charlton slammed into the end zone for the game's only touchdown.

In the game, BC, led by 228-pound tackle John Murphy, held Holy Cross to only four yards on the ground.

Tom "Chick" Murphy ran wild on special teams for Holy Cross. After faking a reverse, he turned in a dazzling 49-yard punt return. Dick Gagliardi, the BC punter, prevented a touchdown by breaking through a convoy of blockers and tackling the elusive Murphy.

The game was a rock 'em, sock 'em affair. John Stephans, a sophomore, was the third quarterback Holy Cross used in the game after two others, Bill Haley and Don Jolie, were forced to the sidelines with injuries.

Holy Cross ended the 1953 season with a 5-5 record including wins over Dartmouth, Colgate, Bucknell, Boston University and Fordham.

Boston College, under third-year coach Mike Holovak, finished 5-3-1 with victories over Fordham, Xavier, Wake Forest, Detroit and Holy Cross.

– 1957 –

Heavy rain turned Fitton Field into a mud bowl and spoiled an expected shootout between two brilliant quarterbacks, Tommy Greene of Holy Cross and Don Allard of Boston College.

Before a crowd of 24,000 soaked-to-the-bone fans, opportunistic Holy Cross sloshed to a 14-0 victory over Boston College.

There were an astonishing twenty-three fumbles in the game. Incredibly, Vince Promuto, the Crusaders all-world lineman and future Washington Redskins' Hall of Famer, recovered eight (yes, eight) of those fumbles.

Greene, Holy Cross' brilliant field general, engineered the victory. He scored one touchdown on a one-yard quarterback sneak and managed the game smartly under horrendous playing conditions. For his cool effort, he was named the winner of the O'Melia Trophy as the game's outstanding player. It was a productive year for the Holy Cross star as he finished second in the nation in total offense that season behind Washington State's Bob Newman.

Defense dominated the game and both teams combined for less than one hundred yards of total offense. Turnovers led to all of Holy Cross' points. Slashing Dick Surrette, the Holy Cross captain, scored the Crusaders second touchdown on a short run. The only other points in the game came on a blocked punt. Watertown's Dick Berardino blocked a BC punt and it rolled out of the end zone for a safety.

It was a frustrating day for Boston College and its prolific passer Allard. The former Somerville High great could not get a potentially potent aerial game untracked because of the foul, nasty weather conditions combined with a stout Holy Cross defense.

– 1958 –

On a cold, wind-swept first Saturday in December, Boston College's pounding ground game battered Holy Cross, and the Eagles posted a convincing 26-8 victory before 26,000 shivering fans at Alumni Stadium.

The tough inside running of Alan Miller, the O'Melia Trophy winner, and Jimmy Duggan led Coach Mike Holovak's team. The hard-driving pair led a potent rushing attack that piled up two hundred and forty-seven yards on the ground. Both Miller and Duggan scored touchdowns as the Eagles led 18-8 at the half and then added an insurance touchdown in the fourth quarter.

On defense, BC, led by the indomitable Larry Eisenhauer, Don Tosi and others, held Holy Cross to only nineteen yards rushing and eighty-six total yards.

Holy Cross scored its only touchdown on a 55-yard pass and run from quarterback Tommy Greene to end Dave Stecchi. On the play, Stecchi caught the football, broke a pair of tackles and then outran the BC secondary into the end zone. Greene, a threat to pass or run, added the two-point conversion on a dandy fake followed by a bootleg sweep into the corner of the end zone.

Captain Jim Healy and tackle Joe Moore were standouts for the Crusaders in defeat.

Holy Cross had won the previous two years, so the win snapped the Eagles' two-year slide against the Crusaders. BC ended the season 7-3, while Holy Cross completed a 6-3 season.

Chuckin' Charlie Maloy

A Potent Field General

HE WAS A COVER BOY QUARTERBACK DURING AN ERA THAT PRODUCED Dick Kazmaier (Princeton), along with 1962 Heisman Trophy winner Terry Baker of Oregon State, the last of the great single wing tailbacks, Vito "Babe" Parilli (Kentucky), Jack Scarbath (Maryland) and Harry Agganis (Boston University).

Charlie Maloy quarterbacked Holy Cross from 1950-'52. "Chuckin' Charlie" was the engineer or field general of two of the most powerful teams in Holy Cross football history. With Maloy at the controls, Coach Eddie Anderson's Crusaders posted back-to-back 8-2-0 seasons in 1951 and 1952. As a senior in '52, Maloy capped a sensational college career by being named the winner of the George H. "Bulger" Lowe Trophy as the outstanding college football player in New England.

During his junior year in 1951, Holy Cross won eight of its first nine games, averaging a whopping 38.6 points per game. The only loss during that stretch was a 20-14 defeat against the Green Wave of Tulane. Around the same time, Maloy, who had lost twenty pounds, was diagnosed with a stomach ulcer and was sidelined for seventeen days. Otherwise, the Crusaders might have entered the annual slugfest against arch-rival Boston College unbeaten.

In its opening two games, Holy Cross defeated Harvard, 33-6, and Fordham, 54-20. Then, after losing to Tulane, the Crusaders rolled over their next six opponents, beating NYU, 53-6; Brown 41-6; Colgate 34-6; Marquette, 39-13; the Quantico Marines, 39-14; and Temple, 41-7. In its first nine games, Holy Cross outscored the opposition, 348-98.

On December 1, 1951, Boston College, under first-year head Coach Mike Holovak, entered the football game with a 2-6 record. Holy Cross, at 8-1, was a huge favorite.

In the next day's *Sunday Worcester Telegram*, legendary editor and writer Roy Mumpton, described the outcome: "What might have been Holy Cross' finest football season ended in bleak disaster yesterday as Boston College's fighting underdogs rose up and spilled the Crusaders, 19-14, before 38,000 emotionally-exhausted spectators at Braves Field."

The weather conditions were ideal: Clear skies and balmy temperatures, unusual for the first day of December. As happens so often in spirited rivalries, Holy Cross was overconfident and took BC too lightly. The Crusaders were emotionally flat and it was the underdog Eagles who had the fire in their bellies. Boston College led 12-7 at the half. After a scoreless third quarter, Holy Cross, sparked by the bulldog running of Mel Massucco, one of the Cross' all-time greats, drove 88 yards to score the go-ahead touchdown with only three minutes and forty seconds left in the game. Massucco, the Holy Cross captain, smashed off-tackle and scored standing up from the six-yard line. (Massucco hailed from Arlington, Massachusetts and later was the head coach at his alma mater. He was drafted by the Chicago Cardinals of the NFL following college.) After John Feltch's conversion kick was good, Holy Cross led, 14-12.

However, BC was far from finished. As the game clock continued to tick, the Eagles moved the ball towards midfield when a pair of frisky freshmen, quarterback Jimmy Kane and left halfback Tommy Joe Sullivan, detonated an aerial bomb that set up the winning touchdown, unleashing streams of purple rain on the potential Holy Cross victory parade.

Fifty-two years later, Maloy remembers the one play that broke the Crusaders' back. "We got beat on a Hail Mary pass," recalled Maloy. "It was similar to the long pass that Doug Flutie threw years later to beat Miami in the Orange Bowl."

From the BC 46-yard line, Kane, a poised 18-year-old from Weymouth, Massachusetts, waited in the pocket, spotted Sullivan far down field and let the pigskin fly. Sullivan, who had raced behind the Holy Cross secondary, made the catch and was dragged down on the one-yard line, completing a 55-yard gain just short of a touchdown.

There were just ninety seconds left in the game and the clock continued to tick. Twice Boston College tried to pound the football into the end zone, but on back-to-back plays the Holy Cross defense stiffened, denying BC the go-ahead score. On the third try, Joe Johnson, a sophomore right halfback from New Haven, Connecticut, found a crack in the Holy Cross defense and slammed into the end zone for the winning touchdown with only seconds remaining in the game.

Not so fast. With the crowd roaring and BC fans racing onto the field, a flag was spotted in the end zone. The field was partially cleared and the officials huddled for what seemed like an eternity. When the circular conclave ended, the referee emerged from the stack and signaled that an off-side penalty had been called against Holy Cross.

Quickly, BC refused the penalty, the play stood, and, after Dick Zotti's conversion kick, the Eagles had their hard-fought 19-14 upset victory. The win was extra sweet for Head Coach Holovak and his line coach, Gil Bouley, who were teammates on the unbeaten and top-ranked 1942 BC team, which was ambushed by heavily underdog Holy Cross, 55-12.

After the game, Holy Cross head coach Dr. Eddie Anderson fumed over the fact that BC had managed to run three plays without a stoppage in play as the final seconds ticked away. Evidently the Eagles had used their allotment of time outs. He had wanted his team to take more time between plays before lining up and getting set on defense. He felt that if his team had been more deliberate, time would have expired before BC had an opportunity to run three plays.

Once he cooled down, Anderson admitted, "My pride and joy—our defense—let me down. They lost the ball game."

Nevertheless, the high powered Holy Cross offense, one of the most potent scoring machines in the country, turned in a sub-par performance. "I can still remember how much that loss hurt," recalled Maloy. "As a team, we were crushed."

"Chuckin' Charlie," the most prolific passer in the East, actually fired many blanks in the 1951 game against the Eagles. It was not one of his best games. In that one game, he was outplayed by the freshman hotshot Kane. Maloy connected on eight of fourteen passes and had two interceptions for an even hundred yards. He also rushed for a touchdown. Kane clicked on nine of fourteen passes for 167 yards, including the 55-yard bomb to Sullivan that set up the winning touchdown, and no interceptions.

In 1952 Holy Cross bounced back from the loss the previous year and defeated Boston College, 21-7. Jerry O'Leary, whose electrifying 55-yard punt return for a touchdown brought the crowd to its feet, was one of the brightest stars for Holy Cross. Costly Boston College turnovers and a pounding Holy Cross ground game (215 yards rushing) proved to be the difference in the game.

For the second year in a row, the BC defense frustrated the Holy Cross passing attack. Maloy was held to 89 yards passing, but his quarterback keepers kept the BC defense off balance throughout the game. "We used an unbalanced line for the first time that season against Boston College and we had success running the football," Maloy said, remembering the offensive game plan used to exploit the BC defense.

Maloy could have been dubbed the "Rochester Rifle." He hailed from Rochester, New York and he was a star athlete at Aquinas Institute, a Catholic high school in Rochester run by the Basilian Fathers. The school's nickname was "The Little Irish," but there was nothing small about the Aquinas football schedule. "We drew 20,000 or more for our home games," said Maloy. Aquinas Institute played top football schools all over the country, schools such as Bishop Burns in Texas, Mt. Carmel in Chicago, St. Benedict Prep in New Jersey and Boys Town in Nebraska.

Maloy was recruited by Notre Dame, but he was so impressed by the quality of the Holy Cross alums he met that he decided to enroll at the College of the Holy Cross. "I had a chance to meet Holy Cross graduates," he said. "Some were medical doctors. They were quality people, very impressive human beings. It is because of them that I decided to go to Holy Cross."

From the first time he met his college football coach, Dr. Anderson, Charlie said he knew immediately that his football mentor was a uniquely special person. "He was much more than my coach," said Maloy. "He became a lifelong friend. Coach Anderson was a leader. He was dynamic, he instilled great confidence in his players, he was thorough, he got you prepared to play and he had a great attitude about football and about life."

Maloy said that Dr. Anderson had such a keen eye for untapped football talent that he could practically pluck someone out of a chorus line and make that person a solid football player. "He was amazing," said Charlie. "We would meet in the gym before the season started, all of us in shorts just lined up in a row. He would pull someone out of the line and say, 'You are going to be one of my linebackers.' Then, sure enough, once we got out on the field that recruit would turn out to be a starting linebacker."

During Charlie's junior year, Dr. Anderson received word that his father had died just before the Crusaders were about to play Fordham. Maloy remembers how much he and his teammates wanted to play well against the Rams to try and lift the spirits of their coach. "After I completed my first nine passes, I was particularly pleased," he said. On that Saturday against Fordham in 1951, the Crusaders were on fire with filial love for their great coach and they flattened Fordham, 54-20. No pep talk or pre-game speech, even from the mouths of a Rockne or Lombardi, can move people like the experience of sharing bits and pieces of our human condition with others, particularly those we care deeply about. In that Fordham game, Holy Cross could have pitched the play book in the trash and still won.

Following the 1952 season, Maloy was selected to play in the East-West game, although he sat on the bench and did not play. The game was played in San Francisco. Three thousand miles away in Mobile, Alabama, another star college quarterback, who was playing in the Senior Bowl, a second post-season college All-Star game, became upset when he heard that a fellow New England quarterback was snubbed by coaches at the East-West game.

That quarterback was Harry Agganis, the former Boston University great. "That's the kind of guy Harry was," said Maloy. "When I heard that he became upset when he heard that I didn't get to play in the East-West game, I was not surprised by his reaction."

Just months later, Maloy and Agganis joined forces and became assistant coaches on the staff of BU football coach Buff Donelli. "We worked together with the quarterbacks," explained Maloy. "If one of the BU quarterbacks threw a pass for minus one yard, I told Harry, 'He's your guy, your responsibility now.' "

"When I joined the BU staff, Harry welcomed me with open arms," said Maloy. "He was a tremendous person, a great human being. You respected everything about him and what an athlete, too!"

Agganis signed with the Boston Red Sox in 1953 for a $30,000 bonus. He played one full season (1954) and part of a second season with the Red Sox before tragically dying of a pulmonary embolism on June 27, 1955. He was only 26 years old.

Although Maloy admitted that the BC-Holy Cross football series was "a great, great rivalry," he applauds the course or philosophy that his alma mater has followed in regard to intercollegiate athletics. That policy of de-emphasizing athletics, a shift from Division 1-A to Division 1-AA competition, caused Holy Cross to drop Boston College from its schedule, thus ending the 91-year-old series. "Big time Division 1-A college athletics are way out of control," said Maloy. "I don't even watch the games anymore."

However, he does endorse intercollegiate sports played at small colleges, particularly those schools that compete at the Division III level of competition. "Those colleges do it right with the proper balance between academics and athletics," Charlie said, who had a son play linebacker for Division III Hobart College.

At Holy Cross, Maloy majored in English and minored in Greek. He attended Boston University Law School. Then, after a tour of duty in the Army, he completed his law school studies at Temple University in Philadelphia.

Today, he is a retired judge. For eight years, he was a city court judge in Rochester and for twenty years he served as a justice with the County Federal Court. He stays active by working a couple of days each week counseling and advising families that have been victimized by domestic violence. "I have studied the problem in the past, taken courses on it," he said. "As far as finding a cure or solving the problem, it is a study centered on the complexity of human nature. In criminal court, if someone robs a bank, you put that person behind bars. But with families, people have to try and live together. As a society, we must help our families and keep them strong."

He said his beliefs can be traced to his upbringing. "We were taught honesty and the difference between right and wrong," he explained. "Growing up, we knew how important it was to do the right thing and we tried to make right choices."

He met his wife, Teresa, at a dance on campus after his first varsity home game at Holy Cross against Brown, a game the Crusaders won, 41-

21. At the time, she was attending Regis College. Today, the couple has three grown children.

As an athlete at Holy Cross, he was the quarterback of a dream back-field that featured Johnny Turco at left halfback, Mel Massucco at right halfback and Bobby Doyle at fullback. It was one of the finest backfields in the history of Holy Cross football, a showcase for the T-Formation.

"Turco was the speed burner who was very elusive," said Maloy. "Massucco was a tremendous competitor and leader, a real fighter. Doyle was real tough, too, and a hard-nosed football player."

During his three-year varsity career at Holy Cross, he completed 406 passes in 689 attempts, good for 4,074 yards and 34 touchdowns, and after all these years is still third on the all-time Holy Cross list for career touchdown passes.

He is right up there among the greatest quarterbacks in the history of Holy Cross football along with Pat McCarthy, Tommy Greene, Jeff Wiley, Dave Boisture, Tom Ciaccio, and Jack Lentz.

Vic Rimkus

Always a Competitor

ONCE A COMPETITOR, ALWAYS A COMPETITOR. VICTOR M. RIMKUS, A Holy Cross Varsity Club Hall of Famer and one of the Crusaders' greatest interior linemen, has had two hip replacements as well as reconstructive knee surgery. Yet, he continues to play tennis and senior hockey.

"I don't want to be around when he can't play sports anymore," says Rosemary Rimkus, Vic's wife and the mother of the couple's eight children.

Mrs. Rimkus met her husband shortly after she graduated from St. Michael's Academy, known today as Hudson Catholic. Reflecting on their long life together, Mrs. Rimkus said that her husband is "a steady man and one of the most determined people I have ever known."

Vic Rimkus hails from Hudson, a small central Massachusetts town, population 8,000 during the mid-to-late 1930s and 1940s. After starring in high school for the Big Red Hudson High Hawks, he enrolled at Holy Cross. He excelled at tackle on two of Dr. Eddie Anderson's best Holy Cross football teams. He was the co-winner of the O'Melia Award in 1952 and was invited to play in the prestigious East-West game at Keizar Stadium in San Francisco. Later, he was the head football coach at Hudson High School for 35 years and he is a member of the Massachusetts State Football Coaches Association Hall of Fame.

Rimkus' family roots can be traced to Lithuania. His father owned a sporting goods store in town. He also used the store as a base for his extensive amateur radio operation, which delighted young Vic because he could listen to the golden tones of sports broadcast legend Bill Stern doing the play by play of big-time college football games involving Notre Dame, Ohio State, Michigan and others.

"I used to listen to those games on the radio almost every Saturday during the fall," remembered Rimkus. In fact, one of his earliest memories of the Boston College-Holy Cross rivalry was a radio broadcast of the yearly football battle. "It was the classic 1942 game," recalled Rimkus, "Holy Cross' stunning 55-12 victory on the day of the Cocoanut Grove fire. I was 11 years old. I was working in my father's store that day and I listened to the game on the radio."

Following high school, Rimkus was a heavily recruited lineman. He could have gone to a number of schools, but he narrowed his choices down to two: Boston University and Holy Cross. In addition to his exploits on the gridiron, Rimkus was a superb hockey player, so he entertained thoughts of playing both football and hockey in college. Holy Cross did not have a hockey program, but BU was a college hockey power and he seriously considered heading to the Commonwealth Avenue campus of Boston University and playing both sports for the Terriers.

However, his family, especially an aunt who lived in Worcester and knew several of the priests at Holy Cross, wanted him to attend Holy Cross. Dr. Bill Osmanski, the former Crusader great was head coach in 1948 when Rimkus was a high school senior. Osmanski's younger brother, Joe, a former Holy Cross player and at the time an assistant Holy Cross coach, visited Rimkus' house in Hudson in an attempt to steer him towards Holy Cross. In the end, Vic decided that Holy Cross was the best fit for him and his future plans. However, BU pulled out all the stops in an effort to land Rimkus. It offered solid academic credentials, a fine athletic program and a chance to experience college life amidst the cosmopolitan setting of downtown Boston. Worcester would never be mistaken for Boston, although the city has its merits, not the least of which is the charm and educational opportunities of the College of the Holy Cross.

Buff Donelli, the head football coach at Boston University, arranged for Rimkus to attend a Red Sox game seated in the special box that belonged to Joe Cronin, the team's general manager and Hall of Fame shortstop. To assist in the recruiting effort, Donelli brought along his star quarterback, Harry Agganis, who was nicknamed "The Golden Greek" and was one of the best college football players in the country. In fact, it was Agganis who put Boston University on the big-time college football map. Rimkus thought long and hard about enrolling at BU, but he had already decided that his collegiate future would be dominated by the color purple, not BU scarlet and white.

Following the Red Sox game, he made his choice known. He took Coach Donelli aside, said he was sorry and then told him that he had decided to accept the scholarship offer from Holy Cross.

At 6-foot-1, 220 pounds, Rimkus was considered a big tackle during the era that he played college football. Today, it is rare if big-time college linemen don't tip the scales at 300 pounds or more. In addition to his size, Rimkus was tough. He was also athletic, had quick feet and he was durable, often playing the full 60 minutes. His brother linemen—Mike Cooney, Bob Masterson, Chet Millett (fellow Varsity Club Hall of Famer and *Look Magazine* All-American), Joe Gleason, Bob Dee (former Patriots' defensive end) and Henry Lemire—all weighed no more than 195 pounds, although Dee bulked up for the trench warfare of the old American Football League.

During his junior and senior seasons at Holy Cross, the Crusaders posted identical 8-2-0 records. In fact, his junior year, 1951, Holy Cross wound up tied for nineteenth place along with Clemson in the annual Associated Press poll of the top-ranked college teams in the country. The Crusaders' only other appearances in the top twenty occurred in 1935 (the 9-0-1 Crusaders finished ninth in the polls), 1942 (tied for 20th) and 1945, when the 8-1-0 Orange Bowl-bound Holy Cross eleven, ended up sixteenth in the country. In the Orange Bowl, Miami upset the Crusaders on the final play of the game, 13-6. Thus, Holy Cross ended one of its finest seasons with an 8-2-0 record.

In 1942, despite just a 5-4-1 record, the smashing upset 55-12 victory over previously unbeaten and top-ranked Boston College elevated the Crusaders to nineteenth place in the final Associated Press poll.

During Rimkus' junior year, Holy Cross was led by quarterback Charlie Maloy and Captain Mel Massucco, a slashing running back. The Purple pounded one opponent after another. The Crusaders beat Harvard, 33-6; Fordham, 54-20; N.Y.U., 53-6; Brown, 41-6; Colgate,

34-6; Marquette, 39-13; the Quantico Marines, 39-14; and Temple, 41-7. The only losses were to Tulane, 20-14, and a crushing loss to underdog Boston College, 19-14, at Braves Field. The Eagles, under first-year coach Mike Holovak, limped into the annual battle against the Cross with a 2-6-0 record. The upset victory obviously soothed many of the wounds from a very disappointing Boston College season.

The game against Tulane was played in New Orleans at Tulane Stadium, also known as the Sugar Bowl. What Rimkus remembers best about the game was the heat and the hard, almost concrete-like playing surface. During the game, he struggled with a combination of fatigue and dehydration. Rimkus played 58 minutes. "I didn't realize until I got on a scale after the game that I had lost 20 pounds," he said.

Late in the game, a Tulane back took off on a long touchdown run, zigzagging his way past a string of would be Holy Cross tacklers strewn in his wake, to account for the winning score.

In the BC game, the Eagles' Jimmy Kane and Tommy Joe Sullivan collaborated on an aerial bomb, a clutch pass play to set up the winning touchdown with time running out. With just seconds remaining in the game, BC pounded the football into the end zone to seal the upset victory before a howling, packed house at Braves Field.

Following the game, Rimkus remembered that Holy Cross coach Dr. Eddie Anderson, who at times was known for his acerbic tongue, was livid. "What he was most upset about was that, after the long pass, we lined up on defense too quickly," said Rimkus. "He thought that if we had taken our time, we could have run out the clock and BC would not have had time to run another play."

During his senior year, Holy Cross dropped a 20-19 squeaker to the Orangemen of Syracuse, one of only two Holy Cross losses in 1952. The other loss was to the Quantico Marines, 27-18. The Crusaders ended the season by soundly whipping Boston College, 21-7. In that game, Rimkus and Boston College's Joe Johnson shared the O'Melia Award as the game's most valuable players.

The Syracuse game his senior year stands out in his memory. Under legendary coach Ben Schwartzwalder, the Orangemen shifted down then lined up in an unbalanced line on offense, which put Rimkus nose-to-nose across the line from Syracuse's great center Jim Ringo, an NFL Hall of Famer who starred for the Green Bay Packers and the Philadelphia

Eagles, a player whom Vic called "a great, great football player, tough to handle, a real challenge." Later that same season Syracuse played the Crimson Tide of Alabama in the Orange Bowl and was overwhelmed, 61-6.

Rimkus reminisced about his former coach, Dr. Anderson, a brilliant yet eccentric man who lorded over his sport. "He was a great man," said Rimkus, "a gentleman, a scholar, an impeccable dresser and a refined man-of-all-seasons type of guy. He was a legendary coach and I had great respect for him."

He lauded Coach Anderson for helping his players maximize their abilities. "He was a great motivator," said Rimkus. "I don't know where I would have been without him."

Following his senior season, Vic was invited to play in the East-West Shrine game in San Francisco. Quarterback Maloy, Millett and Boston College lineman Lou Florio were also selected to play for the East squad, which was coached by Clarence "Biggie" Munn of Michigan State, Andy Kerr of Colgate, Dr. Anderson and others. The starting quarterback for the East was Tommy O'Connell of Illinois, who later played for the Chicago Bears and Cleveland Browns, backing up the great Otto Graham. Maloy, although a genuine star, never got into the game. "For some reason the coaches didn't play Charlie and to this day I have no idea why," remarked Rimkus.

One of the big stars for the West was Billy Vessels, the All-American running back for Coach Bud Wilkinson's Oklahoma Sooners, the architects of a record 47-game winning streak.

At the outset, the West moved the ball at will. Rimkus didn't start the game, but after a tackle from Ohio State got pushed around, the coaches replaced him with Rimkus to steady the line, which is exactly what he did as the East rolled to a runaway victory.

While still in college, Rimkus was selected in the tenth round of the NFL draft by the Green Bay Packers. He made it through training camp but was cut following the final preseason game. After a hitch in the Marine Corps, he played briefly with the Chicago Bears. While in the service, he played football for the Quantico and Parris Island Marines, two tradition-rich service football programs.

At the Cross, Rimkus soaked up all that a Jesuit-based education had to offer, including the 500-year-old Catholic tradition of Jesuit spirituality. During his senior year, he converted to Catholicism. "At that point in my life," he said, "I decided I wanted to become a Catholic." He picked friend, teammate and fellow lineman for the Purple, Chet Millett, to be his sponsor at his baptism.

Like many, Rimkus was disappointed when the BC-Holy Cross football rivalry ended in 1986. Throughout much of the series, Holy Cross more than held its own. The 1978 game stands out in his memory, when Brockton's Peter Colombo led Holy Cross to a thrilling 30-29 victory over winless Boston College. "I was sitting in the stands that day at BC's Alumni Stadium," recalled Rimkus. "At one point, I remember shouting out loud, 'By golly, we are going to win this game.' "

That win was the Crusaders second straight victory over the Eagles. The previous season Holy Cross prevailed, 35-20, in a huge upset. BC went 6-5-0 in 1977, Holy Cross 2-9. It was a double loss for Boston College. Popular, mild-mannered Head Coach Joe Yukica, who guided the Eagles from 1968 through 1977 and posted a 68-37-0 record, was fired following the one-point, upset loss to Holy Cross. Soon after he resurfaced as the head coach of the Big Green of Dartmouth.

Like many ex-players, Vic's love of the game propelled him into coaching. When Rimkus became the head football coach at Hudson High School, he succeeded Bobby Sullivan, the great former Holy Cross back from North Andover.

Over the years, Rimkus has remained close friends with many Holy Cross alums and former football players, people such as Joe Harrington, an ex-end and linebacker for the Crusaders who graduated in the Class of 1954.

Vic and his wife Rosemary have eight children and nine grandchildren. Joe Harrington and his wife Alice have nine children and 28 grandchildren. The two families gather together every year around Christmas to celebrate their many blessings, beginning with a combined legacy of 17 children and 37 grandchildren.

Now those are numbers worth really shouting about, from the top of Mount St. James at Holy Cross or the Heights of Boston College.

Dick Berardino

Almost a Goat

DICK BERARDINO BELONGS TO A LONG LIST OF ITALIAN-AMERICAN athletes who have excelled in athletics at Boston College and Holy Cross. He comes from Watertown, played football and baseball for the Holy Cross Crusaders and has spent the past 35 years working for the Boston Red Sox.

Watertown, like so many cities and towns in Eastern Massachusetts, has cultivated its own Boston College-Holy Cross rivalry. Superb athletes from the town are graduates of both institutions. Jerry York, the current BC hockey coach, a former hockey player for the BC Eagles, is also from Watertown. He and Berardino are two of the many athletes from Watertown who have gone on to play sports at Boston College and Holy Cross.

Berardino played in the final Boston College-Holy Cross football game that was held at Fenway Park. The year was 1956 and the Crusaders nipped the Eagles 7-0 on a fourth quarter touchdown pass with only seconds remaining in the game. The play covered 25 yards. Billy Smithers of Somerville, who was also recruited by Boston College, spiraled the winning TD pass to halfback Paul Toland of South Boston.

Berardino, who was a second string sophomore end for the Crusaders, was on the field during the game-winning drive. In fact, he caught a hook pass from QB Smithers that was good for 15 yards and a first down.

132

Immediately after that play, on his way back to the huddle, Berardino said that he heard Henry Sullivan, the BC captain, scream at Jim Colclough, the Eagles' defensive back whose job it was to cover the hook area: "Get up on him. Cover him tight and don't let him catch the ball in front of you."

As he jogged back to the huddle, Berardino filed away the information and put it to good use a few plays later. Breaking off the line of scrimmage, running another pass route, this time he sprinted straight at Colclough, gave him a little juke, but didn't stop. Instead, he dipped to the inside, turned on the jets and ran a quick post pattern, leaving Colclough behind. Then he looked over his inside shoulder for the football. It was right there. Smithers had thrown a perfect spiral. "I remember how big the football looked coming towards me," recalled Berardino. "For a second, it looked like it was spiraling towards me in slow motion. All I had to do was cradle it softly into my hands. During my football career, I had caught a thousand balls just like that."

Prior to that play, there were just 40 seconds left in the game when the Holy Cross center snapped the football. The crowd roared. Time seemed to stand still while the pigskin was in the air. With a chance to make a potential game-winning touchdown catch, Berardino was driven by a reserve supply of adrenaline. However, at one instant, he was on the threshold of euphoria, at the next he faced the cold, cruel reality of despair: Berardino dropped the football. He got both hands securely on it, but dropped it. The pigskin slipped through his fingers and fell to the ground, not any ground, but the turf of Fenway Park.

In the flash of a single moment, Watertown's Dick Berardino had gone from hero to goat. It seemed that instead of reading "Holy Cross beats BC 7-0 on Berardino's clutch catch," the next day's headline on the sports pages would read, "Late Holy Cross drive stalls, Jesuit rivals battle to 0-0 tie."

After dropping the ball, Berardino sheepishly returned to the huddle. However, on the next play, Smithers and Toland rescued the Crusaders and Berardino by teaming up on the game-winning play.

On the game-winning TD pass, Toland beat BC's captain Henry Sullivan, the same player who, just a few plays earlier, had chastised his teammate, Jim Colclough, for not blanketing Berardino and allowing him to catch a hook pass.

One more note about Colclough, a superb athlete and competitor who was blessed with only average speed at best: He went on to play for the Patriots and he was highly respected in the old AFL as an excellent possession receiver.

In 1957, Holy Cross won its second straight over BC, blanking the Eagles for the second year in a row. The final score of that game was 14-0. The game was played at Fitton Field. It had rained hard that week and it continued to rain on the day of the game. The field was a muddy mess. BC coach Mike Holovak wanted the game postponed, but Holy Cross coach Dr. Eddie Anderson insisted that the game be played. Holovak thought that the muddy conditions would neutralize the advantage that the heavily favored Eagles carried into the game. In that game, Berardino remembers blocking a BC punt with the Crusaders clinging to a 7-0 lead. Holovak's pre-game fears were justified. The Crusaders posted a big upset. Entering the Holy Cross game, Coach Holovak's Eagles rode a seven-game winning streak into the annual showdown against the Crusaders. The two wins capped identical seasons, in terms of wins and losses, for the Crusaders. Both seasons, Holy Cross ended up 5-3-1. BC ended up 5-4-0 in 1956 and 7-2-0 in 1957. Two years later, in 1959, he was fired following a 5-4-0 season and replaced by Ernie Hefferle, the former head coach of the University of Pittsburgh Panthers.

Berardino pointed out an impressive fact about Holy Cross teams during the era he played for the Crusaders. Holy Cross beat Eastern power Syracuse two years in a row, nipping the Orangemen, 20-19, in 1957 and again beating Syracuse, 14-13, in 1958. The following year, 1959, Coach Ben Schwartzwalder's Orangemen went undefeated, beat Texas, 23-14, in the Cotton Bowl and won the national championship. The great Ernie Davis, who was only a sophomore on the national championship team, won the Heisman Trophy in 1961 as a senior. The number one pick of the Cleveland Browns, he died of leukemia shortly after that. In 1957, not only did Holy Cross upend Syracuse, but the Crusaders nearly knocked off Penn State, too. In that game, Holy Cross drove inside the Nittany Lions' five-yard line late in the game. Penn State held and escaped with a hard-fought 14-10 win. Today, many have no idea about the caliber of football the Crusaders played during the heyday of Holy Cross football.

During his Holy Cross football career, Berardino remembers an incident that forced him to the sidelines more vividly than any single play or game during his college career. It occurred during his junior year. One day, he was late for practice and Dr. Anderson benched him.

"I had to take a makeup exam in philosophy," recalled Berardino. "The only alternative would have been to sign up for summer school and retake the course at . . . Boston College."

Rather than commit academic treason, Berardino decided that he better take the test and risk the consequences of being late for practice. He paid a stiff price, too, for being tardy and ended up sitting his fanny on the bench for much of the remainder of the season.

Ironically, Berardino actually did take a couple of summer school business courses at Boston College during the years he pursued a college degree. "I took the courses at BC to try to lighten my academic load at Holy Cross because I knew I had tough Philosophy courses to take the following fall," he explained.

The legendary Dr. Anderson was hardly the warm and fuzzy type. He was a dictator who ruled his football dominion with an iron hand. Like many coaches from that era, he was the boss and no one dared challenge his authority.

"I'll never forget him benching me," said Berardino. "I thought I had a legitimate excuse. You didn't dare approach him and you did what you were told. Period. He was like that, though, a little bit aloof and distant. He smoked cigarettes out of one of those fancy gold, British cigarette holders. Dr. Anderson could be very intimidating."

At Holy Cross, Berardino was a two-sport star. He was an end in football and a swift, hard-hitting center fielder in baseball. During the spring of 1958, he helped lead the Crusaders into the College World Series. In fact, Holy Cross upset top-seeded Southern California, coached by the legendary Ron Dedeaux, in the first round of the double elimination tourney, 3-0. "Dedeaux thought he could get away with throwing his third best pitcher against us in the first round," said Berardino, "but we shut them out." The Trojans were loaded with stars including future L.A. Dodgers' first baseman Ron Fairly. Despite the loss in the first round, USC went on to win the College World Series. Six years earlier Holy Cross beat Missouri 8-4 in the finals to win the College World Series Championship.

Jack Barry was the Holy Cross baseball coach. A legend in his own right, he once had been a member of Connie Mack's and the Philadelphia A's infield gloriously nicknamed, "The million dollar infield." Al "Hop"

Riopel, another illustrious name from Holy Cross' rich sports past, was the assistant baseball coach. In addition to Berardino, four teammates also signed professional baseball contracts. The list included catcher Larry Rancourt (Reds), pitcher Jim Farino (Tigers), pitcher Hal Dietz (Braves) and infielder Ron Liptak (Braves).

During the early summer of 1958, Dick signed a professional baseball contract with the New York Yankees. He was scouted by a string of teams including the Red Sox and Cleveland Indians. In fact, the pen was almost in hand for him to ink a pact with the Red Sox. Berardino remembers the day well. Red Sox scout Neil Mahoney had scouted him, made an offer and invited him to come to Fenway Park to close the deal. It just so happened that on that same day Jim Bunning of the Tigers, the future U.S. Congressman, threw a no hitter at the Red Sox. In the end, however, the Yankees offered Berardino more money so he ultimately signed with the Bronx Bombers instead of the Red Sox. Joe Page, the legendary hard-throwing and hard-drinking Yankees' right-handed relief pitcher, scouted Berardino and was ready to sign him. However, Page suffered a heart attack and died before he could get Dick's signature on a contract. So Lee McPhail and Jerry Coleman had to step in and complete the transaction. As part of the deal he signed with the Yankees, the ball club agreed to pay for Dick to return to Holy Cross during the off season and complete his college education. And that's what he did. He returned to school, picked up the credits he needed and graduated from Holy Cross in 1959.

Berardino played eight seasons of minor league baseball in the Yankees' chain, hitting a solid .295 and advancing to the Triple A level in the New York system. He said that the most home runs he ever hit during a single season was twenty. However, he couldn't make the jump to the big club and never made it to New York. In those days, it would have been difficult for any ball player to unseat the Yankees' regular center fielder, a future Hall of Famer named Mickey Charles Mantle.

In addition to Mantle, Tom Tresh, the son of former big league catcher Mike Tresh, was a promising young player in the Yankees' system. He could play both the infield and the outfield. He even filled in at shortstop for the Yankees after Tony Kubek was summoned into the military.

After the Yankees traded for Roger Maris, who hit 61 home runs in 1961 to break Babe Ruth's single season record, Maris took over in right field. Tresh wound up in left field. However, with a little bit of luck, Berardino might have won that left field job.

Years later, at a reunion at Fenway Park, Dick ran into Ralph Houk, former Yankees as well as Red Sox manager. At the time, he kidded Houk be telling him, "The biggest mistake you ever made was cutting me and not giving me a chance to play left field for the Yankees."

Dick said that Houk, the former Marine, smiled and admitted he could have erred when he sent Berardino back to the minor leagues rather than retaining him on the New York roster.

"Everything in life is timing," said Berardino, remembering how close he came to playing in the same outfield with Mickey Mantle and Roger Maris.

In high school, Berardino played baseball at Watertown High School for George Yankowski, a former big-league catcher who played briefly with the Philadelphia A's and Chicago White Sox. Later, Berardino taught business courses and coached baseball at Watertown High School for many years.

During his long post-playing career with the Red Sox, he has worked for the organization as a minor league manager, big league coach and roving instructor. Currently, he is a player development consultant and spring training coordinator for the Red Sox.

Neil Mahoney, who had scouted him as a young player, helped him land a job with the Red Sox after he retired as a player. Berardino managed the Red Sox minor league affiliate, the Lowell Spinners, for two seasons and the club instituted a "Dick Berardino 33 (the number he wore as manager) Alumni Award." The first recipient is the World Champion Anaheim Angels' pepper pot shortstop David Eckstein, a former Red Sox farmhand who played for the Spinners but was left unprotected and was wisely picked up by the Angels. Eckstein received the award at a banquet held on December 5, 2002.

Berardino, a lifelong supporter of amateur baseball, is a recipient of the "Thomas A. Yawkey Sportsmanship Award" which the Boston Park League annually presents to a person in the community who has contributed the most to the game of baseball.

When he remembers his college athletic career, the BC-Holy Cross football rivalry stands out. "It was a great, great rivalry," he said. "It was an honor and a thrill just to play in the game."

For an ex-football player, the most cherished memories are thoughts about former teammates and that special bond of playing on the same team. In Dick's case, that means thinking about men such as Smithers, Toland, Dick Arcand (captain of the 1956 team) Dick Surrette (captain of the 1957 team), Carlin Lynch, Gerry O'Leary, Anthony "Wally" Bavaro and so many others.

Bavaro was a tackle at Holy Cross. He passed away in 2002. He is the patriarch of quite a football family. His son Mark, who starred at Notre Dame, was an all-pro tight end with the New York Giants. Another son, David, a hard-hitting linebacker for the Syracuse Orangemen, also made it to the National Football League with the Patriots among other NFL teams.

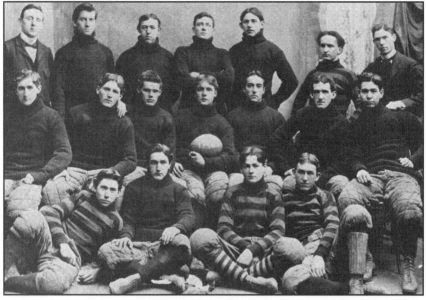

The 1896 Boston College Football Team.

The 1897 Holy Cross Football Team.

Louis Sockalexis "The Jim Thorpe of Mount St. James."

Bill Osmanski of Holy Cross was
called the finest back in the country.

Joe McKenney captained the 1926
Boston College football team.

John Lowney helped Boston College to a 17-14 victory over Holy Cross in 1916.

BC 19, Holy Cross 0 - 1928.

Boston College vs. Holy Cross, 1916: John Lowney scores first BC touchdown.

Dr. Eddie Anderson, Holy Cross coach.

Frank Leahy, BC coach 1939-1940.

Ten seconds remain as Joe Johnson smashes his way over the goal line to give 20-point underdog BC a 19-14 victory over the Cross in 1951.

Chet Gladchuk, BC 1940.

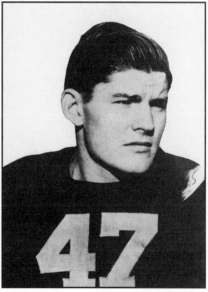

George Kerr, BC 1940.

The 1942 Program
Holy Cross upset Boston College, 55-12.

Right halfback Johnny Grigas scores one of his two touchdowns as Holy Cross crushed BC in the 1942 upset.

Holy Cross coach Ank Scanlon waves his hat triumphantly in the locker room after the huge Holy Cross 55-12 upset of Boston College in 1942.

Holy Cross coughs up the ball in the 1977 game.

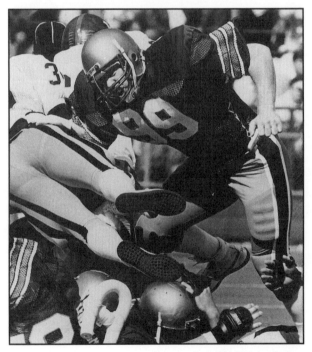

Steve DeOssie, on defense for BC, hated to play Holy Cross. He was later to win a Super Bowl ring with the New York Giants.

Holy Cross quarterback Pat McCarthy on a roll out.

Holy Cross' Gordie Lockbaum takes a break.

Doug Flutie is escorted off of Fitton Field after the 1984 Boston College-Holy Cross game. A helicopter was waiting to take him to New York to receive the Heisman Trophy.

Worcester Telegram photo by Steve Lanava

The Sixties

1960: Holy Cross 16-12

1961: Holy Cross 38-26

1962: BC 48-12

1963: Holy Cross 9-0

1964: BC 10-8

1965: BC 35-0

1966: Holy Cross 32-26

1967: BC 13-6

1968: BC 40-20

1969: no game

A hepatitis epidemic wiped out all but the first two games on the Holy Cross schedule.

IN 1960, JOE "THE JET" BELLINO OF WINCHESTER, MASSACHUSETTS won the Heisman Trophy playing for Coach Wayne Hardin and the Midshipmen of Navy. After fulfilling his service commitment, he played briefly with the Boston Patriots. He could have played pro baseball, too. He was a great catcher. The 1960s was a decade featuring stylish, big-play quarterbacks at both BC and Holy Cross—Jack Concannon, Eddie Foley and Frank "Red" Harris for BC and Pat McCarthy and Jack Lentz for Holy Cross. Dr. Eddie Anderson coached his final game for Holy Cross in 1964, a heartbreaking 10-8 loss to BC. After twenty-one seasons at Holy Cross, his record was 129-67-8. In 1968, Joe Yukica took over as head coach at BC. In ten seasons, his record was 68-37-0, including a near-perfect 9-1-0 against Holy Cross. During the 1960s, BC accelerated its football program and began to assert its dominance over Holy Cross. Although Holy Cross won three of the first four games during the 1960s, BC came on strong and finished the decade with a 5-4 advantage over Holy Cross. However, wins and losses paled in comparison to the terrible hepatitis epidemic which hit Holy Cross so hard that all but two games in the 1969 season had to be cancelled.

– 1961 –

The lightning quick whiz kids of Holy Cross ran wild against a beefier but slower Boston College team and raced to a 38-26 victory before an overflow crowd of 24,000 at Fitton Field.

The Crusaders were led by a bright and shiny Purple backfield, one of the most talented in Holy Cross football history, featuring quarterback Pat McCarthy, halfbacks Al Snyder and Tom Hennessey and fullback Henry Cutting.

Snyder, a dazzling pass receiver and kick returner, rocked BC in the first quarter when he slithered his way around and through the Eagles' defense for the game's first touchdown on a brilliant forty-two-yard punt return. Later in the game, he broke another punt return forty-eight yards to set up a Holy Cross touchdown. The junior from Baltimore, Maryland also caught eight passes in the game. For his efforts, he was awarded the O'Melia Trophy as the game's outstanding player.

Quarterback McCarthy, who won the O'Melia Trophy the previous year in a 16-12 Holy Cross victory, engineered the triumph by connecting on sixteen passes, good for two hundred and sixteen yards and two touchdowns, both to Barry Tyne. McCarthy, from Lawrence Central Catholic High School, rushed for fifty-four yards and scored a touchdown on a one-yard plunge. Cutting and Hennessey also scored touchdowns for the Crusaders.

Co-Captain Jack Fellin, co-Captain Jack Whalen, John Timperio, Ed Lilly and sophomore Jon Morris, who would go on to star for the New England Patriots, Detroit Lions and Chicago Bears in the NFL, all played hard-nosed football for the Crusaders completing a solid 7-3-0 season.

– 1962 –

Jack Concannon, a double threat as both a passer and a runner, put on a clinic as the junior quarterback led Boston College to a 48-12 rout over Holy Cross before 27,000 at Alumni Stadium.

For the game, Concannon completed sixteen of twenty-six passes, good for one hundred and ninety-four yards and three touchdowns. An elusive ball carrier and threat to run out of the pocket and pick up big yardage, nimble Jack also rushed for 84 yards in the game. His double-barreled performance earned him the O'Melia Trophy.

Art Graham, the Eagles' captain, hauled in two of Concannon's touchdown passes. Both Graham and Concannon, former number one draft choices, went on to star in the NFL. Graham was a wide receiver and deep threat for the Patriots, and Concannon played quarterback for the Philadelphia Eagles, Chicago Bears, Green Bay Packers and the Detriot Lions.

The lopsided victory was the most points that BC had scored against Holy Cross since the 1949 game when the Eagles trounced the Crusaders, 76-0.

The win gave first-year coach Jim Miller a huge win and it snapped BC's two game losing streak against Holy Cross.

– 1965 –

On a rainy day at Fitton Field, forcing the rivals to play in mud up to their ankles, a balanced offense enabled Boston College to overpower Holy Cross, 35-0.

Brendan McCarthy, the Eagles' tough inside runner, won the O'Melia Trophy. In a *Worcester Telegram* story, sports editor Roy Mumpton described McCarthy as "215 pounds of lightning and thunder." McCarthy carried the football twenty times, gained 139 yards powering off tackle and scored a touchdown. His backfield sidekick, Terry Erwin, who was only a sophomore, scored three of Boston College's five touchdowns.

Senior quarterback Eddie Foley, whose son Glenn would develop into a record-setting quarterback for Boston College, engineered the victory with his heady play.

Following the game, Mel Massucco, first-year Holy Cross coach and a former star back for the Crusaders, said, "We just couldn't stop McCarthy. Boston College was too strong up front."

– 1968 –

In a smashing show of offensive might, Boston College piled up 609 yards of total offense and the Eagles crushed Holy Cross 40-20 before 26,500 at Alumni Field.

Over land and through the air, BC's overpowering offense operated on all cylinders against the outgunned Crusaders. Dave Bennett, who rushed for 154 yards and scored a pair of touchdowns, was awarded the O'Melia Trophy. Sidekick running back Fred Willis, the first BC back to rush for one thousand yards in a season and who went on to play in the NFL for the Houston Oilers, also had a huge game for the Eagles. He even passed for a touchdown, a surprise halfback option pass that resulted in the game's first touchdown.

Frank "Red" Harris, BC's sophomore quarterback from Malden, Massachusetts, connected on sixteen of twenty passes, good for 193 yards and one touchdown. End Barry Gallup hauled in two touchdown passes, a forty-five yarder from Willis and a fourteen yarder from Harris.

For Holy Cross, quarterback Phil O'Neil, running backs Steve Jutras and Tommy Lamb and end Bob Neary stood out for the Crusaders, a gritty team that battled back and refused to quit after spotting the Eagles a 21-0 first-quarter lead.

For first-year Boston College coach Joe Yukica, it was the first of his eight straight victories over Holy Cross.

Pat McCarthy

Cordial and Competitive

PERSONABLE PAT MCCARTHY IS A STANDARD BEARER OF HOLY CROSS football, a heady, brilliant all-around athlete and one of the finest quarterbacks ever to play for the Crusaders.

Number 18 in purple hails from the Bradford section of Haverhill, Massachusetts. At Lawrence Central Catholic High School, he was a three-sport star and he was recruited by a string of colleges including Navy, Brown and Boston College.

Today, McCarthy is the Director of Alumni Relations at Holy Cross, a position he has held for the past thirty-five years. He was recruited to play football for the Crusaders, not by coaches, but by two members of the esteemed medical profession, both Holy Cross alumni.

"It was after a football game against Archbishop Williams High School," recalled McCarthy. "Dr. John McDonald and Dr. Charley Kickham, two well-known and highly respected physicians, approached me and asked if I had considered attending Holy Cross."

The head coach at Holy Cross was the legendary Dr. Eddie Anderson, himself a medical doctor. A very wise man, he might have been the only coach in the history of college football who ever recruited a team of physicians to help lure a talented student-athlete to his college or university.

McCarthy, considering his options as a high school senior, made a visit to the campus of Brown University in Providence, Rhode Island. "When I returned from the visit to Brown," he said, "I made the mistake of raving about fraternity life, the party scene and all of that. My parents thought that my priorities were not in the proper order and, although Brown is a fine academic college, they thought I should attend Holy Cross."

At Holy Cross, the extended family atmosphere of college life is legendary. Pat said that during a visit to the college, his parents were impressed by what they discovered beyond the many side and back doors of the cozy campus. "We were taken right into one of the kitchens," he said. "We got to see sparkling utensils, rows of produce that had come straight from the market and freshly baked bread being taken out of the oven. It was almost like being at home."

If there was any doubt about where Mr. and Mrs. McCarthy's son would be attending college, it was quickly dispelled as soon as Mom learned how well her son and only child would be fed at the College of the Holy Cross.

As a sophomore, he made his varsity debut for the Crusaders in the opening game of the 1960 season against Harvard. The Crimson were quarterbacked by a slick South Carolinian quarterback named Charley Ravenel, who was nicknamed, "The Riverboat Gambler." Harvard won the game, 13-6. Each time the Holy Cross offense came off the field, McCarthy said that Coach Anderson pulled him over and instructed him to watch and learn from the way the Harvard quarterback managed the game.

"The Harvard quarterback was a smart cookie and a great competitor," recalled McCarthy. "He always seemed to call the right play. If our defense was spread, he would hit us inside. If the defense bunched up to stop the inside game, he'd hit us at our flanks. And he even used a 'jump pass' to cross up the defense. Remember the old jump pass?

"When Harvard had the ball, I stood beside Coach Anderson and listened as he pointed out all the little things the Harvard quarterback was doing for his team. It was his way of teaching and it helped make me a better quarterback."

As a sophomore, McCarthy led Holy Cross to a 16-12 victory over Boston College and in the process he won the O'Melia Trophy as the game's outstanding player. Yet, late in the game he fumbled an exchange from the center. Boston College recovered and the Holy Cross defense had to hold on to preserve the win.

"After I fumbled, I went to the bench with my head down," he recalled. "For a few minutes, I thought the entire world was about to collapse."

He also said that he made sure that he stood far away on the sideline from Dr. Anderson, wanting to avoid his steel-eyed glare that—like Superman—could penetrate thick walls and deflate the human psyche.

At the end of his junior year, McCarthy led the Crusaders to a 38-26 victory over Boston College. He passed for two touchdowns and the high-powered Holy Cross offense, led by McCarthy, Tom Hennessey, Al Snyder, the O'Melia Trophy winner, and Henry Cutting, rolled to its second victory over the Eagles in as many years.

His senior year, Coach Anderson, for some reason, backed off from a formula that in the past had proven successful against Boston College. "He always put in a special wrinkle for Boston College," explained McCarthy. "He didn't put in anything special for the Boston College game my senior year, and we got blown out."

The year was 1962. The final score: Boston College 48, Holy Cross 12. As a coach, Dr. Anderson was not the buddy-buddy, backslapping type. He was reserved, distant and often very much aloof. Maybe preoccupied might be a better word, considering the fact that he was a master of two demanding professions: a medical doctor as well as head football coach at a major college. He was the boss. Everyone on the team knew it, yet he was highly respected by his players. However, come game day, he had confidence in his game plan and he let his players play. He didn't micromanage like so many coaches do today. "I called my own plays," said McCarthy, which is surprising considering the makeup of Dr. Anderson.

McCarthy said that Coach Anderson also could be stubborn. One time, an assistant coach wanted to use the term "umbrella defense" to describe a particular defensive set up. However, Anderson didn't like the term. Briefly, the two coaches argued, but Anderson got his way and "umbrella defense" was folded up, put away and never used again. During the era that McCarthy played football at Holy Cross, he pointed out that all of the assistant coaches had to work side jobs just to make ends meet. "I think one of our assistant coaches, Jim Harris, who had played at Notre Dame, actually had a job with the Worcester Highway Department during the off season," pointed out McCarthy.

McCarthy said that Coach Anderson stressed fundamentals and that he often quizzed the team on aspects of the game such as clock management. "He made sure that we all knew every way that the clock could be stopped to preserve time at the end of a half or at the end of the game," said McCarthy.

Pat also said that Coach Anderson never ran the score up in the fourth quarter when Holy Cross had a big lead. "If there was a chance of running up the score, he would rather have us punt on first down and give the football back to the opposition instead of keeping the football and piling up unnecessary points," said McCarthy.

In 1959, when Pat enrolled at Holy Cross, freshmen were not eligible to play on the varsity. Nevertheless, that season McCarthy had an opportunity to observe one of the greatest linemen in the history of Holy Cross football, one stallion of an Italian named Vince Promuto, who later played eleven seasons for the Washington Redskins and today is a member of the NFL club's Hall of Fame.

Promuto grew up in New York City. He was tough, talented and he had an ornery presence about him. "You couldn't miss him," said McCarthy. "Everyone knew who Vince Promuto was, even in the dining hall. He arrived at Holy Cross wearing big boots and a black leather jacket with the collar turned up. What a football player! Vin was fast, too. When you saw him run down the field, he looked like a human steamroller."

When the street wise-kid from the Big Apple arrived at Mount St. James, his presence on campus had a dramatic impact.

During the 1950s and 1960s, Holy Cross produced many quality linemen. Among the best were Ken "Jocko" Desmarais, Jim Healy, captain of the 1958 team, Jack Whalen, co-captain of the 1961 team, John Timperio and Jon Morris, just to name five. Desmarais, who McCarthy said was as tough as any player he ever played with, was killed in an automobile accident on Cape Cod while returning a rental car to Hyannis Airport.

As a starting quarterback, McCarthy faced Coach Ben Schwartzwalder's powerful Syracuse Orangemen three times during his varsity career. Although Holy Cross lost all three games (15-6, 34-6 and 30-20), two of the contests were highly competitive. When the rival Eastern colleges clashed, the confrontations were particularly colorful with Syracuse outfitted in orange and Holy Cross decked out in purple uniforms. "When we played Syracuse, the clash of colors on the field made the game look like it was played inside a Popsicle factory," laughed McCarthy.

McCarthy set a host of records during his varsity career and he remains among Holy Cross' all-time leaders in scoring (176 points), touchdown runs (25), total offense (4,534) and passing yards (3,289). In 1960, he rushed for six two-point conversions, which ties the all-time NCAA record. During his career, he rushed for thirteen conversions and passed for nineteen more—astonishing numbers.

As a roll out quarterback who was a threat to pass or run, McCarthy said that he always favored the run. "Most of the time," he said, "I was looking to run before I was looking to pass."

After graduating from Holy Cross, Pat served five years in the Marines, saw combat duty in Vietnam for thirteen months and rose to the rank of captain. During his years in the Marines, he also played football with the Quantico Marines. In 1963, the year after he graduated from college, McCarthy and his Quantico Marines earned a bittersweet 7-6 victory over a Holy Cross team captained by Jon Morris, the future NFL great lineman. McCarthy and Tom Singleton, a former Yale player, shared the quarterback duties for the Quantico Marines.

At Lawrence Central Catholic High School, McCarthy played football for Coach Dick Moynihan, a former college football star for the Villanova University Wildcats. As a youth, Pat played all sports. He was a superb baseball player and he played Legion ball with Mike Ryan, the former Red Sox catcher from Haverhill.

Living along the northern rim of the state, far removed from either Boston College or Holy Cross, McCarthy said that the full impact of the Boston College-Holy Cross football rivalry didn't really strike him until he got to college and personally experienced the intensity of the rivalry.

During his four years at Holy Cross, the rivals split four games. McCarthy remembers the rivalry as always being "cordial and competitive."

As the years rolled by and major changes took place at the two schools, McCarthy said the once great rivalry began to unravel. "It had always been a great series," he said. "But that had all changed by the 1980s. The entire picture of the series had changed. It was a meltdown, never to be the same again."

McCarthy's son, Patrick, experienced the meltdown of the series first hand. He was a punter and a quarterback for the Crusaders, graduating in 1986, the year the 91-year-old series ended after 82 games and buckets of purple, maroon and gold memories.

Art Graham

Close to Home

ART GRAHAM, CAPTAIN OF THE '62 BOSTON COLLEGE FOOTBALL TEAM, inherited his natural speed from his father, Arthur "Skinny" Graham, who was so fast that there wasn't enough land in his native Somerville to keep him contained within city limits.

The elder Graham, in baseball, was an outfielder whose combination of speed and natural athletic instincts enabled him to track and shag fly balls with ease, even the ones that appeared to be shot out of a cannon. He played 14 seasons of minor league baseball and also had a brief stint with the Boston Red Sox in 1934 and 1935. He saw action in a total of only 15 games for the Red Sox, who were managed by Bucky Harris in '34 and Joe Cronin in '35.

In 57 at-bats, Graham hit .246. He collected 14 hits, including two doubles and a triple. He also stole three bases. But he struck out 16 times, which probably explains why he toiled in the minor leagues for so many years; he couldn't hit the breaking ball.

The elder Graham, who was 5-foot-7, 162 pounds in his prime, sadly died on July 10, 1967, during one of the most glorious summers in Red Sox history—The Impossible Dream American League Championship season.

While beating the dusty trails of the minor leagues for so many years, the former BC football captain said that his father used to pick up pocket change by winning races that were staged before games, part of an end-less line of promotions that have been associated with minor league base-ball since its inception.

Like his father, Art Graham could run almost as soon as he took his first steps as a toddler. After starring at BC, he played for the Boston Patriots from 1963-'69, a terrific receiver and former AFL All-Star.

At one time, Graham held the Patriots' record for the most receptions in a single game with 11. Probably the greatest individual play he ever made occurred while he was playing on special teams. It was against the San Diego Chargers on the road. Lance "Bambi" Alworth, the ex-University of Arkansas Razorback and NFL Hall of Famer, was streaking down the far sideline headed for a runaway touchdown. Suddenly, a blur was seen darting across the television screen. It turned out to be Graham, who had run all the way across the field, caught Alworth and knocked him out of bounds before he reached the end zone.

The game was televised by NBC. The announcers were Curt Gowdy and Paul Christman. While watching the game, I remember Gowdy shouting, "What a play. Did you see that! Where did number 84 Graham come from?"

Graham developed his considerable athletic talents on the playgrounds and basketball courts of Somerville. At Matignon High School in Cambridge, he was a three-sport star.

Graham and two of his classmates at Matignon, Don McKinnon and Jack Daly, were heavily recruited high school athletes. Matignon, during that era, produced many gifted athletes, stars such as Jack Concannon, who quarterbacked BC and later played for the Eagles, Bears and Packers in the NFL.

Art pointed out that in one high school game in which he played—Matignon vs. Watertown—there were five future pro football players on the field that day. They were Graham, McKinnon and Concannon for Matignon and Bob Cappadona (Notre Dame, Northeastern, Patriots) and Dave O'Brien (BC, Vikings, Cardinals, Giants) for Watertown.

McKinnon, who later played for the Patriots and became a starting linebacker until an injury ended his career prematurely, wound up attending Dartmouth. Like Graham, Daly ended up at Boston College. Graham and McKinnon were recruited by several colleges, including Holy Cross, and both made recruiting visits to the Mount St. James campus of the Crusaders. McKinnon visited Holy Cross first and Artie made an official visit to Holy Cross a few weeks later.

"You have to remember," mused Graham. "Back then, I didn't have a driver's license, let alone a car. I lived in Somerville. Holy Cross was 40 miles away. I didn't want to get stuck that far away from home." Something else bothered Graham about Holy Cross. He thought the school's dominant color, purple, captured the mood he detected on campus. "Everyone was so serious," he said, recalling his recruiting visit. "It was gloomy, a cloak and dagger type atmosphere. Or so I thought."

Consequently, when BC contacted Graham, he didn't waste any time telling the coaching staff, "I'm coming!"

During Graham's college career at the Heights, BC split four games with Holy Cross, winning in 1959 (14-0) and 1962 (48-12) and losing in 1960 (16-12) and 1961 (a 38-26 barn burner). In 1962, Graham captained the BC team that posted an 8-2-0 record, the Eagles' best record since the 1954 team went 8-1-0.

Interestingly, when Graham thinks about the BC-Holy Cross football rivalry during his years at the Heights, one game stands out: a freshman football game at Fitton Field.

After the game, Holy Cross prepared a feast for both teams. Thick, juicy steaks were served family style. "At BC, we ate in the regular cafeteria with the rest of the students," recalled Graham. "When the meal was served my teammates and I just looked at each other and shook our heads."

Art went on to say that if Holy Cross had given him a glimpse of that side of college life for athletes at Mount. St. James, he might have ended up enrolling at Holy Cross instead of Boston College.

In those days, familiarity helped intensify the BC-Holy Cross football rivalry. Many of the athletes on both squads lived in the Greater Boston area and had played against each other in high school. Or if they hadn't played against each other, they certainly were aware of their rivals' athletic exploits.

Graham and Tommy Hennessey, Holy Cross' great back, are a good example: Graham from Somerville, Hennessey, who played two seasons with the Patriots (1965-'66) from Brookline. "We all read the papers," said Graham. "Everyone knew who the really good athletes were from other schools. It was not uncommon to meet the top athletes who lived in nearby or surrounding towns."

At Boston College, Graham ran track his freshman year and played baseball, in addition to football. In baseball, like his father, he was an outfielder. In the College World Series, Art hit over .300 for Coach Eddie Pellagrini's Eagles. Graham graduated from Boston College in1963. It was a special graduation indeed. The featured speaker was President John F. Kennedy, who agreed to give the commencement address in conjunction with the 100th Anniversary of Boston College (1863-1963).

When Graham graduated from college, the AFL and the NFL had yet to merge. As a result, the rival leagues were at war vying for college talent. The white flag didn't go up until the New York Jets signed Joe Namath away from the NFL for $425,000, which, along with the AFL's lucrative TV deal with NBC, led to the merger of the two leagues.

The Boston Patriots of the AFL made Graham their number one pick. The Philadelphia Eagles, Minnesota Vikings and New York Giants of the rival NFL had all expressed interest in Graham. In fact, the Giants let the word get out that they were going to make Art their first round pick. At the time, Graham had a job working for the City of Somerville that paid him $75 a week.

He remembers the night he received a telephone call from Billy Sullivan, owner of the Patriots. "I was a 20-year-old kid," reminisced Graham. "When I received the telephone call from Mr. Sullivan, I almost hung up on him."

There were no agents in those days so Graham did his own negotiating. However, around draft time, he sought the advice of Art Donovan, an ex-BC player, stalwart defensive lineman for the Baltimore Colts and a future NFL Hall of Famer. Donovan, a gruff but big-hearted straight talker, told Art that a first-round draft choice, 40 years ago, should be able to command $25,000, a $15,000 bonus and a $10,000 first-year salary. So when the Patriots offered a $5,000 bonus and a $10,000 salary, Graham refused the offer, telling Sullivan he wanted a package totaling $25,000. Enter the Cleveland Browns, who had drafted Art in the eleventh round. Learning that the Browns had drafted him came as a surprise because he hadn't heard a peep from them prior to the draft. Nevertheless, they quickly offered him a $10,000 bonus and a $10,000 salary.

So Graham, sure that he could get at least a total package of $20,000, relayed the Browns' offer to the Patriots. Reluctantly, Sullivan, who did not have deep pockets, agreed to up the ante to $25,000, a $15,000 bonus and a $10,000 salary, which is what Graham had wanted in the first place.

Around the same time, the Browns came back with a better offer: a $20,000 bonus to go with a $10,000 salary. Immediately, Art telephoned Sullivan and told him that the Browns had trumped the Patriots by increasing the offer.

For several moments, Graham heard only silence on the other end of the telephone. When Sullivan finally spoke in an edgy voice, he told Art: "We had a verbal agreement. You have a moral obligation to sign with the Patriots, to sign with us."

"What should I do?" Arty remembers thinking to himself. "I could sure use the extra $5,000, but would it be dishonorable to accept the extra money?"

At the time, Graham decided he would do what any good Catholic and recent Boston College graduate would do. He sought advice from his dormitory prefect at Boston College, Jesuit Father James L. Monk.

What did the priest advise? "He told me I had made a verbal commitment to the Patriots and Mr. Sullivan and that I had a moral obligation to sign a contract with the Patriots at the terms the team offered," said Graham, recalling his role in the bidding wars between the AFL and the NFL.

That's how Graham ended up playing for the Patriots and not the Browns with $5,000 less in his wallet. During the early years of the AFL, there was a definite maroon and gold tinge to the Boston Patriots' red, white and blue colors. Former Boston College football great and Coach Mike Holovak led the Patriots from 1961 through '68 and many ex-BC players dotted the Patriots' roster. In addition to Graham, a long list of ex-Eagles played for the Patriots. The list included Butch Songin, Don Allard, Larry Eisenhauer, Harry Crump, Alan Miller, Joe Johnson, Jim Colclough and Ross O'Hanley, a tremendous competitor and one of the finest people ever to play college or pro football. The highly respected O'Hanley died suddenly in 1971. His death saddened everyone who knew him.

If he had gone to Holy Cross, instead of BC, maybe the good Jesuit Fathers at Mt. St. James could have, by being creative without sacrificing moral principles, figured out a way for him to have extracted a little extra from Mr. Sullivan, just for travel expenses, dry cleaning or support for the foreign missions.

Graham, who ended his playing career after a brief appearance with the Miami Dolphins, following his release by the Patriots, worked in the Massachusetts Court System for many years. Today, he is retired and he lives on the Cape. Over the years, his knees have held up to the battering he took during his athletic career, he maintains his weight at or close to the 205 pounds he carried as a player and regularly he runs and plays tennis.

For a long time, he stayed involved in sports by working as a high school basketball official. He also coached high school football at Waltham High School for a short time along with Emerson Dickie and Cliff Poirier, two former BC football players.

During the one season he coached at Waltham High, future BC and Buffalo Bills' smash-mouth defensive lineman, Fred Smerlas, was a freshman. "He was a skinny kid back then," recalled Graham, about a boy who grew up to become a physical hulk as a man, plus one whale of a football player.

Graham got the most out of his considerable, God-given athletic ability, which is a credit to his dogged competitiveness. Today, he cherishes the friendships he has made over the years with teammates and opponents alike, including a select group who pride themselves in the fact that they competed for Boston College and Holy Cross in one of the greatest college football rivalries ever. Other rivalries received more national exposure, but the BC-Holy Cross rivalry was every bit as spirited as any of the great college football match-ups.

Jack Lentz

A Miracle Play

THE DATE WAS SUNDAY, NOVEMBER 27, 1966. NOT SURPRISINGLY, THE kid from Baltimore, a excellent student, was deep in thought reading a book entitled *Economic History of the United States*. The day before he had engineered a thrilling 32-26 comeback victory over Boston College at BC's Alumni Stadium and in the process captured his second O'Melia Trophy in three years as the game's outstanding player.

Relaxing in his room at Mulledy Hall on campus, Holy Cross senior quarterback Jack Lentz was approached by *Boston Globe* sports writer Roger Birtwell for an interview. Lentz, a ferocious competitor, wore a battle scar from the spirited battle. In the game, he got poked in the eye and wore a pirate-like black patch to protect damaged blood vessels from glaring light. The eye injury sent Lentz to the sidelines late in the first half but he returned in the second half to lead the Crusaders to a dramatic comeback victory.

Injuries had bothered Lentz during his varsity football career at Holy Cross. As a sophomore, the former Loyola High School standout played much of the season with cracked ribs, yet he won the first of his two O'Melia Awards in a 10-8 loss to Boston College in Dr. Eddie Anderson's final game as the head football coach at Holy Cross.

Lentz was optimistic prior to his junior season at Holy Cross. Mel Massucco, one of the Crusaders' all-time greats, had been hired to replace Dr. Anderson as head coach, but a knee injury and subsequent surgery forced Lentz to miss the entire 1965 season. Throughout his career at Holy Cross, Lentz had been locked in a battle just to earn playing time at quarterback. As a freshman, he had been a starter on defense, but number two on the depth chart at quarterback behind starter Mike Cunnion. As a sophomore, Lentz and Cunnion, who were close friends, shared the signal calling duties. Cunnion was a purer passer, but Lentz was a superior runner and field general.

In the interview with Birtwell following the comeback victory in 1966, Lentz praised the Holy Cross defense. "Our defense was great," he said. "And it carried us the first half of the year."

At the same time, he spoke critically about his own play and admitted that multiple injuries had reduced his quickness and ability to cut sharply. "In our attack," said Lentz, "I was the weak spot. I had lost some of my speed. I had lost my timing. I didn't know when to cut."

However, like all warriors, he fought through the eye injury just as he had overcome rib and knee injuries during his sophomore and junior years at Holy Cross. On the game-winning drive against Boston College, he completed four passes as the Crusaders drove to the BC 39-yard line with only eighty seconds remaining in the game. From the thirty-nine, Holy Cross faced third down and six yards to go for first down, trailing 26-25.

On the game-winning play, Boston College "pinched" its corner backs expecting Holy Cross to run a short eight or nine-yard sideline or out pattern in an attempt to pick up the first down. At the time, Lentz thought only about getting his team to within field goal range with an opportunity to kick a potential winning field goal.

Lentz collaborated with senior end and Captain Peter Kimener for the deciding touchdown. Kimener was jammed by a BC defender just as he was about to make his cut, so instinctively he altered his pass route. Instead of breaking toward the sidelines, he sped straight down the field and got behind the Eagles' defense. Lentz quickly spotted him and let the football fly. Kimener looked over his shoulder, nestled the spiral into his arms and raced into the end zone with the winning touchdown. In the post-game newspaper accounts of the game, the pass and catch were called a "miracle."

Kimener, the second oldest of 12 children and son of a career Naval officer, spent his youth living all over the world. By the time he reached high school age, his family had settled in Maine and he attended Bishop Chevrus High School in Portland. Coming out of high school, both Kimener and Lentz were interested in enrolling at Boston College, although both wound up at Holy Cross. "My old high school coach, Tracy Mehr, was an assistant coach at Boston College," said Lentz. "He is a great coach and a great man. I also had a lot of friends at BC, but they only offered me a partial academic scholarship and they said I could try out for the football team. I needed a full scholarship, so I went to Holy Cross."

As for Kimener, in another *Globe* story written just after the 1966 game, he said: "There was only one college I wanted to go to. Boston College was the only place for me."

However, the Boston College coaching staff felt that the Maine schoolboy football star was too small to play Division 1-A football and he was not offered a scholarship. Spurned by BC, like Lentz, he accepted a scholarship to play football at Holy Cross.

"I wonder what they think now," Kimener was quoted as saying after his game-winning touchdown catch had toppled the Eagles, 32-26.

The victory over BC enabled Holy Cross to complete the 1966 season with a 6-3-1 record, while the loss dropped Coach Jim Miller's Eagles to a 4-6-0 final record.

By winning the first of his two O'Melia Awards in 1964, Lentz became the first member of a losing team to win the coveted trophy. In that 10-8 loss to BC, Lentz rushed for 83 yards, which gave him 802 for the season and a new school record. Since then, the single season rushing record has been shattered by numerous Holy Cross backs. Woburn's Andy Clivio was the first to crack the thousand yard barrier for a single season. He rushed for 1,073 yards in 1982. The current Holy Cross single season rushing record is held by Jerome Fuller, who rushed for 1,465 yards in 1991.

Following the 1964 game, Dr. Anderson was quoted as saying: "He [Lentz] is a courageous boy. He has played with painfully sore ribs since the fourth game of the season and he re-injured those ribs when he was hit on the first play of the game today. For the rest of the game, he could only run to his left as he tried to protect those ribs."

After graduating from college, Lentz made the difficult transition from college football to the pros and played free safety for the Denver Broncos of the NFL in 1967 and 1968. After the Broncos cut him in 1969, he played one season for the Montreal Alouettes in the Canadian Football League before retiring from pro football. As an NFL rookie in 1967, Lentz fondly recalls one game against the New York Jets at Shea Stadium. In that game, he intercepted two Joe Namath passes in a 33-24 Broncos victory and was named defensive player of the week. "I had a pretty good game," recalled Lentz. "It was extra special because my parents were at the game and they saw me play at Shea Stadium."

Lentz called the Boston College-Holy Cross football series "a great rivalry." "It was the focal point of the entire season and every year we pointed toward that game," he said. "It was always intense and hard-hitting."

Today, he is managing director at Lehman Brothers, Inc., a Wall Street investment banking firm. Lentz' journey has taken him from college quarterback to trustee at his alma mater.

Going from a college player to the NFL is one thing, but rising from graduate to trustee of the oldest Catholic college in New England is an entirely different climb. But that is exactly what Lentz has done. He served a six-year term as Chairman of the Board of Trustees at the College of the Holy Cross. Father John Brooks, S.J., president emeritus of Holy Cross, praised Lentz for his many accomplishments since the day he first set foot on the Holy Cross campus. "Jack Lentz is bright, he was a terrific student, a great competitor as an athlete and over the years he has been extremely dedicated to Holy Cross," said Father Brooks.

Lentz grew up in the West Baltimore town of Catonsville, Maryland. He is the middle child in a family of three children. His father was an F.B.I. agent for 25 years and later worked in the office of the Maryland Attorney General. Lentz and his wife, Pat, have two sons, Chris and Mark.

In the 1964 game, Boston College junior quarterback Eddie Foley, whose son Glenn would later become a star quarterback at BC, pitched a 16-yard touchdown pass to end Jim Whalen for the winning score in a 10-8 victory. In high school, the elder Foley, as a senior, led Woburn (Massachusetts) High School, to an unbeaten and untied season. His son Glenn, who quarterbacked the Eagles from 1990 to 1993, is BC's all-time career leader in touchdown passes with 72. He is second in career passing yardage with 10,039. Doug Flutie is the all-time leader in career passing yardage with 10,579. Foley also played several seasons in the NFL with the New York Jets and Seattle Seahawks.

Boston College's 10-8 win in 1964 spoiled the final game in the great career of Holy Cross coach Dr. Eddie Anderson, whose career record as a college football coach was 201-128-15, including 129-67-8 during two tenures at Holy Cross (1933-1938 and 1950-1964). Holy Cross finished 5-5-0 in 1964, while BC ended up 6-3-0. In that 1964 game, Bob Hyland, the great Boston College center who was only a sophomore, might have been the best pure football player on the field. From 1967 to 1977, he put together several All-Pro seasons in the NFL while playing for the Packers, the Bears, the Giants and the Patriots.

Following his final game, Dr. Anderson admitted. "I am not a sentimental person, but I hated to see that one get away."

However, in the post-game locker room, one of his sons, Nick, put the loss into prospective by hugging the great college Hall of Fame coach and saying, "You are a great father. God bless you!" Another son, Jerry, caught up in the moment, added, "I'm glad it is over. We want him at home. He is a great man!"

1969

The Year of the Plague

IN 1969 INFECTIOUS HEPATITIS SWEPT OVER THE HOLY CROSS FOOTBALL program like a mini-plague, infecting seventy-five football players. Most of the Crusaders' season was cancelled, and the very existence of the football program seemed threatened.

The symptoms of the highly contagious disease are jaundiced skin, dark urine, weakness, loss of appetite and the whites of the eyes turning yellow. Medical experts pinpointed the source of the infection to be a water faucet in a shed on the practice field. To prevent further spreading of the disease, all those who were infected had to be quarantined.

The season opened for Holy Cross with a 13-0 loss to Harvard. The disease peaked around the time Holy Cross played its second game of the season, losing to Dartmouth, 38-6. Shortly after that game, the remainder of the 1969 schedule was canceled.

Head Coach Bill Whitton, in his first year as coach of the Crusaders, became infected himself. He would coach only a part of one season and a full second season at Holy Cross, without a single victory. A victim of bad luck, the former Princeton coach never had a chance.

The first indications of the disease struck the squad in September prior to the team's opening game against Harvard. Holy Cross lost 13-0 and "looked sluggish" in defeat. Whitton was the first to praise his athletes. "To hang in there like they did, as sick as so many of them were, took tremendous courage," he said. "I have never been around such a group of dedicated athletes."

Tom Lamb and Bill Moncevicz were co-captains of the ill-fated 1969 Holy Cross team. The Crusaders were so shorthanded by the time they played Dartmouth that Lamb had to switch from his normal position, fullback, to tailback for the game. "We didn't have any tailbacks left," he said. "They all were sick, including the starter Steve Jutras, so I had to step in and play the position."

Lamb recalled that he didn't have a fever and he was not nauseous. "I just felt weak and my skin turned yellow," he said. "But I got hit with a double whammy. Just as I was recovering from hepatitis I came down with mononucleosis."

In a touching gesture, Sacramento State dedicated its season to Holy Cross, wore the Crusaders' purple jerseys in a game against Puget Sound and flew co-Captains Lamb and Moncevicz out to California for the game. Sacramento State flanker Mike Carter was presented an honorary O'Melia Award following the game.

Lamb was a two-time captain at Holy Cross. He also captained the 1970 squad, which limped through the season with a 0-10-1 record. Only a 20-20 tie against Connecticut prevented the Crusaders from losing all eleven games.

"I have the distinction of being the Holy Cross captain with the most losses," shrugged Lamb, who was a tough, hard-nosed football player and is one of the most respected and successful high school football coaches in the state.

Lamb comes from Cheshire, Massachusetts, a tiny town of 2,500 north of Pittsfield. He was recruited by a number of colleges but selected Holy Cross after watching Jack Lentz and Pete Kimener team up to topple Boston College 32-26 in 1966 on a touchdown pass with less than a minute remaining in the game.

"That was a thrilling game," exclaimed Tom. "As soon as it ended, there was no doubt in my mind that I was going to Holy Cross."

Lamb was Doug Flutie's coach in high school and he played a major role in Boston College awarding Flutie its final football scholarship in 1981. As the hour of decision approached and the signing deadline inched closer, Lamb sent all of Flutie's game films to BC for the football staff to pour over. It was a Saturday. The next day, after spending all day

Sunday looking at the films, Lamb got a telephone call. The message from Coach Jack Bicknell and his staff was clear: "We are going to take him; Boston College will offer Doug Flutie a scholarship." So the stage was set in 1981 for New England and college football in general to come under the hypnotic spell of "Flutiemania."

Flutie was also recruited by Holy Cross. In fact, one of the first tasks Coach Carter undertook as soon as he arrived at Holy Cross was to travel to Natick High School and speak to Flutie personally.

"I remember meeting Coach Carter when he came to the high school," recalled Lamb. "I remember how intense he was that day, serious, all-business. He and Doug were about the same size and about the same height. I don't think, at the time, Holy Cross had much interest in recruiting him."

Between 1990 and 1994, Lamb left high school coaching to become the offensive coordinator on the staff of Head Coach Barry Gallup at Northeastern University. Today, Gallup, a star player and assistant coach at BC, has returned to his alma mater as Assistant Athletic Director for football operations. After leaving Northeastern and college coaching, Lamb became head coach and athletic director at Norwood High School before returning to Natick as both AD and head football coach.

Lamb has never forgotten the lessons he learned on the football field. "Losing is ugly," he said. "But you learn much more about yourself as a person from losses than you do when you are winning. But I don't like to lose. Maybe that is why I work so hard. Losing is no fun!"

Over the years, Lamb has observed a change in the approach that many coaches bring to the game. In many cases, he says that the regimented, military style; the gruff, no nonsense, drill sergeant in-your-face mentality has faded away. "Years ago many of the great coaches came from military backgrounds," said Lamb. "That is no longer true. Today, for the most part, you see an entirely different style of coaching."

Woody Hayes and Vince Lombardi, just to name two legendary coaches from the past, must be turning over in their graves at the mere thought of anyone daring to tinker with the coaching philosophy that drove them to greatness.

The Seventies

1970: BC 54-0

1971: BC 21-7

1972: BC 41-11

1973: BC 42-21

1974: BC 38-6

1975: BC 24-10

1976: BC 59-6

1977: Holy Cross 35-20

1978: Holy Cross 30-29

1979: BC 13-10

OKLAHOMA, NEBRASKA AND ALABAMA, EACH WINNERS OF TWO national championships during the decade, dominated college football during the 1970s. In 1974 and 1975, Ohio State running back Archie Griffin became the only two-time winner of the Heisman Trophy. In 1976, BC stunned Texas 14-13 in the opening game of the season at Alumni Stadium. It was a huge win for the Eagles and a sign that the BC football program was ready to tackle the "big boys" of college football. Neil Wheelwright became Holy Cross head coach in 1976. During his five seasons as head coach, Holy Cross gave BC fits, winning two games against the Eagles and losing two others by a total of four points. That was after losing the first game he coached against BC, 59-6.

In 1978, BC went winless, 0-11, under first-year Head Coach Ed Chlebek, who lasted just three seasons at the Heights. In the season finale, Holy Cross nipped BC, 30-29. Nevertheless, BC flexed its muscles during the 70s and won eight of the ten games the Jesuit rivals played during the decade.

– 1973 –

Mike Esposito, Boston College's record-breaking ground gainer from Wilmington, Massachusetts, was one of many stars for the Maroon and Gold in a 42-21 victory over Holy Cross before 22,500 at Fitton Field.

Esposito rushed twenty-one times for 192 yards and a touchdown, a 45-yard romp that was a thing of beauty. His heroics earned him the O'Melia Trophy as the game's outstanding player.

Mel Briggs, a fleet flanker, scored three touchdowns in the game. Boston College erupted for 535 yards of total offense, 389 on the ground and 146 through the air. Both quarterbacks, Gary Marangi of Boston College and Peter Vaas of Holy Cross, treated the fans to aerial shows in the annual battle.

It was a day that saw records tumble one after another. Briggs broke the BC record for most receptions in a career (88). Esposito set the BC career rushing record for attempts and yards. He also set the Eagles' single season record for touchdowns (17). Vaas was one of the most prolific passers in Holy Cross football history. He set records for most yards passing in a season, most pass completions in a season and equaled the record for the most pass completions in a game, tying the mark set by Charlie Maloy in 1952. Holy Cross' Jerry Kelley also set a new school record in points by a kicker in a season (41) and during a career (80).

In the game, Vaas, the Purple passer with a velvet touch, completed 24 of 42 passes, good for 292 yards and a touchdown.

– 1974 –

A balanced running game and pinpoint passing powered Boston College to a 38-6 rout over Holy Cross, the Eagles' seventh straight victory over the Crusaders.

Mike Kruczek, a junior quarterback from Fairfax, Virginia, won the O'Melia Trophy. Kruczek, who is the offensive coordinator for the NFL Denver Broncos, connected on nine of twelve passes, good for 124 yards and a touchdown.

Keith Barnette and Earl Strong led a Boston College ground game that riddled the Holy Cross defense by piling up 357 rushing yards. Barnette rushed for two touchdowns, giving him twenty-two for the season. (In 1974, he led the country in scoring.) For the game, he rushed for 109 yards on twenty-three carries. Strong, filling in for injured BC star Mike Esposito, ground out ninety-nine rushing yards on thirteen carries.

Early in the game, BC used a smartly executed screen pass to confuse the Holy Cross defense and open up the running lanes for a relentless ground game.

For Holy Cross, quarterback Bob Morton and big-play receiver Dave Quehl took to the airways in an attempt to get Holy Cross back into the game. With seven receptions, Quehl tied the New England college record for most catches in a single season with sixty-two.

Following the game Holy Cross coach Ed Doherty, a former BC quarterback, said, "Anything I say will sound like sour grapes. BC is a great team. For us to have won, they would have had to make a lot of mistakes. That didn't happen."

A Huge Holy Cross Upset

Peter Colombo; Fred Smerlas

A GUTSY 5-FOOT-7, 167-POUND QUARTERBACK, BLESSED WITH THE right athletic genes and a fabulous sports lineage, orchestrated the biggest upset in the Boston College-Holy Cross football rivalry in 35 years, one of the most shocking turnarounds in the 91-year series.

The date was Saturday, November 26, 1977. The place was Fitton Field in Worcester. Holy Cross entered the game with a 1-9 record. BC was 6-4 and had come close (a 24-18 loss) to beating Tennessee in Knoxville. Holy Cross, a 28-point underdog and beaten 59-6 the previous year, stunned Boston College, 35-20. It was the Crusaders' first victory over the Eagles in eleven years (Holy Cross 32, BC 26 in 1966) and it was the biggest upset in the historic series since 1942.

Peter Colombo, the little field general with the heart of a lion, was an unlikely hero. The former Brockton High School star was a walk-on to the Holy Cross football team. Jack Whalen, the head baseball coach and assistant football coach, recruited him for baseball and offered him a half-scholarship to play shortstop for the Crusaders.

In 1975, Colombo's freshman year, Holy Cross limped through a 1-10-0 campaign, but Peter got his first taste of varsity action. He played solidly against Furman (a 21-14 loss) and actually fired a touchdown pass to crack wide receiver Dave Quehl, an All-New England performer who caught 63 passes good for 959 yards and five touchdowns in 1975, in a 24-10 loss to Boston College.

In 1976, Colombo's sophomore year and Neil Wheelwright's first season as head coach, Holy Cross struggled through a disappointing 3-8-0 season. In Coach Wheelwright's "Dial a Quarterback" offensive scheme, Peter was part of the QB rotation, and played well in a tough 26-24 loss to Army, but did not play again after the third game, a 45-7 blowout loss to Dartmouth.

Heading into his junior year, Colombo had fallen to fourth on the depth chart, behind starter Bob Morton, who had missed part of the previous season because of academic difficulties, and two red-hot freshman recruits, Neil Solomon of Dartmouth High School and a kid from Chicago who didn't pan out.

As the 1977 season approached, Colombo faced an uphill battle just to earn playing time. The lowest point of his athletic career at Holy Cross occurred after the publicity department sent out a release, which was published in Peter's hometown newspaper, the *Brockton Enterprise*, stating that Colombo would be used during the upcoming season only as the "holder for extra points and field goals."

A tremendous competitor, Colombo vowed to himself, "I'll show them," and he worked even harder during the summer to prepare for his junior season of football at Holy Cross.

One person who believed in him and his athletic abilities all along was his wife, Jane Walker Colombo. The couple has known each other since the time both were students at South Junior High in Brockton. Growing up, they lived just streets apart in the same neighborhood and they began dating in high school. Today, they have two children, Caitlin, a mathematics major at Holy Cross and Peter, Jr., a hockey star at Milton Academy.

Jane Colombo recalls how discouraging the press release was, indicating for all intents and purposes that Peter would not be given an opportunity to compete for the starting quarterback position. "When that press release was published in the *Brockton Enterprise*, Peter was hurt," remembered Jane. "It was probably the best thing that ever happened because it only made him more than ever determined to show everyone that Holy Cross was wrong in writing him off."

For Peter, it was time to tap into his reserve strength, that burning Colombo-Marciano spirit. As many know, Peter's uncle, his mother's brother, is the late Rocky Marciano, the undefeated heavyweight boxing champion and pound-for-pound maybe the hardest hitter in the history of boxing. Marciano weighed only 185 pounds, but he became a great champion through the combination of an iron will and the type of determination that drove him to train harder than any and all opponents. He died on August 31, 1969 in a single engine airplane crash near Newton, Iowa.

"I was only thirteen when he died. I remember him well. He had a huge influence on my entire family. It makes me particularly sad to think how young he was and how much living he should have had ahead of him," Peter said.

Heading into his junior year and the 1977 season, Peter Colombo prepared for the upcoming football campaign with the type of zeal that characterized his uncle's preparations for a fight. All that work paid off. After the starting quarterback, Morton, got hurt in the third game of the season, a 17-14 loss to Dartmouth, Colombo got his chance to start.

In 1977 special care went into the Crusaders' preparation for the Holy Cross-BC game. Tender loving care. Holy Cross, which entered the game with a 1-9 record after beating the University of Connecticut 14-3 for its only win in the final game before tackling BC, mapped out an elaborate game plan just for the Eagles.

Coach Wheelwright and his staff, according to Colombo, planned to run their regular offense, the Wish-Bone attack, but the offensive brain trust also put in variations of the Wish-Bone, a Wing-Bone offense—with a back in motion—similar to the offense made popular by the Air Force Academy Falcons and other colleges.

"Our goal was simple," recalled Colombo. "We wanted to run the ball, control the game clock and keep the high-powered BC offense, one of the most explosive offenses in the nation, off the field. Despite our record, we were confident we could run the football against BC."

Early in the first period, it appeared to be the same old sorry story for the Crusaders against the Eagles. BC struck first in lightning quick fashion, driving 87 yards on just a few quick-strike plays and jumping ahead 6-0 on a five-yard run by fullback Dan Conway with only 4:25 gone in the first quarter. But Holy Cross fought back and led 21-13 at the half.

In the third quarter, with Holy Cross clinging to a 21-20 lead, BC drove to the Holy Cross three-yard line, where the Crusaders stiffened on defense and forced a missed field goal try. The gallant goal line stand might have been the biggest series of the game. On defense, Jay Howlett, Mike Hanne and Bob Roncarati, who teamed up for two big sacks of BC quarterback Ken Smith on that all-important series, stood tall for the Crusaders.

In the fourth quarter, with Colombo using audibles and running the offense perfectly, Holy Cross frustrated BC with its pounding ground game. The Crusaders put the game away by scoring two touchdowns on short runs by Steve Hunt and Brian Doherty.

After the game, Colombo was quoted in the *Worcester Telegram* report on the game, saying, "I thought we could run the option on them. We would flank our backs out and spread their defense a little . . . "

Winning Coach Wheelwright said, "This is the biggest win I have ever had. The kids just kept getting stronger as the game went along."

BC coach Joe Yukica, who had won eight straight against Holy Cross, was gracious in defeat. "Their offense executed," he said. "That was the key." The mild-mannered Yukica, a true gentleman, was let go by BC after the loss to Holy Cross after ten seasons and a 68-37-0 record. The next year he resurfaced as the head football coach at Dartmouth. He was the head coach of the Big Green from 1978 to 1986, won the 1978 Ivy League Championship and posted a 36-47-4 overall record.

To the victors go the spoils. Colombo and Steve Hunt, an undersized fullback from tiny Littleton, Massachusetts, were co-winners of the O'Melia Award as the game's outstanding players. Hunt rushed for a career-high 102 yards on 21 carries and scored a touchdown. Colombo ran for 69 yards, including a 14-yard scamper for Holy Cross' first touchdown, passed for 61 yards and ran the offense with aplomb, using his head as well as his physical skills. For the game, Holy Cross outgained BC 365-329, gaining 296 yards on the ground.

During the decade leading up to the 1977 BC-Holy Cross game, there had been much speculation in the media that the series was doomed and that it was only a matter of time before it was discontinued. Consequently, following Holy Cross' smashing victory in 1977, ending an 11-game drought against BC, one of the most stinging post-game comments was attributed to Reid Oslin, Director of Sports Publicity at BC. He said: "I hope you guys [Holy Cross] are not going to drop us now!"

The unsung heroes for the Crusaders in the 1977 upset were the team's embattled offensive line, a unit comprised of Mark Bates, Bob Hurley,

Jack McGovern, Joe DeSisto and Jim Pendergast. In the *Worcester Telegram* report of the game, it was written that Hurley, outweighed by some 30 pounds, "manhandled BC tackle Fred Smerlas."

Smerlas, a 6-foot 4-inch, 280-pound behemoth of a defensive lineman, disputes that claim. Known to be both crude speaking as well as tough, he put together a 14-year career in the National Football League after starring for Boston College. In response to the suggestion that he was manhandled by Hurley or any other Holy Cross lineman, he snapped, "I split his eye open. I have the films to prove it. I kicked him in the balls and then spit in his face. I kicked the shit out of him."

Throughout his career, Smerlas had a reputation as a dirty player, hounded by a "bad boy" reputation similar to the tag that has been hung on linebacker Bill Romanowski (1984-1987), another great former Boston College player who has won four Super Bowl rings playing for the San Francisco 49ers and Denver Broncos. In 2003, he was denied a fifth Super Bowl ring after the Tampa Bay Buccaneers trounced the Oakland Raiders 48-21 in Super Bowl XXXVII.

In college, Smerlas got kicked out of one game against Villanova. His senior year, in 1978, Boston College went winless, going 0-11-0 under first-year coach Ed Chlebek, who coached BC for only three seasons and wound up with a 12-21-0 record. Smerlas was tri-captain of the 1978 Eagles along with Paul McCarty and John Schmeding.

Despite losing his final 12 college games (BC ended up 6-5 in 1977), the experience toughened Smerlas and made him a better nose tackle in the NFL. "In college, I got double and triple teamed every game," he said, recalling the wars he fought in the college football trenches.

The burly ex-defensive lineman expresses nothing but disdain for Holy Cross. "We hated them," he said. "It was a rivalry and we absolutely hated them. They hated us, too!"

In one college game against the Navy Middies, Smerlas was credited with 28 tackles, two sacks and a fumble recovery, yet he was beaten out by a rival player for the ECAC defensive player of the week honor. "That week," said Smerlas, "the award went to some player from Holy Cross. I can't even remember his name. It was a joke."

Any time Holy Cross defeated Boston College, Smerlas considered it a fluke. "Let all those guys like Dan Shaughnessy of the *Boston Globe* and Channel 5's Clark Booth (both Holy Cross graduates) stand on the sidelines wearing their little purple beanies and white tee shirts and watch us kick Holy Cross' ass. If we played them again today, we'd beat them up, whip their butts."

Smerlas is from Waltham. As a youth, Smerlas said that he felt inferior to his older brother, Pete, Jr., who was a natural athlete, but lost interest in sports and never really developed his abilities. As a result, Smerlas said he was an introverted, angry kid by the time he reached puberty.

He had no interest in football until he reached high school and weighed 190 pounds, but he said he broke out of his shell by learning how to handle himself on the streets of Waltham. "There were six housing projects near where I lived," he recalled. "I learned how to use my fists in street fights. If you couldn't defend yourself, you didn't survive."

In high school, he lifted weights, discovered hidden athletic abilities and bulked up to 250 pounds. "I could ski, skate and I had good hand-eye coordination," he said. By the time he was a Waltham High School senior, he had developed into a monster lineman, a high school All-America in both football and wrestling who was recruited by practically every major college football program in the country. He narrowed his choices down to Notre Dame, Penn State and Boston College, although his father wanted him to attend an Ivy League school such as Harvard or Dartmouth. Smerlas selected BC for a very parochial reason: he wanted to remain close to his friends. "The dorms we lived in were "mods" better than many apartments in the area," he said. "I loved to cook. My father owned a grocery store and he regularly brought over bundles of food. It was great."

Following his senior year, Smerlas was selected to play in several All-Star games including the Senior Bowl and he excelled. "I quickly learned that I could push around All-American linemen from big-time schools like Oklahoma and Nebraska," he said. "I ate their lunch."

As the NFL draft approached, Smerlas' stock was on the rise, although his reputation as a "bad boy" continued to follow him. "I had this reputation of being uncontrollable," he shrugged. "If it hadn't been for that, I would have gone even higher in the NFL draft."

As it was, he was the thirty-second player selected, the fourth pick in the second round of the draft by the Buffalo Bills. Smerlas played eleven of his 14 seasons in the NFL with the Bills and he is enshrined in the team's "Wall of Fame." During his NFL career, which included stints with the San Francisco 49ers and New England Patriots, he set an NFL record by starting 200 games at nose tackle. During one stretch, he started 156 straight games for the Bills, a team record. Five times he was selected to play in the NFL Pro-Bowl and three times he was an alternate.

As a player, he was a beastly lineman; he could bench press 500 pounds and he ran the 40-yard dash in 4.9 seconds. A combination of quick feet and brute power made him a force in the NFL. "Forget about speed," said Smerlas. "It is quickness that counts." Looking at today's game, he has soured on the offensive line play in the NFL where the linemen get away with so much holding. Drive blocking, so important to the running game, seems to be a thing of the past. "With all that grabbing and holding, they don't have the balance," said Smerlas. "That is why so many linemen have so much trouble with the outside pass rush."

He also said that two pro football Hall of Famers: Dwight Stephenson, a center for the Miami Dolphins, and John Hannah, a guard with the New England Patriots, were the two best offensive linemen he faced in the NFL.

Today, Smerlas runs a successful business "All-Pro Productions." He also is regularly heard on WEEI Sports Talk Radio and he works as a studio television host for a New England Patriots pre-game show, along with Glenn Ordway and Steve DeOssie, another former BC great (1980-1983) who played ten years in the NFL and won a Super Bowl in 1991 with the Giants.

On radio and television, Smerlas draws on his vast football knowledge while alternating between a trash talker and a comic, perpetuating his in-your-face, bad guy image. That's not the real Fred Smerlas, only a persona he has grown into, a made for TV and radio act that stems from his career as a rowdy, let's get down and dirty, all-pro defensive lineman.

Smerlas is a family man trying to make a living off what he knows best: football, some business sense and his celebrity status as an ex-NFL player. Smerlas did not graduate from Boston College. He said he left school to prepare for the NFL draft just one semester away from earning his degree. He and his wife, Kris, have three children. Smerlas said that he considers himself a "non-denominational Christian" and he regularly attends services at Grace Chapel in Lexington.

As for Colombo, after concluding the 1977 season with a huge emotional victory over Boston College, he quarterbacked the Crusaders to five straight wins to open the 1978 season. Counting the victories over Connecticut and BC at the end of the 1977 season, that gave Holy Cross a seven-game winning streak en route to a 7-4-0- season in 1978, capped off by another thrilling win over Boston College, this time by the score of 30-29. In that game, Holy Cross rallied from a 23-9 deficit. Defensive end Jeff Fisher returned a blocked field goal attempt 73 yards for a touchdown. Jay Howlett intercepted a screen pass and returned it for a touchdown and O'Melia Award winner Glenn Verrette deflected a two-point conversion pass that could have won the game for BC, which ended the season winless. Holy Cross won, although the Eagles pounded the Crusaders on the ground. Anthony Brown rushed for 164 yards on 37 carries. Dan Conway piled up 116 yards on 22 carries and even quarterback Jay Palazola got into the act. He gained 75 yards on 15 carries. However, in the end, turnovers cost BC the game.

In high school, Colombo quarterbacked Brockton to the first two Super Bowl wins, a 16-14 victory over Newton North and a 41-0 blowout over Revere. However, as a senior, Smerlas and the Waltham High Hawks had the last laugh, trouncing Brockton on Thanksgiving Day, 46-6.

Today, Colombo is the assistant head coach and offensive coordinator at Brockton High School where his father, Armand Colombo, is the head coach and the winningest football coach in the history of Massachusetts high school football with 316 wins and counting. The elder Colombo graduated from Stonehill College in the same class with former Boston Red Sox general manager Lou Gorman.

Being a coach's son gave him insights into the nuances and philosophy behind the game's strategy. He knew Xs and Os backwards and forwards. He understood football with the mind of a coach and that increased his confidence as a player and made him a wiser competitor. "Others might have had more ability, but I had great confidence in myself as a leader," he said.

The Eighties

1980: BC 27-26

1981: BC 28-24

1982: BC 35-10

1983: BC 47-7

1984: BC 45-10

1985: BC 38-7

1986: BC 56-26

THE 1980S WERE FILLED WITH TRIUMPH AND TRAGEDY FOR BC AND Holy Cross. Jack Bicknell was hired as head coach at BC in 1981 and he promptly put BC back into the national spotlight. It was the fabulous Doug Flutie era at BC. In 1982, the Eagles made their first bowl appearance since 1943, losing to Auburn in the Tangerine Bowl, 33-26. In 1984, Cinderella finally did get to go to the ball. BC posted a 10-2 season, beat Houston 45-28 in the Cotton Bowl, finished fourth in the national polls, and the fresh-faced, boy-next-door from Natick, Massachusetts, Doug Flutie, won the Heisman Trophy.

In 1986, BC won its second bowl game in three years, storming from behind to beat the Georgia Bulldogs 27-24 in the Hall of Fame Bowl. Forty miles up the road in Worcester, the Holy Cross football program experienced a nightmare. Popular and highly successful football coach Rick Carter took his own life in 1986, which stunned and saddened everyone who knew him. In five seasons, Carter compiled a 35-19-2 record and led the Crusaders into the Division 1-AA playoffs. The challenge was to climb off the deck and push forward, which is what the Holy Cross football family did. Mark Duffner took over as head coach on February 8, 1986, just six days after Carter's death. In six seasons, Holy Cross posted a 60-5-1 record and won five league titles after joining the Patriot League in 1986.

The BC-Holy Cross series had been in trouble for years. By eliminating scholarships and joining the Division 1-AA Patriot League, the ancient rivalry was doomed. The final game of the great series was played in 1986. Holy Cross entered the game with a 10-0 record, but BC battered the overmatched Crusaders in the final game, 56-26. Shortly after that game, Holy Cross notified BC that it was terminating the series. By the time the series ended, BC had won eight of the last ten and seventeen of the last twenty games between the rivals.

– 1981 –

In one of the most thrilling games in the 91-year history of the series, Boston College thwarted a last-minute drive by Holy Cross and held on for a 28-24 victory before 22,500 at Fitton Field.

The game featured an aerial duel between a pair of passing wizards, Doug Flutie of Boston College and Dave Boisture of Holy Cross. Flutie, who was only a freshman, won the O'Melia Trophy as the game's outstanding player. He completed twelve of seventeen passes, good for 251 yards and two touchdowns. Boisture, the son of former Holy Cross coach Tom Boisture, hit seventeen of thirty-nine passes, good for 241 yards. He was intercepted three times in the game, Flutie once.

With only nine seconds left in the game, Holy Cross stormed to the BC four-yard line, but a fourth down pass fell incomplete and the heavily favored Eagles managed to hold on to a four-point win.

Holy Cross dominated the game by running ninety-five plays to only fifty-five for Boston College. Mark Covington of Holy Cross gained eighty-seven yards on the ground to lead both squads in rushing.

After the game, Holy Cross coach Rick Carter said, "I am very proud of my team. Our kids played their hearts out."

As for Boston College, Coach Jack Bicknell breathed a sigh of relief. He said, "Holy Cross did an excellent job. It is obvious the rivalry is alive and well."

It might have seemed so after the 1981 game, but just five years later, in 1986, the Jesuit college football series ended. It was over after ninety-one years, eighty-two games and a flood of memories that will never completely fade.

November 29, 1980

The Fumble

THE YEAR WAS 1980. THE DATE WAS NOVEMBER 29. THE SITE WAS BC's Alumni Stadium and two of the featured combatants were Boston College running back Leo Smith and Holy Cross linebacker Curt Bletzer.

Early in the fourth quarter of a close game, Smith received a quick pitch from quarterback John Loughery on a toss sweep play, turned the corner and accelerated. Bletzer sprang from his linebacker position like a cat, squared his shoulders and prepared to drill the BC running back. Suddenly, before Bletzer could make contact, the football, as if it were a slab of butter, squirted out of Smith's grasp and popped straight into the air. In a flash, Bletzer grabbed the fumbled ball in mid-air and took off. Without breaking stride, he burst 20 yards into the end zone for a Holy Cross touchdown. That electrifying score temporarily gave the Crusaders a 26-14 lead in a barn burner of a football game. The Eagles, by scoring 13 points with the clock running down in the fourth quarter, eventually won, 27-26.

In the next day's newspaper report of the game, Bletzer was quoted as saying, "I was just going to make a tackle and, boom, the ball is up in the air and I grabbed it at full stride. I couldn't believe it for a second but I just kept running until I ran out of lines."

In the stands behind the end zone, Holy Cross fans cheered wildly while BC partisans had stunned expressions on their faces. One fan was filled to the brim with mixed emotions. He was the Honorable Conrad Bletzer, former Newton District Court judge, a graduate of BC Law School and the proud father of opportunistic Holy Cross linebacker Curt Bletzer.

"When I ran into the end zone, I was so excited I raised the football high above my head," recalled Curt. "Then, I looked immediately into the stands and saw 'the old man'—my father. That was pretty special."

He didn't say, however, if his dad, a diehard Boston College loyalist, cheered or cried at that critical moment during the game. Conrad Bletzer attended BC, had his education interrupted by military service in the Army during the Korean War, enrolled in BC Law School after completing his military obligation, graduated in 1957, passed the bar exam and started his own law firm. Two of Curt's siblings are Boston College graduates: Conrad, Jr., who, like Curt, is a lawyer and works for the family law firm, and Paula, who works in athletic development at BC.

The family has maroon and gold in its veins. How, then, you might ask, did Curt end up at Holy Cross?

"I wanted to go a different route," he explained. "After I visited Holy Cross, I decided to go there. At the time, I thought it was right for me, the best fit."

He also said that his college football coach, Neil Wheelwright, a graduate of Springfield College and former head coach at Colgate, was not only a classic gentleman, but "an excellent recruiter and salesman."

Bletzer and Smith, bitter rivals on the field, got to know each other and became friends following their never-to-be-forgotten, highlight reel encounter on the gridiron.

Following the thrilling game, the first time they met was at a BC hockey game. Smith spotted Bletzer first as they entered McHugh Forum, and immediately he blurted out, "you're welcome," before Curt even had a chance to say "thank you" for coughing up the football and providing him the opportunity for a golden moment of glory. Then, before the college hockey game, the two relived "the Fumble" and shared a laugh together about a play that will link them whenever people talk about memorable moments from the crackling 91-year rivalry.

Curt Bletzer grew up in Brighton and he is a graduate of Boston Latin. In high school, he played football and hockey. In fact, he was a teammate and played defense along with Jack O'Callahan, a star defense man at BU and a 1980 Olympic gold medalist who also played for the Chicago Black Hawks in the NHL.

Coming out of high school, he was recruited by BC, Holy Cross, the University of New Hampshire, the University of Massachusetts and many of the Ivy League schools before deciding on Holy Cross.

At Holy Cross, he redshirted his sophomore year and graduated in the Class of 1981. He attended both Boston College and New England Law School, earned a law degree, passed the bar exam and is a partner in the family law firm in Brighton. He also was an assistant football coach at Boston College for six seasons on the staff of Head Coach Jack Bicknell.

One final note about the brotherhood of linebackers: Linebackers are a special breed. Lining up behind the line, fighting off burly blockers who outweigh you by 50 pounds or more and knocking heads makes for a close fraternity, especially if you are teammates, such as Bletzer and fellow Holy Cross linebacker Kevin Harrington. The two ex-linebackers are such close friends that both named their first born sons after each other.

The elder Bletzer, the Honorable Conrad J., reported that the final BC-Holy Cross football game in 1986 (BC won, 56-26) was in the capable hands of a fellow member of The Bench. The Honorable David Harrison, a Gloucester District Court judge, was the referee of the final BC-Holy Cross football game.

———

Growing up in Weymouth and graduating from Boston College High School, the 6-foot-2, 205-pound Smith was a heavily recruited running back. He was a high school All-American and he could have gone to a number of name colleges, all of which played big-time college football. Ultimately, he chose a scholarship offer to play college football for the UCLA Bruins. However, things did not work out for him on the west coast, so he transferred to Boston College, sat out a year and resumed his college football career playing running back for the Eagles. "It was too far away from my family and friends," he said, recalling the reason he transferred. "I wanted to get back home to my roots."

Sunny southern California, beautiful Westwood and the sprawling UCLA campus was not for him, despite its balmy weather and many attractions.

Boston College entered the 1980 game against Holy Cross as a 23-point favorite, although the Crusaders had won two of the previous three games. BC entered the game 6-4, Holy Cross was 3-7. Following the game, both coaches—Wheelwright of Holy Cross and Ed Chlebek of Boston College—were fired.

Entering the game, Smith recalled that he and his BC teammates expected a dog fight. "We knew it was going to be a tight, tough battle," he said.

During his football career at the Heights, Smith enjoyed many memorable games, including a 100-yard rushing effort in a big victory over the Aggies of Texas A&M. He was a sophomore in 1980. He remembers that Coach Chlebek ran a system featuring "tailback by committee," which means that several players shared the top running back position.

As for the Fumble, he said: "Curt was a solid football player, but in about a second I provided him with a gift, an instant reel of highlight film. To his credit, he took advantage of it."

In the end, however, Smith had the last laugh. Later in the game, he hauled in a pass from quarterback Loughery that covered 30 yards and set up the eventual winning touchdown, a five-yard keeper by QB Loughery. On the key pass play, Smith received a cut on his chin that required stitches. Following the tying touchdown, kicker John Cooper booted the extra point to give the Eagles a one-point victory, 27-26.

Loughery was awarded the O'Melia Trophy as the game's most valuable player. He completed 11-25 passes for 212 yards and one touchdown. In a losing effort, Holy Cross quarterback Dave Boisture was brilliant. He connected on 20-34 passes for 242 yards and two touchdowns. Many felt he deserved to win the O'Melia Award.

Today, Smith is an executive with the Putnam Investments Co. He and his wife, Brenda, have four children. Growing up, he said that his parents, faith-filled people who taught him proper values, and veteran BC High football coach Jim Cotter influenced his life the most. "I have great admiration for Coach Cotter," he said. "He is a tremendous example of Christian manhood and no one has ever worked harder to get his student-athletes into a good college. I can't say enough about him."

One of those student-athletes, Smith, a superb athlete who also was an excellent high school pitcher and outfielder in baseball, coughed up a huge fumble. But Smith and BC fought back, rallied and won the game. There was no real loser that day, and the game itself was a winner.

Steve DeOssie

But Not Holy Cross

STEVE DEOSSIE, TRI-CAPTAIN OF THE 1983 BOSTON COLLEGE FOOT-ball team, and his coach, Jack Bicknell, had much in common, including their mutual dislike of having had to play Division 1-AA Holy Cross.

Before the ancient rivals met on November 19th of that year at Foxborough Stadium, home of the NFL New England Patriots, DeOssie said that the normally even tempered Bicknell blew up in the locker room before the game. "He really went off," said DeOssie. "It wasn't like him, but Coach Bicknell was angry. He told us he hated the Holy Cross game, hated having to play it and he wanted us to take it to them; to bury them."

Which is exactly what the Eagles did. Division 1-A Boston College, which would play Alabama (20-13 win) and Notre Dame (19-18 loss) in the Liberty Bowl during the final weeks of the 1983 season, toyed with their little Jesuit Patriot League brothers from Worcester, crushing Holy Cross, 47-7. Following that rout, the teams played each other only three mores times and the series was discontinued after the 1986 game, another BC blowout, this time 56-26.

As for DeOssie himself, he called the annual game against Holy Cross "boring." "It was a waste of time playing Holy Cross," he said. "I loved playing the big games, games against Alabama, Penn State, Notre Dame. Those were the schools we wanted to play, not Holy Cross."

Interestingly, before he had a chance to loosen the pads following the 47-7 shellacking of the Crusaders, the media asked DeOssie not only about the game, but about the decline in the once great rivalry. "I told the press that I wanted to beat those guys so badly that we would get a phone call from their athletic director [Ronnie Perry] telling us that Holy Cross was canceling the series," said DeOssie. "That's exactly what I said. I wanted no part of playing Holy Cross."

Words travel, sometimes faster than the speed of light, and acrimonious, incriminating statements sometimes take on a life of their own. Before too long, Coach Bicknell got wind of what his outspoken tri-captain had gushed to the press, and he called his star linebacker into his office.

"Coach Bicknell was furious," said DeOssie. "He screamed at me. He was really mad. All I did was repeat what he had said to us in the locker room before the game, but he insisted that his comments were meant only for the team and should have been kept within the football family."

DeOssie, like any linebacker worth his salt, didn't become a tough, solid football player by worrying about making politically correct statements to the press or to anyone else.

(Another former BC and NFL star linebacker is Bill Romanowski, who played with Doug Flutie at Boston College and was also a four-year starter for the Eagles. Romanowski, a 16-year NFL veteran, was a finalist for the Dick Butkus Award as a BC senior. He has played in five Super Bowls, collecting four Super Bowl rings, two while playing for the San Francisco 49ers and two with the Denver Broncos. In 2003 he played for the Oakland Raiders in Super Bowl XXXVII, losing to Tampa Bay, 48-21. Off field, Romanowski and his wife, Julie, started an education fund to help support and inspire needy children.)

DeOssie also said that in his comments he meant no offense to the Holy Cross football players. "They were tough guys, scrappers," he said. "No matter how much they got slapped around, they fought back and never quit. They would kick, scratch and bite. Playing Holy Cross was like playing in one of those neighborhood games when you were a kid. It was a local thing and many of the players on the two teams knew each other from high school."

DeOssie grew up in Brighton, Massachusetts, a middle class section of Boston. His father, Bob, comes from French extraction. He spent twenty years in the military, serving in both the Air Force and the Army. "We lived all over the world until I was six," Steve explained. His father worked for the Boston Water and Sewer Department. Steve said that his father was a hard-worker who sometimes held down as many as three jobs. DeOssie's late mother was from Germany, which is where his father and she met. He said his mother had light brownish-blonde hair, green eyes, stood four-feet-eleven inches and weighed ninety-seven pounds. "She was born in Germany, had only an eighth grade education, but she was one of the smartest people I ever met," he said. DeOssie is the third born in a family of four children.

In the seventh grade, he attended prestigious Boston Latin—briefly. "I got kicked out of Boston Latin," he remarked matter-of-factly.

In high school, DeOssie enrolled at Don Bosco Technical High School, which was operated and staffed by the Salesians, a Roman Catholic religious order of priests and brothers. The school has since closed. St. Don Bosco (1815-1988) founded the religious order in Turin, Italy. He spent his life educating neglected boys, building them into the type of men who would be leaders in the Church and in society. The great nineteenth century saint, a rugged athlete himself, would have been especially proud of a rough and tumble no-nonsense guy like DeOssie.

At Don Bosco, a school with just a few hundred students, DeOssie developed his abilities and with the help of Coach Bob Currier became passionate about the game of football. "Along with my father, Coach Currier had more influence on me than anyone," said DeOssie. "When I first started playing football, I was just a big guy who ran around and made plays. But after listening to him, I learned to love the physical part of football, the hitting and the violence."

At six-foot-three, 235 pounds, Steve played linebacker on defense and many positions on offense, including quarterback. By the time he was a senior, he had bulked up to 245 pounds and he was a red-hot college recruit. He could have gone to many of the big name colleges including Notre Dame, the University of Southern California, the University of Miami, and the University of Colorado among others. For a long time, he didn't even consider Boston College.

Boston College was too close to home. For DeOssie, there was no mystery, no sense of adventure about the school. "When I was a kid growing up in nearby Brighton, we went to Boston College's Alumni Stadium every Sunday morning after a BC home game," he said. "My buddies and I would search under the stands and find all kinds of stuff. One time I found a miniature bible with a $20 dollar bill sticking out of it."

BC tried to recruit DeOssie, but he never made an official visit to the school. When he finally met Ed Chlebek, the BC coach at the time, he did not like him. "I thought he was a wormy kind of guy, very insincere," said DeOssie.

Around the same time, a high profile scholastic magazine projected that DeOssie would make an excellent center in college. However, Steve had no intention of playing center; he wanted to play linebacker and he would not commit to a college unless he was guaranteed an opportunity to play linebacker.

Without the efforts of Barry Gallup, at the time BC's recruiting coordinator, DeOssie never would have ended up at Boston College on a football scholarship. "Barry was straight forward and he told me the truth," said Gallup. "He also was relentless and he wouldn't take no for an answer."

Gallup first arrived at Boston College during the mid-1960s. Since then, except for the years he served as head football coach and athletic director at Northeastern University, he has been a vital component of the Boston College football program as a player, assistant coach and administrator. Currently, he is an assistant athletic director for football operations.

Gallup, who was instrumental in landing Doug Flutie and countless other recruits for Boston College, sold DeOssie on the college, the area and the football program. "He was sincere and he knew what buttons to push," said DeOssie. "When I was in high school, my father came to every practice. He would stand under a goal post and smoke Pall Malls. Gallup convinced me that if I went to college out of state, my father would seldom get a chance to see me play."

Before DeOssie agreed to enroll at Boston College, he wanted two guarantees: he didn't want to redshirt (sit out a season to gain an extra year of eligibility) and he wanted a chance to start at linebacker as a freshman.

He got both, although Gallup had to come to his rescue when the BC coaching staff entertained thoughts of switching him from linebacker to center.

In 1980, when he was a 17-year-old freshman, DeOssie made his first varsity start against the University of Pittsburgh, a close hard-hitting contest the Eagles lost, 14-6. The Panthers went on to post an 11-1-0 season, beat South Carolina 37-9 in the Gator Bowl and ended up ranked number two in the country behind the National Champion University of Georgia Bulldogs.

Prior to his first game, DeOssie was issued number 99. However, his jersey was misplaced, and never made it to Pittsburgh, so he had to wear number 66 against the Panthers. Throughout the rest of his college career, he wore number 99.

"Number 66 belonged to Tony Jones, a tackle from Syracuse, New York who didn't dress for that game," said DeOssie. "Later, I watched the replay of the game and when I made a play the announcer credited Tony Jones with making the tackle."

As a freshman linebacker, he made an auspicious debut. "I'll never forget my first varsity play," he said. "I came flying around the corner, hit the Pittsburgh fullback, the football popped into the air and we recovered the fumble."

Following his freshman year, Boston College changed football coaches, replacing Chlebek with popular Jack Bicknell, who quickly revived what had been a slumbering football program. "Coach Bicknell surrounded himself with good people," said DeOssie. "He knew how to delegate. He let his coaches coach and his players play."

During his junior and senior seasons at BC, the Eagles won seventeen games, lost six and tied one and played in back-to-back bowl games, losing to Auburn 33-26 in the Tangerine Bowl in 1982 and dropping a 19-18 decision to Coach Gerry Faust's Fighting Irish of Notre Dame in the Liberty Bowl in 1983, a game played in Memphis, Tennessee on a frozen field amidst bitter cold and howling winds.

Following his senior year, DeOssie played in two All-Star games, the Hula Bowl and the Senior Bowl. In the Hula Bowl, he injured a knee when mammoth defensive lineman Reggie White of the University of Tennessee, the future NFL great, landed on his leg. He arrived at the Senior Bowl on crutches, picked up a check for $1,500, but got delayed making connections to Boston. The delay, through no fault of his own, cost DeOssie dearly because his mother, who had been battling cancer, died before he could make it to her bedside. "I wanted to see my mother before she died, but she passed minutes before I could get there," said DeOssie, remembering the anguish he felt at the time.

In the 1983 pro football draft, DeOssie was selected in the first round by the New Jersey Generals of the defunct USFL and in the fourth round by the Dallas Cowboys of the NFL. He signed with the Cowboys and played twelve seasons in the NFL, five seasons with the Cowboys, four and one-half seasons with the New York Giants, two seasons with the New England Patriots and half a season with the New York Jets.

In the NFL, DeOssie played middle linebacker at 250 pounds. Although he was tough and loved to hit, he said that he had to work extra hard to earn a spot in the NFL. "I was a slow, fat, white guy," he quipped. "So I did everything it took—watching extra film, learning the defensive reads, picking up as many tips as I could, pushing as hard as I could— to make myself a valuable NFL player."

With the Giants, he earned a Super Bowl ring in 1990 after the team's thrilling 20-19 victory over the Buffalo Bills on Matt Bahr's fourth quarter field goal. In the final seconds, kicker Scott Norwood had a chance to win it for the Bills but his field goal attempt sailed wide right.

DeOssie, who as a youth used to roam under the stands of Alumni Stadium looking for lost dollar bills, profited financially beyond his wildest dreams from his career in pro football. The ex-kid from Brighton picked up a cool $130,000 for playing on a Super Bowl winning team and his salary in the NFL peaked at $700,000 per annum.

With both the Giants and Patriots, he played for Coach Bill Parcells, whom he said "was the best coach I ever played for and I played for some good ones, coaches such as Tom Landry and Dan Reeves."

"Parcells worked as hard if not harder than any of his players," said DeOssie. "He is a fabulous communicator. He even thrives on the banter that goes with dealing with the press. With him, it is all about winning. Nothing but that matters and he allows nothing to get in the way of winning."

DeOssie also said that the genius of Parcells stems from his approach to the game, breaking a complicated, highly sophisticated game down to a common denominator. In other words, pitch all the hype in the trash barrel. Football is first and foremost about blocking and tackling. "He wants players who are tougher than the player in front of them," said DeOssie. "His philosophy centers on beating the player opposite you physically one play at a time. If you win those individual battles, you will win the bigger battle which is the game."

DeOssie is divorced with three children, including twins. Today he works in television and radio. He does a Patriots pre- and post-game show and other television spots. He also is a regular on WEEI all-sports radio.

He was brought up a Congregationalist. He graduated from Boston College with a degree in communications and he is proud of the Jesuit education he received at BC. "You can't grow up in the Boston area and not be influenced by the Catholic Church," he concluded. "I have probably attended more Catholic services than many Catholics. The discipline and structure of a Jesuit college education helped make me who I am today."

Doug Flutie

On the Road to the Heisman

It was the "sweetest" pass he ever threw, although by no means the most accurate. He tossed it on December 1, 1984 in his final regular season game against Holy Cross at Fitton Field in Worcester.

Leading 24-10 in the third quarter, Doug Flutie connected with his freshman brother Darren on a 30-yard touchdown pass to give the Eagles a commanding 31-10 lead. Sparked by a 28-point third quarter, BC went on to demolish Holy Cross 45-10 on one of the most magically thrilling days in Boston College football history. Later that same day, Doug Flutie was awarded the Heisman Trophy, the most prized individual trophy in all of sports, as the outstanding college football player in the country.

For Natick's own Flutie, the touchdown pass to his brother was the final jewel in his crown. "It was something he really wanted to do," said Reid Oslin, BC sports information director at the time. "The one thing he hadn't done."

On the play, Doug Flutie said he broke the huddle, noticed the Holy Cross defensive alignment and immediately called an audible, changing the play at the line of scrimmage. "The Holy Cross defense dictated an automatic check off," he said. "At the time, I didn't even realize Darren was out there."

Flutie said he dropped straight back into the pocket, pump faked once to draw the Holy Cross safety back towards the middle of the field, spotted a receiver all alone deep outside the coverage, stepped up and let the pigskin fly. He said he didn't realize he was throwing to his brother until after the football was out of his hand.

"I actually under threw the football," Doug remembered. "I babied the throw and didn't put enough into it. I was so fired up when I realized it was Darren out there. Darren had to come back to make the catch, but he was so wide open he had plenty of time to adjust his route and come back to the football."

Darren Flutie easily caught the football, made one nifty cut to the inside and rambled untouched into the end zone for a touchdown. Immediately, Doug said he was seized by the emotion of the moment and he sprinted toward his brother in the end zone to congratulate him. "Earlier in the game, I landed on a shoulder and slightly separated it," explained Doug. "So when I went to high five Darren, I had to reach across my body with my left hand."

The touchdown was one of two Darren scored in the game. He also scored the next BC touchdown, making the score 38-10. On the play, an inside reverse, Darren broke two tackles and raced 19 yards into the end zone for his second touchdown. "When he scored that second touchdown, I was thrilled for him because he did it all on his own, bouncing off two tacklers, then turning on the speed to get into the end zone," Doug said. For the game, Darren rushed twice for 31 yards and a touchdown. He also caught three passes, good for 83 yards and a touchdown. Doug, who admitted, "I played a sloppy game," completed 13-25 passes for 276 yards and three touchdowns. He also was intercepted twice by the Crusaders.

Following the game, when it came time to award the O'Melia Trophy, five votes were cast. Two went to Doug, two to Darren. The final and deciding vote simply said "D. Flutie." It was determined that the voter who marked D. Flutie on his ballot intended to vote for Doug Flutie, so that is how Doug won the O'Melia Trophy.

Years later, Doug says, "I still think Darren should have won it."

The atmosphere surrounding the 1984 BC-Holy Cross football game was unlike anything anyone had seen or would see in the 91-year history of the great series. The media coverage was so intense that BC Sports Information Director Oslin handled news related to the Heisman Trophy and he delegated an assistant, John Conceison, to handle the flow of news from the game itself. Following the game, as darkness fell over Fitton Field, absolute pandemonium broke out on the field.

Flutie said that he was in the midst of doing a post-game television interview when the network had to break for a commercial. He could hardly breathe, crushed on all four sides by fans, many of whom were shouting, "Doug! Doug! Doug!" State and Worcester police worked to control the crowd. Luckily, Flutie said he spotted his girl friend, now his wife, Laurie, being jostled by the crowd. Before she was knocked down and possibly hurt, Flutie rescued her. "She was fighting to get through the crowd so I just reached out and grabbed her," he said.

What happened next turned into a blur of whirlwind activities: a frantic race against time to get to New York City in time for the Heisman Trophy Award ceremonies. There was a police escort, with sirens blaring, to Worcester Airport, a jet flight to the Big Apple and a helicopter ride to the Downtown Athletic Club in the heart of Manhattan. Nineteen years later, Flutie remarked, "I still don't know who paid for the jet. But it must have been an alumni group."

Flutie said that he did not know that he had won the Heisman Trophy until it was officially announced at the Downtown Athletic Club. He didn't know, but Laurie was sure her future husband would win. At one point, during the race to get to New York City, Doug said that Laurie turned to him and said, "Don't worry, honey. They wouldn't be going to all this trouble if you didn't win."

After the airplane landed, a trio consisting of Doug, Laurie and Oslin was whisked into a helicopter for the short flight into the city. Oslin remembered that there was time to spare. So the pilot, the calm amidst a building storm, asked if Flutie and company would enjoy a tour above Manhattan. "The pilot's gesture broke the tension," remembered Oslin. "It was great. For a few minutes, we just sat back and enjoyed a breathtakingly beautiful view of New York City."

Win or lose, the media hype over the Heisman Trophy had become what Flutie called "a monster." He said that it wasn't winning or losing the award that bothered him, but rather how he would have to defend himself if he didn't win it. "By the middle of the season, I knew that I was the favorite to win it," he said. "It was nothing I had to do with. I didn't create all the hype. The media had turned the whole thing into a monster and I had fear about how I would defend myself if I didn't win the Heisman."

Commenting on the BC-Holy Cross rivalry, Flutie said, "They should have beaten us in 1981 [BC hung on at the end by the skin of its teeth for a 28-24 win]. We only led by 17-10 at half-time my senior year. We were always supposed to be bigger, stronger, faster, but Holy Cross always battled. What intensified the rivalry was the fact that many of the players on both teams knew each other and had competed against each other in high school."

Flutie's journey that would ultimately lead to his capturing the Heisman Trophy began in Florida. "We moved from Florida to Natick, Massachusetts when I was 13 years old," he said.

He also said that it was during those early years in Florida, amidst year-round warmth and sunshine, when he had the opportunity to jump-start his athletic career. "What I remember most about that time in my life is that we were outside all the time playing one game or another," he said. "We never stopped playing until it was dark and time to go to bed."

Doug Flutie's name is synonymous with the position of quarterback. Yet, Flutie has always considered himself an athlete first and a quarterback second. "I have always loved all sports," he said. "Football in the fall, basketball during the winter and baseball during the spring and summer. I like to think of myself as an athlete before I was a quarterback and I define myself as an all-around athlete, not just a quarterback."

At Natick High School, Flutie was a three-sport star: a guard in basketball, second baseman and shortstop in baseball and, of course, a quarterback in football. Over the years, his height, or lack thereof, has always been a topic of interest and controversy. "How tall are you, anyway?" he was asked. "I'm the same height now that I was when I was a sophomore in high school," he said, "5-foot-9 and 7/8 inches. "Today I weigh about 180 pounds. Back then, I weighed 165 pounds."

When it came time for Flutie to select a college, he thought about attending Harvard or Brown University, where his older brother Billy, a star third baseman on the Brown baseball team, had gone. He also had scholarship offers to attend the University of New Hampshire and Holy Cross. "New Hampshire was the only school that guaranteed me a shot at playing quarterback," he said.

Looking back, it seems improbable, considering his size, that he would end up at Boston College. Tom Lamb, his high school football coach, and Barry Gallup, an assistant football coach at BC, were sold on his abilities and were instrumental in his receiving a scholarship offer to play football at BC. Between the end of the 1980 season, the year Flutie graduated from high school, and the beginning of the 1981 season, Boston College had changed football coaches with Jack Bicknell replacing Ed Chlebek, who had won just 12 games in three seasons (1978-1980). Luckily for the Eagles, Flutie was awarded one of the final football scholarships BC had to offer that year.

"Although I thought it might be over my head, I always wanted to take a crack at playing Division 1-A college football," said Flutie, explaining why he jumped at the opportunity to play football at Boston College.

High school coach Lamb, who believed in his abilities, played a major role in convincing the Boston College football staff that Flutie was indeed capable of competing at the Division 1-A level of college football.

Bicknell enjoyed a marvelous run as the head football coach at BC (1981-1990) and went on to be head coach of the Barcelona Dragons of NFL-Europe. "The first time I saw Doug play in a high school All-Star game, I knew he could play quarterback at the Division 1-A level," Bicknell said.

Flutie said that he was confident in Coach Lamb's ability to sell him and his multiple talents. "He knew me," said Flutie. "He understood the subtleties of the game, the things you can't coach: all-around athletic ability, natural instincts, presence on the field and leadership potential."

"I love playing the game," he said. "It's all about competing on the field, taking over on offense late in the game with your team down by four points and having a chance to win.

"That's what it is all about for me. It has nothing to do with 80,000 people being in the stands or being able to watch the highlights later that night on SportsCenter. It is the same feeling I get when I'm playing pick-up basketball, the first team to score eleven baskets wins, and I have the ball in my hands with a chance to win the game."

Doug Flutie is an original. One of the intangibles that has made him so consistently good for so long is his ability to focus on the present. "I don't worry about the future," he said. "It will take care of itself. I concentrate on the moment, what is happening in my life right now. If I'm playing basketball, I focus on the game, not on what I have to do later in the day."

Flutie is a wealthy man. In the Canadian Football League alone, one three-year contract he signed with the Calgary Stampeders paid him five million dollars. That figure does not even come close to the amount of money he has made during his pro football career, beginning with the bonus he received from the New Jersey Generals of the USFL when he signed to play in the doomed pro football league coming out of college in 1985.

Flutie is grateful that he has more than enough money to take care of his family. However, as for the fame and celebrity status that comes with being a star professional athlete, he would give it away if he could. "It means nothing," he said.

Then, he added. "Be very careful what you pray for because you might get it. I have the same day-to-day problems as other people. My athletic career is not a fair or true indicator of who I am as a person. Not even close."

As for his number one blessing, without a doubt he said it is his family: his wife, Laurie, and his two children, Alexis, who is 15, and Doug, Jr., who is 11, plus his father, mother, brothers and sister, aunts and uncles, nieces and nephews.

As a parent, he knows the concerns of caring for a child with special needs. Since birth, Doug, Jr. has been challenged by autism, also known as infantile autism, which, among other things, causes flights of fantasy and the inability to grasp the moment or live in the present. As a father who desires nothing but the best for his son in the future, Flutie compassionately yet honestly commented that, "my son will be dependent on my wife and me for the rest of his life."

Doug said that his son is a loving boy blessed with a mild and sweet disposition. "He is the happiest kid I have ever been around," said Flutie. "When he comes into a room, he just lights it up."

In 1998, when he played for the Buffalo Bills, Doug and Laurie started "The Doug Flutie, Jr. Foundation For Autism." Fundraisers alone have raised almost $4 million dollars for the foundation. Much of the money goes toward education, increasing public awareness and services to families to help them care for autistic children. "Children with autism need long hours and many years of one-on-one tutoring," explained Flutie.

Federal funding has provided additional funds for research and services. "The greatest blessing is that my son will be in a position to help others," Flutie said.

The Fluties are a closely knit family who stick together through good times and bad. Doug says that he gets his competitive drive from his father, Richard, and his athletic ability from his mother, Joan, who at one time was "a strong defensive specialist in girls' basketball. "For years, my father played the keyboard with a dance band and he taught himself to be a pretty good golfer. He is very competitive, very driven in his own way."

Older brother Bill, in addition to playing baseball, was a starting wide receiver for the Brown University Bruins football team. Sister Denise, the oldest of the Flutie siblings, was a star girls' basketball and softball player in high school.

Doug is comfortable being a "townie." Twenty years from now, he will be happy just as long as he can shoot baskets in his driveway or play shortstop for a softball team in a Natick Men's League.

Flutie was a long way from Natick on New Year's Day 1985, just weeks after beating Holy Cross and winning the Heisman Trophy, when he sparked BC to a 45-28 victory over the Houston Cougars in the Cotton Bowl at Dallas, Texas on a rainy and windy day. That win locked up a dream season: a 10-2-0 record, fourth place ranking in the final national polls and a second straight Lambert Trophy, emblematic of Eastern college football supremacy. The team was led by Flutie, nose tackle Mike Ruth, who was awarded the Outland Trophy as the outstanding interior lineman in college football, junior running back Troy Stradford and an overachieving class of senior football players who got the most out of their collective abilities. The bowl victory was Boston College's first in forty-four years, or since the 19-13 victory in 1941 over Tennessee in the Sugar Bowl.

At the end of his college career, he amassed a flood of records. He is the all-time BC leader in career passing yards (10,579, which at the time was an NCAA record. It has since been broken.); passing yards during a season (3,454); most passing yards in a single game (520); total yards (11,318); touchdown passes in a single game (6); and a single season (27). His 67 career touchdown passes are second behind Glenn Foley, who threw 72 TD aerials.

Flutie never owned a car until he signed with the New Jersey Generals. Then he bought a maroon Porsche, which stood out like a sore thumb in the BC parking lot. When he purchased the luxury car, he had never driven an automobile with standard transmission so he had to learn how to shift gears.

Life changed in other ways for Flutie. His communications professor received a note from Flutie saying he could not attend class on a given day because "he would be appearing on the Today Show." In an aside the professor remarked, "What do I have to say about communications to someone who is appearing on the Today Show?"

In the NFL, Flutie has played for the Bears; the Patriots; the Bills, where during his three seasons (1998-2000) in Buffalo he helped lead the foundering Bills back into contention; and the Chargers, where in 2003 he was expected to tutor and back-up starter Drew Brees, the young QB from Purdue. Mike Ditka, the former coach of the Bears, was a big Flutie supporter. However, Raymond Berry, who coached him when he joined the Patriots in 1987, was prejudiced against him, didn't stick with him and as a result his stint with his hometown NFL team was less than fulfilling.

From 1990 through 1997, he enjoyed his greatest success in Canada playing in the CFL. He played for three teams: the British Columbia Lions, the Calgary Stampeders and the Toronto Argonauts. In eight seasons playing in the CFL, he won six Most Outstanding Player awards and three Grey Cups after leading teams to the CFL title.

Flutie is the fourth leading career passer in the history of the CFL with 41,355 yards, 270 touchdowns and 66 rushing touchdowns. Interestingly, Darren Flutie, who recently announced his retirement after playing twelve seasons in the CFL, is the league's all-time leader in career pass receptions with 972. He also is second in career pass receiving yardage with 14,359 yards, just 532 yards behind the leader, Allen Pitts, who played college football at Cal State Fullerton, and racked up 14,891 yards during eleven seasons playing in the CFL. Darren also had 66 career touchdown catches in the CFL. The Flutie brothers actually played on the same CFL team for one season, 1991, when both Doug and Darren were members of the British Columbia Lions.

Darren and his wife, Terri, also have two children, a daughter, Taylor, who is eight, and a son, Troy, who is seven.

Terri, as a wife and daughter-in-law, has experienced the closeness of the Flutie family. "Darren and Doug just enjoy being with each other," she said. "That is true of the entire family. They are very supportive and Darren is just as proud of what Doug and Billy have accomplished as he is of anything that he has done."

As for the role that football has played in her relationship with her husband, Terri said, "I didn't know anything about football when I met Darren. The only things I cared about is that he is a good person and he has a great heart."

Billy McGovern

Facing Superior Talent

BILLY MCGOVERN IS AN ASSISTANT FOOTBALL COACH AT BOSTON College on the staff of Head Coach Tom O'Brien. Back in 1984, he was a free safety on defense and co-captain of a Holy Cross football team, along with quarterback Peter Muldoon, that faced a Herculean task when it tangled with arch-rival and Cotton Bowl-bound Boston College on Saturday, December 1, 1984.

The game was the third to last meeting between the rivals. Over 25,000 fans packed cozy Fitton Field in Worcester to witness the coronation of Doug Flutie, who later that same day would be named the winner of the Heisman Trophy as the top college football player in the country. There was so much interest in the game because of the Heisman Trophy hype that the game was regionally televised.

The Division 1-AA Crusaders entered the game with a solid 8-2 record. However, Boston College, which played a Division 1-A schedule, was in the process of putting the finishing touches on one of its greatest seasons ever. While Coach Rick Carter's Crusaders had racked up wins against the likes of Harvard, Dartmouth, Colgate and Brown, Coach Jack Bicknells's Eagles had beaten Alabama, North Carolina, Syracuse and one week earlier, the UMiami Hurricanes, 47-45, at the Orange Bowl, in one of the most thrilling endings in the history of college football: Doug Flutie's 48-yard "Hail Mary" pass to Gerard Phelan for the winning touchdown as time expired. During the past nineteen years, the average college football fan has seen a replay of that last-second heave and miracle catch at least one hundred times or more.

During that 1984 season, Holy Cross lost to Boston University, which has since dropped collegiate football, 16-12, and New Hampshire, 14-13. Boston College, on the other hand, entered the 1984 Holy Cross game with an 8-2 record, ranked eighth in the country and only eight slim points away from an unbeaten season. The only blemishes on the Eagles' record were a 21-20 loss to West Virginia and 37-30 defeat against the Beast of the East, Penn State.

Realistically, Holy Cross had no chance against BC entering the 1984 game. The best chance that the Crusaders had was to "hang around," keep the game competitive and hope that Boston College would be flat emotionally, operating on cruise control after its huge win over Miami and gearing for a Cotton Bowl match-up against the Houston Cougars.

For the first half, Holy Cross hung tough and trailed by only seven points at the half, 17-10. However, in the third quarter, three costly Holy Cross turnovers (two interceptions and a fumble) opened the floodgates. BC struck for 28 points en route to a 45-10 win and it was time for the Maroon and Gold to don ten-gallon hats and get ready for a trip to Texas. In the game, Flutie connected on 13 of 25 passes for 276 yards and three touchdowns. He was intercepted three times, and his normally sure-handed receivers also dropped six of his passes. Otherwise, Flutie's final passing statistics would have been even more impressive.

Almost two decades following the game, Billy McGovern can look back at the game with a degree of detachment. "In the second half, their superior talent just took over," he said, speaking by telephone from the Boston College football offices.

Although lapses in pass coverage resulted in at least one BC (Darren Flutie's 30-yard reception) touchdown, McGovern played solidly. He was credited with six tackles and an interception, his eleventh of the season which led Division 1-AA. Entering the 1984 BC game, Holy Cross was already a cranky football team on edge. The previous season the Crusaders qualified for the Division 1-AA NCAA playoffs, losing to Western Carolina, 28-21.

Around the time of the BC game, Father John Brooks, S.J., president of Holy Cross, announced that because the dates of the Division 1-AA playoffs conflicted with the dates of final semester exams at Holy Cross coach Carter's team would not be participating.

"As a team, we were very disappointed," recalled McGovern. "It particularly hit us seniors hard. That decision meant that the Boston College game would be our final college football game."

Today, McGovern remembers the intensity that surrounded his final college football game. Yet, at the same time, with all the Heisman Trophy hype in the air, McGovern said, "It was a carnival-like atmosphere, unreal, like nothing we had ever experienced."

As for the Heisman coronation that took place later that night at the Downtown Athletic Club in New York City, Billy contributed to the myth and magic that surrounds the award when he said, "I helped win the Heisman Trophy for Doug Flutie. He completed more passes over my head than anyone else."

"Seriously," McGovern continued, "Doug is a great, great player. I should consider myself lucky that I made it into some of his highlight films."

Nevertheless, make no mistake about one fact: William McGovern was one tough football player, a consensus Division 1-AA All-American as a senior and All-East as both a junior and senior. After college, he had a brief tryout with the New York Giants. At 6-foot-1, 200 pounds, an athletic defensive back who was clocked in the 40-yard dash in 4.6 seconds, McGovern was no Deion Sanders. McGovern was not as fast or as gifted as Sanders, but he was far tougher. Billy was a bone-rattling hitter and during his college football career he rattled the cage of many a running back.

McGovern looks like a football player. Every inch and pound of him. With his skin haircut and a face that looks like a clenched fist when he scowls, he would need no resumé to qualify as a Marine drill sergeant, lumberjack or a bouncer.

This son of a trucker comes from Oradell, New Jersey. He is the middle child in a family of nine, six brothers and two sisters. "My father, Howard, is tough," Billy said. "But my mother, Terry, is even tougher. Growing up, I remember that she had a wicked left cross."

In high school, at Bergen Catholic, McGovern excelled in three sports. In football, he not only made All-State but he was selected to the Bergen County All-Century team. When it came time to select a college,

McGovern had a little "inside help" getting into Holy Cross. At the time, his mother's brother, Father Earle Markey, S.J., was Dean of Students at the College of the Holy Cross. In football, without a scholarship, Billy proved his grit by making the varsity and starting as a freshman walk-on.

A week before the BC-Holy Cross game, the day after Thanksgiving in 1984, McGovern was home and watched the BC-Miami game on television with his brother Jack. At the conclusion of Boston College's dramatic win over the Hurricanes, McGovern remembered that his brother Jack turned to him and said after watching how hard it had rained in Miami during the game, "You better hope that Flutie comes down with a bad cold."

He also remembers the letdown feeling he felt coming off the field after the 45-10 loss to BC. "There was a huge celebration going on. Flutie was being carried off the field. I looked up at the scoreboard and it was not the score I had wanted to see."

At the time, he remembered Steve Raquet, a defensive end, who played his final game the previous year, a 47-7 pasting by BC, telling him how painful the realization was, when it sunk in, that you had played your final game.

"I didn't want to leave the field," he said. "And it was difficult having to take the uniform off."

There is something downright painful—if you love the game, revel in the feeling of delivering a square, big blow, absorbing a hard, solid hit yourself and the special camaraderie of the team experience—about knowing you have played your last football game. I wondered how McGovern had expressed his emotions after his final college game. "Did you have tears in your eyes?" he was asked.

"No nothing like that," he said, setting the record straight. "A true Irishman only cries over the last drop of beer."

What about his upbringing, the middle son growing up in a large, middle-class family in Northern New Jersey? How much affirmation did he receive from his parents and his father in particular? McGovern said that although his father is a rugged, man's man type of guy, a typical Irishman not prone to displays of emotion, especially in regard to feelings of affection, he said he and his siblings come from a loving family. "It was understood," he said. "All of us knew that we were loved and our parents were proud of each of us."

Billy said that many of the Boston College and Holy Cross football players come from similar family backgrounds. "The football players come from New Jersey, Pennsylvania, Illinois, Massachusetts, Ohio, New York and other places," he said. "The families are hardworking. They sacrifice and do whatever it takes so that their children will get a good education."

His sister, Patricia, the oldest in the McGovern family, was, as Billy says, "the first to leave the house." She headed to New England and enrolled at Boston College. After her, four brothers—Jack, Tom, Billy and Rob—all came East and enrolled at Holy Cross. Jack and Rob both played football for the Crusaders. Rob, like Billy, was a consensus Division 1-AA All-America. A fifth brother, Jim, intended to enroll at Holy Cross. However, instead he accepted a golf scholarship to the University of Arkansas and later played on the PGA tour.

McGovern tells a humorous story about his brother Jack, who was a rugged offensive lineman for Holy Cross and played a major role in the Crusaders 35-20 upset of Boston College in 1977. In that game, the strategy, when double teaming Boston College's one-man wrecking crew of a defensive lineman, Fred Smerlas, was to attack him from the waist down; to hit him low because of his tremendous upper body strength and power.

"Late in the game," McGovern said, "Jack told me that he got cocky and tried to go high at Smerlas, hitting him around the chest, sticking him on his upper body."

That boldness, straying from a strategy that had been somewhat effective throughout much of the game, proved to be a mistake.

"Jack said that Smerlas simply picked him up like a pillow or rag doll and smashed him to the ground on his head," said McGovern, laughing as he retold the story.

What about the intensity of the rivalry? Did you guys hate BC? "That is the wrong choice of a word," said McGovern. "It was a very intense rivalry but we didn't hate them. BC represented the pinnacle of success in college football in New England. They were the best. We wanted to be where they were, although we were heading in an opposite direction. I would say that most of the football players at Holy Cross respected Boston College."

McGovern has coached at Pennsylvania, Holy Cross, UMass, Pittsburgh and Boston College during his college coaching career. He has

Mike Ruth

An Elite Lineman

IN 1985, THE YEAR AFTER DOUG FLUTIE HAD GRADUATED AND MOVED on to the pros, Boston College senior nose tackle Mike Ruth won the prestigious Outland Trophy, given each year to the best college football interior lineman in the country.

By winning the award, he joined an elite inner circle comprising many of the greatest college linemen in the history of the game, giants such as Jim Parker (Ohio State), Alex Karras (Iowa), Tommy Nobis (Texas), Bruce Smith (Virginia Tech), Lee Roy Selmon (Oklahoma), George Connor (Notre Dame), Ron Yary (Southern California) and Mike Reid (Penn State).

The award is named in honor of its benefactor, Dr. John H. Outland, who was a graduate of the University of Kansas. On the football field, Ruth had much in common with other Outland Trophy winners. Off the field, especially in terms of academics and college classroom experience, Ruth stands alone. At Boston College, he majored in religious studies— a claim that no other Outland Trophy winner can make.

"At Boston College, we had a great religious studies program," Ruth said, "the best in the country. In fact, my senior year we were tied with Notre Dame for the top program for undergraduate students majoring in religion."

The Outland Trophy was instituted in 1946. In the 58-year history of the award, Ruth is one of only two linemen to have captured the Outland Trophy despite playing on a losing team. He is also the only nose tackle to win the award. The fact that he set the Division 1-A NCAA record for career sacks (29) for an interior lineman was certainly a factor in his being honored.

In 1985, the BC football program tumbled back to earth after the Eagles' meteoric rise the year before climaxed by Doug Flutie winning the Heisman Trophy; a 45-28 victory over the Houston Cougars in the Cotton Bowl; a 10-2 record; and a fourth place finish in the national polls.

Coach Jack Bicknell's Eagles opened the 1985 season by losing to Brigham Young 28-14 in the Kick Off Classic at Giants Stadium in East Rutherford, New Jersey. In that game, Ruth staked an immediate claim for the Outland Trophy. He was a disruptive force on defense and he chased Brigham Young quarterbacks all over the field.

Boston College lost four games in a row: West Virginia, 13-6; Cincinnati, 24-17; Penn State, 16-12; and Syracuse, 41-21, before ending the season by blasting Holy Cross, 38-7. The loss to Joe Paterno's Nittany Lions of Penn State was particularly painful because BC outplayed Penn State for much of the game. After a glorious season in 1984, Boston College fell to 4-8-0 in 1985.

"Heading into the season we knew it was going to be a tough season," said Ruth. "You can't lose someone like Flutie and not be hurt by it. He was the best athlete and finest person I have ever been around."

In 1985, Ruth was tri-captain of the Eagles. The other captains were Troy Stradford, a two-time captain, and Shawn Regent. Ruth and BC never lost to Holy Cross during his four years at the Heights. In fact, BC outscored the Crusaders, 165-34. Ruth, who expressed respect for rival Holy Cross football players, said that depth was the major difference between the two programs. "Every year, they had ten to fifteen football players who could play for anyone," he said. "But by the end of the first quarter, we knew we were going to win and that the game was over. Holy Cross just didn't have the number of quality football players to compete with us."

Ruth also praised the quality of the education that students receive at both schools. "Some of the best people I have ever met played football for

Boston College and Holy Cross," he said. "Not one of them is a wimp. They received a solid education; they speak well, write well and all them have been very successful in their own fields."

Ruth, who played at 6-foot-2 and between 265 and 275 pounds, was known for his intensity on the field as well as his brute strength. On a regular basis, he bench pressed 580 pounds. He wound up at BC, but he came very close to accepting a scholarship to play football for the University of Arizona Wildcats.

"I had a great recruiting trip out to the University of Arizona," he said. "But it came down to academics and the fact that Boston College is a Catholic college."

Before he accepted the scholarship offer from Arizona, Ruth wanted to know what their graduation rate was for football players. School officials were reluctant to tell him it was thirty-six percent. When he heard that, he immediately called the BC coaching staff and said that he had changed his mind and if the scholarship offer was still on the table, he was coming to Boston College.

"At Boston College," he said, "even if you only play one series of downs as a freshman and never play again, the graduation rate for football players is ninety-three percent. At the time, I was looking at the big picture and life after football. As soon as I heard that I started packing my bags; I was going to BC."

Ruth comes from Morristown, Pennsylvania. In high school, he was a star offensive tackle at Methacton High School. He is the youngest of three children. When he was in the ninth grade, his parents separated and eventually divorced. Back then, he said, divorce was not nearly as accepted as it is today. As a result, there was an ugly stigma attached to it and the sons and daughters of divorced parents were seen as outcasts. "At the time, myself and another student were the only ones in the entire school who saw their parents go through a divorce," he said. "By the time I graduated from high school, more than half of the parents at the same school were divorced."

Around the time that Mike was heading to college, his late mother's rheumatoid arthritis condition worsened. Ruth said she suffered greatly and at one point underwent four major operations. "In the span of four weeks, my mother had four surgeries, two hip replacements and two knee replacements," he said. "With all those surgeries in such a short period of time, she set a medical record in this country. It had never been done before—a rheumatoid arthritis patient having that many operations in such a short period of time. My mother was the toughest person I have ever known."

Any mention of Ruth the person would be inaccurate and incomplete without including his spiritual depth. For years, he said, he only attended Mass twice a year, at Christmas and Easter. Then, during high school, he read a book about the Fatima apparitions (The Catholic Church affirms that in 1917, at Fatima, Portugal, Mary, the mother of Jesus, appeared to three children numerous times).

Ruth said that the book dramatically changed his life and that reading it triggered a personal conversion experience. "After reading that book, I had to know more about it," he said. "I absolutely had to know if it was true, because if it was I knew that I would never be the same again."

Soon after reading the book, Ruth said that he took a forty minute bus ride into Philadelphia and went straight to the main library. "I asked the librarian to get me everything that has ever been printed in a major newspaper about the apparitions," he said.

Over a period of time and many trips to the Philly library, Mike said that he read reports about the apparitions in New York, Chicago and London newspapers. "I read everything I could get my hands on," he said. "When I was finished reading the accounts of the apparitions in secular newspapers, I became convinced that the apparitions had happened and what the Church says about them is true."

And from that moment until today, Mike Ruth has been a changed man, examining every aspect of his life, past and present. As a youth, he said that he has come to believe he may have been afflicted with ADD (Attention Deficiency Disorder). "Football was an important part of my life, but it is by no means my entire life," he said. "Number one in my life is my relationship with Christ."

During his football career, stories surfaced in the secular press that Ruth intended to study for the priesthood. "I was very serious about it," he explained. "I kept going back and forth on the subject; I'm going in the seminary; I'm not going in the seminary."

Eventually he decided that he was called to be a Catholic layman and to marry and raise a family. Today, Mike and his wife, Judy, are the parents of six children, three boys and three girls. "I really struggled with the celibacy issue," said Ruth. "I am grateful that God eventually showed me the path he wanted me to travel and I'm especially blessed because my wife Judy is absolutely the greatest person in the world!"

From the moment Ruth walked onto the BC campus, he made his commitment to the Catholic faith known; he did not hide his light under a bushel basket as it says in Sacred Scripture. Instead, he let it shine for all to see.

Reid Oslin, former sports information director at Boston College, told a couple of stories about Ruth standing up for his beliefs even on the football field.

"Once Coach Jack Bicknell went on a tantrum on the practice field, swearing and throwing his hat because things weren't going well," Oslin said. "Mike went right up to him and said, 'Coach, you shouldn't swear like that.' Jack is known as a gentleman and immediately he turned towards Ruth and said: 'You are right, Mike. I shouldn't be using that kind of language.' "

The night before games, the BC football team ate a big meal together and often watched a movie. "One night, the particular movie was racy with a lot of foul language and violence," remembered Oslin. "Ruth got up and walked out of the room. He didn't want to be separated from his teammates, so instead of going back to his room, he pulled up a chair and sat in the hallway outside the room where the movie was being shown until it was over."

Today, Ruth travels around the country speaking to Catholic men's groups. Several years ago, he spoke in Lowell, Massachusetts before a crowd of two thousand men from all over New England. He was on the dais along with the late Bishop John McNamara, former auxiliary bishop of Boston and Chief of United States Navy chaplains. At the conference, Mike told all in attendance: "The world is loaded with wimpy men. The Church needs bold, courageous men. It takes real guts, real courage to stand up for your faith by living what you believe. By being the best fathers and the best husbands we can be, we will rebuild the family, reform the culture and change the world."

Following his Outland Trophy-winning senior season, Ruth was drafted in the second round by the New England Patriots. After two years and two knee operations, the Patriots released him and he gave pro football one last try with the Houston Oilers as a free agent. He performed well during training camp and it looked like he would earn a spot on the regular season roster, but another injury, his third in as many years, ended his playing career and forced him to retire.

Today, Ruth is an independent contractor in the insurance industry. His specialty is providing coverage for businesses. The insurance industry attracts many ex-college football players. Gordie Lockbaum, the ex-Holy Cross great, has settled into a career in insurance. And so have Brian McNally, a former UMass quarterback, and John Daniel, a former Brown University lineman, just to name four. It must have something to do with the intense nature of sales and the insurance industry. The combination gets the old competitive juices flowing in ex-college football players.

The Darkest Day

Rick Carter

PERHAPS THE DARKEST DAY IN THE HISTORY OF HOLY CROSS FOOTBALL was February 2, 1986.

On that day, popular and highly successful head football coach Rick Carter took his own life. The previous night, a Saturday, he had left the football offices at Holy Cross, appearing to be in good spirits. Early the next morning, at 8:14 A.M., he was found hanging in a hallway of the family's West Boylston home by his 21-year-old son, Nick, a Holy Cross student. Medical examiners ruled the death a suicide. No suicide note was found.

The news of his death devastated the Holy Cross football family like nothing that has ever happened to the football program before or since. The entire campus was in shock. The expressions of grief were all filled with sentiments of disbelief. "He was so full of life, enthusiasm and energy," they said.

For the 42-year-old Carter, the sky appeared to be the limit. He had compiled a 137-58-7 career record. Before coming to Holy Cross in 1981, he had coached at Hanover College, Earlham College, his alma mater, and at Dayton University, where, in 1980, he led the Flyers to a 14-0 record and the Division III NCAA Championship. For his efforts, he was named Division II and III Coach of the Year. In his five seasons at Holy Cross, he had a 35-19-2 record, including a 9-2-1 record in 1983 when he was named Division I-AA Coach of the Year. That season Holy Cross lost to Western Carolina, 21-28, in the NCAA Division I-AA playoffs. Coach Carter took that loss hard. He stewed and fretted over every loss.

All who knew him admitted that he was a driven man, a perfectionist, a person who had to be the best at whatever he did, regardless of whether it was coaching football, playing racquetball or even filling a glass jar with loose change. Once, he observed a friend tossing change into a jar and commented about it. Immediately, Carter went out, got his own jar and starting filling it with change as quickly as he could and was not satisfied until the jar overflowed with coins. Then, gleefully, he announced to his friend that "he had beaten him" by being the first to fill the jar "to the top" with nickels, dimes and quarters.

In a probing story written by Jackie MacMullan of the *Boston Globe*, following the death of Carter, the late Edward Bennett Williams, the former chairman of the board of trustees at Holy Cross, was quoted as saying this about Carter: "He was a driven, compulsive man. He had tunnel vision. He was unable to see anything but his own career. He had no friends in the sense that most people did. He had no one to share his joys and troubles with."

Williams, who described Carter as a clone of George Allen, the great Washington Redskins' coach, who also was restless and driven, was instrumental in bringing Carter to Holy Cross from the University of Dayton. It was he, too, who refused to let Carter out of his contract when the coach wanted to entertain other coaching opportunities.

Carter was a brilliant coach, a superb judge of talent, a master organizer and man who knew how to assemble the quintessential coaching staff. He surrounded himself with many of the brightest and best young coaches in the country, men who have climbed the coaching ladder such as: Mike Sherman (head coach of the Green Bay Packers), Mark Duffner (former Holy Cross head coach and current Green Bay Packers assistant coach), Tom Rossley (Green Bay Packers offensive coordinator), Peter McCarty (Stanford Defensive Ends Coach), and Dan Allen (former Boston University and the current Holy Cross head coach). The list goes on and on.

Fellow coaches were attracted to his clinics and practices like bees to honey. Tom Lamb, athletic director and head football coach at Natick High School, was a two-time captain at Holy Cross in 1969 and 1970.

Speaking of Carter, he said, "He had an excellent grasp of the game. All football teams run reps or plays in practice [sometimes called signal drill or dummy scrimmages]. But his reps were all quality reps. You would stand on the sidelines watching and just marvel at it."

In 1985, Carter and Holy Cross suffered through a 4-6-1 losing season. His father died the previous summer and his father's death had hit him hard. The two were close, "two of a kind," many said. Pleasing his dad, making him proud, was a big part of what drove Rick Carter. After his father's death, Carter had briefly sought treatment for his own depression. His mother also was in poor health. In fact, at the time of his own death, his wife, Deanne, was in Ohio visiting family, including his seriously ill mother.

Reportedly, Carter was also distraught over the Holy Cross decision to de-emphasize football, which included eliminating scholarships by 1989. He was restless, fearful that the shine had faded from his rising star. He was looking for a fresh start, a new opportunity. He wanted to interview for head coaching positions at North Carolina State and the University of Missouri, but Holy Cross refused permission and would not let him out of his contract.

Like everyone else at Holy Cross, the news of Carter's death blindsided Coach Mark Duffner. He said he was unaware that his friend and fellow coach was so distraught. "I wish I had seen some signs, but I really didn't," Duffner said.

Although Carter was a fiery, emotional coach, Duffner said that he was placid and unemotional when it came to his personal life. "He was very contained and low key about his personal life," continued Duffner. "He let it out on the football field, but when it came to his own personal struggles, he kept those feelings to himself."

Duffner played a major role in the Holy Cross football team being able to pull itself off the deck after the terrible tragedy and move forward. He said it never could have been done without the support of everyone at Holy Cross. "Everyone rallied and pitched in to help," he explained. "That's what makes Holy Cross so special; that's what makes Holy Cross such a great place."

From the top all the way down, Duffner said that Holy Cross pulled together like an extended family, and he rattled off a series of names of people who made a huge difference during the worst of times: Father

John Brooks, S.J., the president of the college; Ron Perry, the athletic director; Joe McDonough, the business manager; Father George O'Brien, the team chaplain; Jim Long and John Bresnihan, the grounds crew at Fitton Field; and Henry Roy, a graphic arts manager. The list of names goes on and on.

People, caring people, picking up the broken pieces from a tragedy and moving outside or beyond their own concerns to care about others. "Those people all bleed purple," Duffner said. "They really do, and you see it in the way they care about everyone at Holy Cross.

"I'll tell you something about Holy Cross," he continued, "and I was there for eleven years, six years as an assistant coach and five years as a head coach. Every one of the seniors I coached at Holy Cross passed something special on to the underclassmen."

Duffer said that he admires the Jesuits and that he has deep respect for a college education based on Jesuit ideals. He also said that living in Green Bay, Wisconsin is similar to living in Worcester. "It is the same type of community, even with the weather," said the Packers linebacker coach. "Warm, caring people. A lot of good Catholics and a great place to raise a family."

Ever since the Carter tragedy, Duffner said that he has tried to live in the moment, while not letting himself get too down by realizing that things are never as bad as they may seem. He also said he was forced to make a difficult decision when he left Holy Cross in December of 1991 to become the head coach at the University of Maryland. "I never thought I'd leave Holy Cross," he concluded. "I almost didn't leave. It is just such a great place."

Finally, at the end of the conversation, Coach Duffner left the door partially open to his one day returning to Mount St. James.

"You never know," he said. "Someday I could return to Holy Cross."

———

Steve Southard was one of four captains of the 1986 Holy Cross football team. For him, the year 1986 was a roller coaster ride. First, there was the shocking death of Coach Carter. Next, came the appointment of Mark Duffner as Carter's successor. What followed was a whirlwind unbeaten 10-0 league season and Patriot League Championship, only to be followed by a crushing and humiliating 56-26 loss to Boston College in the final game of the 91-year rivalry. Before moving to Maryland as head football coach, Duffner enjoyed phenomenal success leading Holy Cross to the top of Division I-AA. From 1986 to 1991, Holy Cross had a 60-5-1 record, posted two 11-0-0 seasons, captured five Patriot League titles and four Lambert Cups.

Southard comes from Fairfield, Ohio, not far from where Coach Carter was born and raised. He was recruited by Carter, had deep respect and admiration for him and looked up to the former coach as a hero. So obviously, when Carter took his own life, Steve was deeply saddened, but he and the entire Holy Cross football family were also left bewildered and confused.

"The last time I saw Coach Carter was just before he died," said Southard. "He had just greeted a class of recruits. For him, he seemed subdued. But at the time, I didn't make anything of it."

The news of Carter's death spread like a wildfire. The team's awards banquet, scheduled for that same Sunday night, was canceled. A black cloud enveloped the campus, affecting everyone.

Southard said that the emergency, pastoral response team put into place by Holy Cross prevented a full scale meltdown. Holy Cross rolled up its collective sleeves and pulled together as a family. "Everyone pitched in," recalled Southard, "the coaching staff, priests, faculty members, the entire staff. All of us were given a chance to speak and to vent. Counseling was made available. We all needed to get our feelings out and people were there just to listen. That is how we got through it."

Shortly after Coach Carter's death, Duffner was named the head coach, which provided the team with all-important continuity and stability. Football-wise, the team picked up where it had left off, shook off a terrible personal loss and began preparing for the 1986 season.

Southard remembered that the 1986 season got off to an inauspicious start. "In the spring, we lost the annual Alumni game, 6-3," Southard said. "How bad were we going to be? I remember Denny Golden, Sr., a former coach and player, pulling all of us aside and saying, 'You'll get through this, you are going to be a good team.'"

Although BC's overall superiority eventually overpowered Holy Cross in the 1986 game, resulting in a 56-26 victory, he will never forget the first quarter when Holy Cross bolted into a quick 14-0 lead and the stands at Fitton Field rocked with excitement. "That first quarter was wild," he recalled. "The feeling on the field and in the stands was electric. If you experienced it, you will never forget it."

The 1986 Crusaders performed better than anyone anticipated, winning their first ten games and capturing the Patriot League Championship. Years later, Steve Southard still cherishes the team's thrilling 17-14 come-from-behind win over Army at West Point. "It was the homecoming game for Army," Southard recalled. "Mrs. Douglas MacArthur, the wife of the general, was in the stands. Michie Stadium was packed. The place was going crazy and we stole the game on Bill Young's field goal."

Southard played nose tackle for Holy Cross. At 230 pounds, he was an undersized overachiever. Once, when National Football League scouts came to Holy Cross, he said that one scout took a brief look at him and remarked, "Hey, kid. If I were you, I would head back to the library."

Steve chose Holy Cross over the University of Indiana, where he had been offered a full scholarship to play football for the Hoosiers. His stepfather, Arthur Barraclough, had been an outstanding football player at Colgate and he impressed upon young Steve the value of an education at a top Eastern college. In tribute to both Holy Cross and Colgate, Steve and his stepfather named their commercial cleaning company "Cross Gate" after their alma maters. Today, Steve, his wife, and their four children, live in Nashville, Tennessee.

Steve played in the final BC-Holy Cross football game. It was a bitter defeat and he said that the BC players rubbed Holy Cross' collective noses in the loss. "I don't remember exactly what was said," he recalled. "But there was a lot of talking. The Boston College players made sure we knew how much better they were than us."

When he was a sophomore, Steve remembers the Hollywood atmosphere that surrounded Doug Flutie's final regular season game at Fitton Field, a 45-10 BC win, on the day Flutie won the Heisman Trophy. "I got to touch his jersey," said Southard, remembering an event that was about as close to a coronation as he will ever get.

Today, almost two decades after he played his final game for Holy Cross, Southard said that he remains in touch with many of his teammates. "I loved my experience at Holy Cross," he said. "We were a family."

Gordie Lockbaum

The Stuff That Legends Are Made Of

MRS. MARIE LOCKBAUM, GORDIE LOCKBAUM'S MOTHER, DID NOT know that she was raising a son who one day would be known as "college football's 60-minute man."

"He had his moments," she said, speaking about the second oldest of her seven children. "But he was a good little boy."

Growing up, Gordie was a normal, active boy who, like all youth, occasionally got into mischief. Like generations of boys before and after him, his youthful energy and imagination were channeled into sports. "He was very good at all sports," said his mother.

But where did his rare natural ability come from? The raw, God-given talent that one day would enable him to become maybe the greatest all-around football player in the history of Holy Cross football?

In response to that very question, Lockbaum said, "I don't know. Everything just unfolded."

But what about his genes? Does he come from a family with a history of producing great athletes? "That's something you will have to ask my mother," advised Lockbaum.

So I did.

"Gordie's father was a very good amateur baseball player," said Mrs. Lockbaum, about her late husband, Robert, who passed away on Holy

Saturday in 2000. "But other than that, I can't think of anyone on either side of the family who had special athletic talent."

Gordie Lockbaum. Even if you know nothing about his football exploits, just his name alone draws attention. It is no ordinary name, unlike John Smith or James Jones. It is one of the great football names of all-time, like Steve Stonebreaker or Yale Lary.

At Holy Cross, Gordie's number 17 is as revered as Doug Flutie's number 22 is at Boston College. During their careers, the two super stars, Lockbaum and Flutie, revitalized football at their respective colleges. In 1984, Doug Flutie won the Heisman Trophy. In 1983, when he was a junior, Flutie finished a surprising third in the Heisman balloting behind the winner, Mike Rozier of Nebraska. Gordie Lockbaum, a two-way starter, which is unheard of in today's modern game of specialists, finished fifth in the Heisman Trophy balloting in 1986 behind the winner Vinny Testaverde of Miami and third in 1987 behind Heisman winner Tim Brown of Notre Dame.

Back in the 1950s, an end for the University of Kentucky played the trombone with the band at half-time. One of the major sports magazines ran a photo of him playing the trombone while dressed in full football gear. Lockbaum—who excelled on offense, defense and on special teams, returning punts and kick offs—did everything but play in the band at half-time.

As a football player, Gordie had to be seen to be believed. "I never realized what a great football player he was until I saw him play in person," said Jack Bicknell, the former Boston College head coach who lost hours of precious sleep while thinking up schemes to counter Gordie's explosive abilities. In the final BC-Holy Cross game in 1986, Lockbaum, a junior, caused Boston College fits. His fifteen-yard pass reception and nine-yard run set up the first Holy Cross touchdown. He scored the game's second touchdown on a 22-yard pass from quarterback Jeff Wiley, as undefeated Holy Cross shocked the Eagles by taking a quick 14-0 lead, only to fall victim to BC's overall might, 56-26. In that game, Lockbaum and sidekick Wally Dembowski had big games. Lockbaum caught ten passes for 104 yards and one touchdown. He also rushed three times for 22 yards and piled up over 100 yards in kick off and punt return yardage. Dembowski hauled in eleven passes, good for 151 yards and one touchdown.

To use a basketball analogy, Gordie Lockbaum was the John Havlicek of college football, constantly on the move, personifying perpetual motion. Like Gordie, "Jarring John Havlicek," which was the late and great broadcaster Johnny Most's pet name for the former Boston Celtics' great, also wore number 17. Also like Lockbaum, he was a fine college football player. Havlicek played wide receiver for the Ohio State Buckeyes and was drafted by the Cleveland Browns. After a brilliant college football career, Lockbaum played two seasons in the NFL, with the Pittsburgh Steelers in 1988 and the Buffalo Bills in 1989.

Lockbaum hails from Glassboro, New Jersey. In high school, Gordie was recruited by a string of colleges including Annapolis, Syracuse and Holy Cross. Often, when he visited the campuses of prospective colleges, his parents went with him. On one visit Gordie and his parents traveled to Annapolis, Maryland to visit the Naval Academy.

"His father loved the Naval Academy," said Mrs. Lockbaum. "We were very impressed with the entire scene at Annapolis."

Gordie, however, was not ready to make the type of commitment that attending the service academies requires. "Going to the Naval Academy meant a nine-year commitment," explained his mother, "four years of college and five years in the Navy after graduation. At the time, Gordie was not ready to make that kind of commitment."

When Lockbaum made an official visit to the Holy Cross campus in Worcester, his parents remained at home. However, when he returned home, they picked him up at the airport. "As soon as he got in the car, the first thing we noticed was that he was beaming," said his mother. "His father and I took one look at him and we knew he was heading to Holy Cross and that he had made the right choice for him."

Mrs. Lockbaum said that her son loved everything about Holy Cross: its small size (only 2,700 students), the layout of the campus allowing students to walk to all their classes, the intimacy and the discipline. "In terms of education, we felt that the tradition and discipline so much a part of a Jesuit, Catholic college were important factors to be considered in choosing the right college," said Mrs. Lockbaum.

As for Gordie himself, it was the close and intimate Holy Cross community, an extension of the environment in which he was raised, that sold him on the prospect of continuing his education at Holy Cross. "I was comfortable with everything I discovered after visiting Holy Cross," he said. "I grew up in a close family, a caring neighborhood and a tight community in New Jersey. I found all of that at Holy Cross in the coaching staff, the football players, the other recruits, the students, the faculty. Everyone. When I attended different events and activities, I even found it easy to relate to the students who were not athletes. It was great."

That reach-out-and-touch-someone environment spilled over into varsity athletics, especially home football games at Fitton Field. How could he ever forget the final game against Boston College in 1986? The underdog Crusaders shocked the Eagles by bolting into a quick 14-0 lead. In that game, Lockbaum caught a 22-yard touchdown pass from quarterback Jeff Wiley giving the Crusaders a two touchdown first-quarter lead. "How could I ever forget the exhilaration I felt after that play?" he asks. "The adrenaline was rushing and my head felt like it would explode. The fans are so close to the action at Fitton Field. The place was going crazy after that touchdown and I felt as if I could high-five everybody in the stadium."

Lockbaum said that Holy Cross had "a great game plan" and that he and his teammates felt that they had a solid chance "to beat BC." But in the second half, the frozen turf began to thaw and the Eagles' superior strength and talent took over.

The disappointment of that loss paled in comparison to the shock experienced by the entire Holy Cross football family after Coach Rick Carter took his own life in February of 1986. "A whole bunch of 20-year-olds grew up and became men on the day we heard the news," said Lockbaum.

An emergency team meeting was called on Sunday morning shortly after Carter's body was discovered in his West Boylston home. The team had known, said Lockbaum, that Coach Carter's mother had been seriously ill and many thought that the meeting had been called to announce that she had passed away. Lockbaum said that everyone was stunned when they heard the news. "I just remember how shaken everyone was when I walked into the team meeting and that it seemed odd that so many priests were there," he said.

Gordie praised Coach Carter, who had recruited him, as being a consummate professional. "He was so organized, so professional," he said. "None of us had ever experienced a football situation at such a high level of sophistication. He demanded so much from everyone.

That included the athletes as well as the great staff of assistant coaches he had assembled."

Lockbaum also said that Coach Carter came from the same school of discipline that had produced the likes of Tom Coughlin, former Syracuse player and BC and Jacksonville Jaguars head coach: "Be on time, take off your hat at team meetings, sit up straight in your chairs with both feet on the floor."

Mark Duffner, as assistant coach on Carter's staff, was selected to replace Carter as head coach. "At first we thought that Coach Duffner was too close to us, the players, to be able to run the entire program," said Lockbaum.

Duffner, however, quickly dispelled any doubts about his ability to be a head coach. He enjoyed phenomenal success as the head coach at Holy Cross, posting a 60-5-1 record in six seasons, before moving on to the University of Maryland and later signing on as an assistant coach with the Green Bay Packers. The secret of his success at Holy Cross: He was his own man; he didn't attempt to copy Coach Carter or anyone else.

"Duff implemented what he had been preaching all along. He was more of a backslapper than Coach Carter. He also had a great way of departmentalizing all aspects of life. He taught us there was a time to laugh, a time to grieve, a time to practice, a time to play, a time to study, a time to pray and a time to just be quiet, alone with your own thoughts."

For Lockbaum and his teammates, riding an emotional roller coaster together, not only forced them to mature more quickly than could have been expected, but it bonded them like blood brothers, guaranteeing that the college experience they shared would never be forgotten. As both a student majoring in Economics and an athlete, Holy Cross brought out the best in Lockbaum. On the football field his exploits are the stuff that legends are made of.

In 1986, as a junior, Gordie scored six touchdowns against Dartmouth sparking the Crusaders to a 47-8 rout in their Homecoming game. In 1987, in his final game, he caught fifteen passes, good for 196 yards as Holy Cross crushed Villanova 39-6 on ESPN, wrapping up its first 11-0 season and the number one ranking in the Division I-AA polls. In that game, Lockbaum, set or tied seven school records. The 1980s was a record-breaking decade for the Crusaders. In 1983, Gill Fenerty rushed for 337 yards and scored six touchdowns in a 77-28 blowout victory over

Columbia and in 1987 quarterback Jeff Wiley passed for 414 yards and seven touchdowns in a 63-6 rout of Lehigh.

After the 1987 season, Lockbaum earned a staggering list of post-season awards: He finished third in the Heisman Trophy balloting; second in the Maxwell Trophy voting; he was selected a National Football Foundation Hall of Fame Scholar-Athlete; an NCAA Top Six Award recipient; Touchdown Club of Washington, D.C. All-Purpose Back of the Year; AFCA-Kodak First Team 1-AA All-America; Associated Press First Team 1-AA All-America; Walter Camp Football Foundation 1-AA All-America; and *Football News* Division I-AA Player of the Year. In 2001, Gordie was elected to the National Football Foundation College Hall of Fame.

Today, Lockbaum applies his many talents to the insurance industry. He also coaches wrestling at Worcester Academy. As a father, husband and businessman, he is known for his personal integrity. The person who knows him best, his wife, Denise, says this about him: "Gordie is a man of principle and high moral values," she said. "In every situation, he always does what is right."

Lockbaum settled in Worcester, where he is viewed as a knight (or Crusader) in shining armor. "I love Worcester," he said. "It is a great place to raise a family and I get the same feeling I got growing up in New Jersey; it's almost like never leaving home. I'm lucky. My athletic career just goes on and on. It won't go away because everyone still wants to talk about it."

As for the future, don't bet against Gordie Lockbaum running for political office. The grass roots support for any potential political candidacy is already firmly in place.

During the summer of 2002, Gordie's son, Gordon Joseph Lockbaum (Gordie's middle name is Carl), helped spark the Jesse Burkett Little League All-Stars of Worcester to the Little League World Series in Williamsport, Pennsylvania. Lockbaum's son is a promising young athlete who excels in baseball, football and wrestling. "He's a good athlete," Gordie said. "And he is faster than I ever was."

Each year, network television covers the Little League World Series. As the cameras fanned the crowd, the former Holy Cross football great was spotted and identified sitting on a hill behind the center field fence.

He was far removed from the action on the field, enjoying the game as a father and fan, free from the limelight. He had his day and he made the most of it. That moment, as special as it was, belonged to young Gordie and his Little League teammates.

Like Doug Flutie, Gordie Lockbaum was a special athlete, loaded with natural ability and charisma. Also like Flutie, off the field he is a very appealing person, humble and down to earth. You can not help but like him.

"I have been blessed," he said.

The Final Game

A Different Atmosphere

AFTER EIGHTY-TWO GAMES IN NINETY-ONE YEARS, A CAVALCADE OF unforgettable players, thrilling finishes and shocking upsets, producing a rivalry second to none, the grand Jesuit college football rivalry matching Boston College against Holy Cross ended the way it began: ugly.

In the second game of the series in 1896, fisticuffs erupted late in a game which saw both schools claim victory. And on November 22, 1986—the twenty-third anniversary of President John F. Kennedy's assassination and the date of the final BC-Holy Cross football game— bitter words spewed out of the mouths of some of the participants in the post-game locker room.

As for the game itself, a crowd of 23,271 packed cozy Fitton Field, in Worcester to watch the grand finale of the epic college football series. Holy Cross entered the contest with a 10-0-0 record, yet was a decided underdog against bowl-bound BC, which came into the game with an 8-3 record. The odds makers, rightly so, saw the game as a David vs. Goliath mismatch, Division I-A Boston College vs. Division I-AA Holy Cross.

In the first quarter, Holy Cross, led by wily quarterback Jeff Wiley, who was ill and played despite having a fever, shocked the visitors by jumping out to a 14-0 lead. Wiley scored the first touchdown on a one-yard sneak and he passed twenty-two yards to the irrepressible Gordie

Lockbaum for the second Holy Cross score. Lockbaum, who was a junior, finished fifth in the Heisman Trophy balloting that year and third the next year, demonstrated why he was one of the best football players in the country. In that game, the two-way Crusaders' all-time great rushed three times for twenty-two yards; caught eleven passes good for 151 yards and a touchdown; and he returned seven kickoffs for 107 yards.

But it was not nearly enough. Boston College simply had too many weapons—too much size, speed, depth and talent. The Eagles tied the game 14-14 on a pair of Shawn Halloran-to-Kelvin Martin touchdown passes at the end of the first quarter. Then, Boston College put the contest away by scoring twenty-eight unanswered points in the second quarter en route to a 56-26 lopsided victory. Troy Stradford, who rushed for 128 yards on twenty-eight carries and scored three touchdowns, and Halloran, who torched the Crusaders by connecting on 20 of 27 passes for 281 yards and four touchdowns, led the rout. In the game, the high-flying Eagles piled up 534 yards of total offense, while the Crusaders lit up the airways with a passing game that racked up 359 yards. Wiley completed ten of twenty-three passes good for 123 yards and one touchdown. He also was intercepted three times. A. J. Nieman, the sophomore back-up quarterback, completed 19 of 33 passes good for 199 yards and two touchdowns. He was intercepted once.

The game was played in the muck and mire of Fitton Field on a day better designed for ducks then athletes. After the game, Boston College coach Jack Bicknell talked about the pressure he and his team felt entering every game against Holy Cross. In a story written by Michael Madden, a former *Boston Globe* columnist, Bicknell said, "We know—and I sincerely believe—there is a difference between Division I-A and Division I-AA. And that is not being at all critical of Holy Cross: It's just a fact. And it is like we always have to prove it all over again . . . and over again . . . and over again. And our kids hear a lot of things, that they are as good as us or whatever. And our kids get into it. Our kids get excited."

Consequently, at half-time, with BC leading 42-14, Bicknell did not pull in the reigns. In fact, he encouraged his team, according to Madden's story, to continue to pour it on, to pile up the points.

As a result, both teams became more than a little testy during the second half. Harsh words were spoken and tempers flared. "I don't know exactly why but there is a different atmosphere coming into a game with Holy Cross," Bicknell said. "I don't feel the way I do the morning of any game the way I feel the morning of a Holy Cross game. It's a game we have to win. I can't imagine living the winter after losing to Holy Cross."

Put yourself in the place of the Holy Cross football players, entering the final game against Boston College with a 10-0-0 record. Had the contest not been between Division I-A and Division I-AA programs, the Crusaders would have been heavy favorites to win the game. Instead, BC was favored. Nevertheless, Holy Cross hungered for a win to cap its dream—a perfect season—despite the fact that the undermanned Crusaders faced an uphill battle. So it is perfectly understandable that the Holy Cross football players—proud, competitive athletes—were devastated after the crushing defeat.

In the post-game locker room, Lockbaum could not hide tears. "It was a very disappointing loss, obviously," he told Madden, before pausing and being unable to continue speaking. When he regained his composure, he continued, "Boston College just has bigger people than Holy Cross, but you've just got to believe you're tougher and bigger on the inside than they are on the outside. A lot of times in football, it's who's got more heart."

Holy Cross had no chance of defeating Boston College given the disparity of the two football programs during the final years of the series.

In another corner of the post-game locker room, Holy Cross quarterback Wiley added wistfully, "I was just praying and hoping for the best, just praying for the perfect season . . ."

After Holy Cross jumped out to a 14-0 lead, the Eagles' star running back Stradford accused Holy Cross defensive back Byron Dixon of taunting him. "When they were up 14-0, he started talking trash. He kept talking, so I talked back to him," Stradford told Madden.

By the time the game ended, the players on both teams were caked with mud. The intensity with which the game had been played was palpable. Players were accused of taking cheap shots and purposely trying to injure opponents. BC assistant coach Pete Carmichael was flagged with an unsportsman-like penalty. The Boston College coaches criticized the Holy Cross coaches for running an illegal play—hiding a potential pass receiver near the bench on a punt formation so that it would be difficult for the BC defense to spot the player.

In a story written by John Gearan in the *Worcester Sunday Telegram*, Holy Cross linebacker Scott Rudy made no attempt to conceal his own frustration plus the venom he felt towards BC. "It's so frustrating," he told Gearan. "People think BC is the big bully and they come in here and push us around like we are wimps. But we are not. That is not true."

Rudy was a senior, playing his final game in what for him had been an injury-plagued season. His most vitriolic comments centered on the final game of the 91-year-old series. "As for the BC rivalry, I will say this openly," he told Gearan. "They are the most classless group we have played against. I was held by the face mask and they punched me in the face. They spit at us . . . swore at us. There's no need for that. They are classless on and off the field. I went down to BC one time and we got mauled by a bunch of their players. Bottom line. I hate BC."

Despite the acrimony on both sides, Bicknell, known for his graciousness, win or lose, made a point to praise Holy Cross star Lockbaum. "I never knew how great a football player he was until I saw him do what he did today in the mud," said the BC coach.

At the end of Madden's column, both Boston College president Father J. Donald Monan, S. J. and athletic director Bill Flynn spoke with regret about the end of the BC-Holy Cross football series. "Maybe it is because I'm sentimental," said Flynn, "but this has gone on so long that I feel it should go on and on. I don't want it to end."

As for Father Monan, he, too, expressed his disappointment over the end of the series. "I wish it would continue," he said. "But it will end because the president of Holy Cross wishes it to end."

From a vantage point high above the action, Bob Fouracre, the television and radio voice of Holy Cross sports for thirty-two years, did the play-by-play of the final BC-Holy Cross football game on radio with Holy Cross great Mel Massucco doing the color commentary. He saw his first BC-Holy Cross game in 1951 at Braves Field, a thrilling come-from-behind Boston College 19-14 upset victory. Growing up in Northboro, Fouracre was weaned on Holy Cross sports and he has followed the Crusaders for years. He even saw his all-time favorite Holy Cross football player, Vic Rimkus, play a high school game for Hudson High in 1949. As a broadcaster, his partisanship toward Holy Cross paints nothing but bright purple verbal pictures for his listeners, à la Johnny Most, the legendary radio voice of the Boston Celtics who never uttered a disparaging

A Classic Rivalry Ends

WHAT WOULD TURN OUT TO BE THE FINAL GAME IN THE GRAND, OLD Jesuit college football rivalry had just ended at Fitton Field in Worcester. Boston College had won convincingly, drubbing Holy Cross 56-26. The final cheers had barely faded when Father John Brooks, S.J., the former president of the College of the Holy Cross, took action.

The date was Saturday, November 22, 1986. Almost immediately following the game, Father Brooks called for a meeting of the College of the Holy Cross Board of Directors, the governing board of the college. The Chairman of the Board of Directors was the late attorney, Edward Bennett Williams, an avid sportsman who, during his career, owned the Washington Redskins and the Baltimore Orioles. That weekend the Board met in a hastily called meeting. The future of the Boston College-Holy Cross football rivalry was the main topic of discussion. At the end of the meeting, Father Brooks received unanimous support from the Board to do what he thought he must: Terminate the BC-Holy Cross football rivalry.

That is exactly what he did. Father Brooks pulled the plug on the series. By the end of the weekend, he had written and mailed a letter to Father J. Donald Monan, S.J., the former president of Boston College, "telling him that we [Holy Cross] were breaking the rivalry, ending the series," Father Brooks said, recalling the gist of the letter.

That decision was by no means hasty or impulsive. The future of the series, which BC had come to dominate, winning eight in a row and seventeen of the final twenty games, had been under discussion for years. As early as the previous February, newspaper reports had speculated that the series was finished. The talks had intensified due to two factors. First, the NCAA ruled that Division I-A football programs must have stadiums that seat 30,000 or more (Holy Cross' Fitton Field, a terrific venue to watch football, only seats 23,500). Second, Holy Cross eliminated football scholarships and joined the Division I-AA Patriot League.

"I had no reservations, no second thoughts whatsoever about making that decision," emphasized Father Brooks, who grew up in the Boston area and admitted that he had been a longtime fan of the series. "It had been a great series. But that time was over. It had been great in its day, but that day had gone by."

Father Monan acknowledged receiving the letter from Father Brooks asking that the series be terminated immediately. However, he quickly pointed out that had he not received that letter, he would not have taken action himself to end the series. "I was not going to take any action to end the series," he said. "Holy Cross ended the series. That's what they wanted and the letter made it clear they preferred to end the competition."

Father Monan took umbrage over a comment made about the two colleges heading in different directions. "What does that mean, different directions?" he asked.

Then, he answered his own question. "At BC," he remarked, "we want to be the best we can be in all areas—academics, athletics, our graduate schools and research. That has not and will not ever change."

Nevertheless, there are distinct differences between the two schools. Boston College is a university and Holy Cross is a college. BC enrolls over 8,000 undergraduate students, Holy Cross just 2,700. BC's total enrollment, including graduate students, is just under 15,000. Of the twenty-eight Jesuit colleges and universities in the United States, Holy Cross stands alone in its exclusive commitment to undergraduate liberal arts education. Boston College, on the other hand, lists graduate schools in law, social work, education and nursing that are among the country's best. In terms of revenue, BC's endowment is $1 billion, Holy Cross' endowment is $380 million.

Geography also plays a role in differentiating the two Jesuit institutions. BC is located in Chestnut Hill, on the edge of Boston. Holy Cross is located forty miles west of Boston in Worcester, a much smaller city.

When BC was founded in 1863, it was basically a commuter school, where day students, the sons of immigrants, many of them Irish, worked after school and slept each night in their family home, more often than not located in one of the many and diverse sections of Boston. Holy Cross, on the other hand, located on Mount St. James overlooking Worcester with a panoramic view of the hills of Central Massachusetts, has always been a boarding school. The majority of its students, since the beginning, have traditionally come from outside the city. Today, both schools, which are inundated with applicants every year, draw students from every area of the country as well as many foreign countries. Both are coeducational institutions and half (or more) of its undergraduate students are women.

In the final analysis, competition, or lack thereof, doomed the series. By 1986, the two football programs were not competing on the same level. BC increased Alumni Stadium by 12,000 in 1995 to seat 44,500 and continues to play a Division I-A schedule. The university, which has established a rivalry with Notre Dame, competes in the Big East Conference. Each season BC battles for an invitation to a major bowl game, and on a regular basis, the program aspires to compete for a national championship.

Unlike BC, Holy Cross is content to remain in the Division I-AA Patriot League ever since it made the decision to de-emphasize football. The Patriot League is vanilla ice cream. There is no rivalry among its member schools, particularly in football, that excites anyone. However, if somehow Holy Cross were to join the Ivy League, the possibilities of exciting rivalries are numerous. Holy Cross and Dartmouth and Holy Cross and Harvard are just two examples of a pair of gridiron rivalries that are already rich in tradition. Many believe that Holy Cross would prefer to be associated with the elite Ivy League.

Former Boston College coach Jack Bicknell, who enjoyed an exciting run guiding the Eagles from 1981 to 1990, which included the fabulous Flutie era, hated to play Holy Cross. His BC teams out-manned Holy Cross and were heavily favored each season the old rivals met and playing the Crusaders was a no-win situation for him and his teams. When

BC won, it was never by a large enough score and losing to Holy Cross was unthinkable. Fortunately for Bicknell, he was 6-0 against Holy Cross before the series was terminated.

Nevertheless, Bicknell, the head coach of the Barcelona Dragons of NFL-Europe, regrets that Holy Cross de-emphasized football. "First Holy Cross de-emphasized football and then a few years later Boston University dropped football entirely," said Bicknell. "I don't think college football in New England will ever recover from those two things happening."

The BC-Holy Cross football rivalry ended for one simple reason: Holy Cross could no longer compete with BC on the football field.

When the series ended there was cheering as well as regret. Clark Booth welcomed the decision to end the series. Long a crusader on behalf of Holy Cross' philosophy regarding intercollegiate athletics, over the years Booth has seldom missed an opportunity to rip Boston College. In essence, Booth, a Holy Cross grad and retired Boston television newsman, has repeated the same theme over and over again: Shame on Boston College for daring to pursue excellence in competitive athletics.

In the November 1987 issue of *New England Monthly*, he wrote a story entitled "Requiem for a Mismatch." He wrote: "The severing of the Holy Cross-BC link was a major skirmish in the war between those schools that want football to be simply a part of campus life and those that want it to define their prominence and produce huge revenues . . . "

Booth went on: "You have to give BC credit for pluck. All alone in these parts they hang in there, contesting for ratings, bowls, the pursuit of glory, and yes, profits. It's a bit of a roll of the dice. But when you consider that Doug Flutie reaped them an estimated $9.4 million, you can understand where they're coming from."

Further down in the same story, Booth used Jon Morris, a great former Holy Cross player and an All-Pro center in the NFL who played eleven seasons with the Patriots, to substantiate his views. After viewing the final BC-Holy Cross game, which the Crusaders entered unbeaten, Morris told Booth, "I felt so bad for the Holy Cross kids. It should have been one of the finest years Holy Cross ever had. Instead, it was humiliating . . . " In conclusion, Booth quoted Morris as saying, "Ending the madness was definitely the thing to do. I only wonder why it took so long."

Booth ended the piece by writing: "So the rivalry has ended, but the battle continues. You cannot find two schools more polarized on the subject of the principles and purposes of collegiate sport. And to think for all these many, many years, they were brothers."

Clark Booth is entitled to his opinion, but athletic and academic excellence are not necessarily incompatible. You don't have to have one without the other or sacrifice one to maintain the other.

By eliminating football scholarships and de-emphasizing football, the Holy Cross administration made it impossible for the college to compete against Boston College on the gridiron. That is why the rivalry ended.

In a perfect world, it never would have ended; Boston College and Holy Cross still would be locking shoulder pads and banging heads today. It was a natural rivalry packed with history and tradition: two great Jesuit institutions of higher learning meeting to do battle on the football field. How could it possibly get any better than that?

Since the series' inception, many changes have taken place in the social fabric of our country, in higher education, and in the role of athletics. Perspectives differ. Heraclitus, the ancient Greek philosopher, said that you can not step into the same river twice. Change is constant. The series ran its course for close to a century. But the waters changed. As far as football was concerned, Holy Cross and Boston College were no longer on the same course, and, in fact, had not been for some time.

The end of the football rivalry does not diminish either school.

And although the memories may fade, they will never be erased.

Retrospective

View from the Press Box

SINCE 1989, BOB RYAN AND DAN SHAUGHNESSY, A PAIR OF CLEAR-EYED and hard-hitting columnists, have surgically dissected and analyzed the often zany world of sports for the readers of the *Boston Globe*.

Ryan is a Boston College graduate, Class of 1968. Shaughnessy is a Holy Cross graduate, Class of 1975. Who better to discuss the demise of the Boston College-Holy Cross football rivalry than Ryan and Shaughnessy?

One might expect some controversy, perhaps some discordant notes about the end of the series. But one would be wrong. Both writers took a dispassionate and realistic view of things.

"It was a knee-jerk decision to end it, a no-brainer," Bob Ryan said. "It was no big deal and totally appropriate. Holy Cross tried to keep up, but they couldn't compete any more. It was over. Done. Finished. Football-wise, the two schools were traveling different paths."

For Ryan, it was simple. When it came to athletic competition involving Boston College and Holy Cross, it was all about basketball by the time he arrived at the Heights. Frankly, as a basketball writer who covered the Celtics for years, he broke new ground and had no equal.

Shaughnessy also came right to the point, mincing no words when the subject turned to the end of the series. He pointed to the final game of the rivalry in 1986 as proof positive that the series was axed just in the nick of time. As many remember, Holy Cross entered the 1986 game unbeaten with a 10-0-0 record. "Holy Cross was never going to get any better than they were that day," he said. "Yet, they got waxed [56-26]. It was painful to watch, time to end it. You saw what you didn't want to see. It was like men against boys. It was like a different sport, not football."

And it did indeed end after the 1986 mismatch. Entering the game, Holy Cross had come up dry against BC seven years in a row. Over the previous twenty years, Boston College had won sixteen of nineteen games. (There was no game in 1969 because of the hepatitis epidemic that resulted in Holy Cross canceling the final eight games of that season.) It was obvious that the rival programs were on different plateaus. Holy Cross, en route to a 10-0 record and the Patriot League Championship, defeated the likes of Lehigh, Lafayette, Bucknell and Colgate, the heart of the Crusaders' Division I-AA schedule. On the other hand, BC, which ended up 9-3 in 1986, beat California, Maryland, West Virginia and Syracuse before capping its Division I-A season with a 27-24 victory over the Georgia Bulldogs in the Hall of Fame Bowl.

So for Ryan and Shaughnessy, Father John Brooks, S.J., the former president of the College of the Holy Cross, made a wise, merciful decision when he pulled the plug on the series.

Ryan and Shaughnessy, during their four years as undergraduate college students, have their own memories of the Boston College-Holy Cross football rivalry. Ryan remembers traveling to Worcester and watching a game from the stands ("I have never been in the press box at Fitton Field and I never covered a BC-Holy Cross football game.") that was played in rain and mud. Shaughnessy, on the other hand, said, "We lost to BC all four years that I was at Holy Cross."

Although he had already graduated, Dan, for reasons other than just football, will never forget the 1977 game at Worcester, which Holy Cross won 35-20, snapping a ten-game losing streak against Boston College.

On the day of that game, Shaughnessy and former *Globe* colleague Lesley Visser, a BC graduate, former cheerleader for the Eagles and a writer/reporter who toppled the gender barrier with her pioneer work on network television, traveled by car to Worcester to watch the '77 game. "We drove to the game in an AMC Pacer," recalled Shaughnessy. "There was a big celebration after the game at the Holy Cross field house. During the game, I had been drinking Amaretto in the stands and then

I drank a few beers after the game. On the way home on the Mass Pike we had to stop the car so I could barf. Ever since that day, I can't stand it. It smells like licorice, doesn't it? I have never touched Amaretto since then and I'll never go near it again."

Ryan comes from New Jersey. He is an only child. Interestingly, his late father, Bill, who died when Bob was eleven, once was the assistant athletic director at Villanova University. In addition, at one time, he was the business manager for the Columbus, Georgia Cardinals, a minor league baseball team in the old Sally League.

As a youth, beginning in the eighth grade and continuing through high school, Ryan attended the Lawrenceville School, an elite private school located in a sleepy little town between Princeton and Trenton. Originally, he wanted to become a sports broadcaster. He wrote his first column when he was still Little League age, at eleven. In high school, he played varsity basketball and he was manager of the school's varsity football team.

At Lawrenceville, he also wrote for school publications and he credits the school with providing the tools for him to develop his writing skills. Lawrenceville was founded in 1820 on the classic British house system of education. Language arts were stressed. "There were no multiple choice tests," said Ryan. "We had to read and we had to write. It was great for me because those were my strengths."

After graduating from high school, Ryan was accepted at Georgetown, Boston College and Holy Cross. "If you put all the students at the three schools together and shake them up, you will find the same type of students at Georgetown, Boston College and Holy Cross," he said.

"Holy Cross is a nice little school located up on a hill in Worcester," he said. "You receive a fine education at Holy Cross, but I wanted a big city environment. So, for me, it came down to Georgetown and Washington, D.C. or Boston College and Boston. I decided that BC was the place for me."

At BC, Ryan started out majoring in English, but he switched his major to History. "I didn't like many of the electives so I switched my major to History," he explained.

The outspoken Ryan believes that, at least in his case, the value of a college education is overrated. "Society demands that you must have a college education," Ryan said. "It is one of the biggest rackets in the world. Great. I got a college education, but I was more interested in snack bar city and studying Basketball 101 with Professor Bob Cousy." Cousy, the former Celtics' great, was the head basketball coach at Boston College from 1963 to 1969.

In college, Ryan roomed with Reid Oslin, senior media relations officer at BC and the school's former sports information director. Bob and his wife, Elaine, are the parents of two grown children and grandparents of triplets, named Conor, Jack and Amelia.

A card-carrying sports junkie, Ryan, at a moment's notice, can produce a ticket stub from the 1964 BC-Holy Cross football game at Alumni Stadium. The date was November 28, 1964. At that game, Ryan sat in Section O, Row 22, Seat 46. Boston College won, 10-8. The previous week, the Eagles defeated the University of Detroit 17-9 in the final football game the Midwestern school ever played.

Shaughnessy, the youngest of five children, grew up in bucolic Groton, Massachusetts. "When I was growing up, there were four thousand people living in Groton," said Shaughnessy. "Since then, the population has doubled, but you can still drive through town without hitting a traffic light."

Dan said that at a very young age, he became acutely aware of the BC-Holy Cross football rivalry. His late father, William, was a Boston College graduate, Class of 1936. "At BC, he was in the same class as Tip O'Neill," said Shaughnessy.

Shaughnessy said that, although he was unmoved by the end of the BC-Holy Cross football rivalry, he was more than a little bit annoyed when Holy Cross joined the Patriot League. "Holy Cross was beginning to develop rivalries with Ivy League schools like Harvard, Dartmouth and others," he explained. "I can't get excited when they play games against Lehigh, Bucknell and Lafayette. That bothers me more than Holy Cross not playing BC anymore."

In high school, the 6-foot-2 Shaughnessy played varsity basketball, baseball and ran cross country. Both at Groton High and in college, he also was a writer/editor for the school newspapers. Like Ryan, Shaughnessy was accepted at both Boston College and Holy Cross. He selected Holy Cross for several reasons, including basic economics. "There was no on-campus housing at BC at the time," he said. "Plus, Holy Cross offered me a small academic scholarship."

From 1977 to 1981, Dan was a beat writer covering the Baltimore Orioles for two newspapers, the *Baltimore Sun* and the *Washington Star*. It was during that time in his life when he met his future wife, Marilou, who worked in the personnel department of a Chicago retail chain.

The couple met in a restaurant/bar at the Western Hotel in the Windy City. At the time, Shaughnessy was seated at a table with a person no one would mistake for the love god Cupid, chain-smoking Earl Weaver, the crusty former manager of the Baltimore Orioles, a curmudgeon of the first order.

Seated beside Weaver, who looks much more like pug-nosed and square-jawed former Yankees' right fielder Hank Bauer than he does dashing movie legend Clark Gable, it was easy for Dan to appear to his future wife as if he were Prince Charming. The date was April 11, 1980. "We hit it off right away," mused Shaughnessy. "The timing was right for both of us and we got married less than two years later, on February 20, 1982."

The Shaughnessys have three children. One of their children, Kate, developed cancer when she was only eight, courageously fought the disease and licked it with the help of prayers and expert medical attention. She was captain of the girls' softball team at Newton North High School in Newton, Massachusetts and graduated in June, 2003. "She is doing very well," said Dan. For parents of a seriously ill child, like Dan and Marilou, "cancer survivor" are the two most profoundly meaningful words in the English language.

Same Press Box;
Different View

JOHN GEARAN IS A RARITY: A SPORTS WRITER WITH A LAW DEGREE.
For 35 years, Gearan, a graduate of Holy Cross and Suffolk University
Law School, wrote about the games that we love for the *Worcester
Telegram & Gazette*. For the last twenty-one years of his career, before
retiring in 2001, he was a columnist known for his dry, Irish wit and bit-
ing tongue-in-cheek humor. A personable man, he delights in telling stories. His favorite tales are colored purple, centering on Holy Cross athletics and Holy Cross football in particular.

John grew up in Fitchburg, the second youngest in a family of two
boys and two girls. Both his father, Paul, and his brother, Paul Vaughn,
graduated from Holy Cross and became lawyers. In fact, his father, Paul,
Holy Cross Class of 1927, was a mover and shaker in Holy Cross alumni affairs for years. Not only that, but he played a major role in bringing
Coach Eddie Anderson back to Holy Cross from the University of Iowa
to begin his second term as head coach of the Crusaders in 1950.

In a story that has been told and retold many times over the years,
when Holy Cross deliberated over bringing Anderson back to Mount St.
James, Attorney Paul Gearan forged the signature of the Holy Cross
treasurer on a check and mailed it to Dr. Anderson to pay for his traveling expenses back to Worcester. Then, at the eleventh hour in the unfold-

ing drama of who would be the next Holy Cross football coach, Attorney Paul Gearan told the board of trustees who had assembled for a vital meeting to reach a conclusion on the subject, "You better either arrest me for forgery or get someone to the airport in a hurry because Dr. Anderson is arriving in two hours."

That story is classic.

Of the many people Gearan interacted with during his career as a sports journalist, none was bigger than the late Roy Mumpton, the Grantland Rice of sports reporting in the Greater Worcester area. "Between 1927 and 1987, Roy Mumpton saw fifty-nine out of sixty BC-Holy Cross football games," said Gearan. "I think the only game he missed was because he had to attend a wedding."

During his career, Gearan loved to good naturedly ruffle the feathers of readers and even colleagues. In 1984, Doug Flutie's final regular season game against Holy Cross at Fitton Field, the same day he was awarded the Heisman Trophy, the real drama occurred after BC's 45-10 win. Who would win the O'Melia Trophy as the game's outstanding player, Doug or his younger brother, Darren Flutie? After the votes were cast and counted, the balloting was deadlocked; each of the Flutie brothers received the same number of votes.

Gearan, for his part, wrote "D. Flutie" on his ballot. Frantically, all the other sports writers quizzed each other, wanting to know who marked their ballot D. Flutie. Sheepishly, John fessed up; he was the culprit. Immediately, he heard a chorus of shouting, "John, John, who did you mean to vote for, Doug or Darren?"

Gearan, calmly, sat back and let the tension rise before informing his fellow scribes that he meant to vote for Doug Flutie to win the O'Melia Trophy.

"The funny thing about it," said John, "most of the writers were disappointed that I had voted for Doug because if Darren had won the award, it would have made for a much better story."

Speaking of controversial stories, prior to Flutie's final regular season game against Holy Cross, Gearan wrote a piece comparing the rival quarterbacks, Flutie of BC and Peter Muldoon of Holy Cross. Gearan analyzed the statistics compiled by the two quarterbacks and he wrote, just by looking at cold, hard numbers, that Muldoon was the more efficient passer.

A night or two later, Gearan received a telephone call at his Leominster home from none other than Dick Flutie, Doug's father, complaining about the story.

Gearan listened to the elder Flutie go on and on about what he thought was an unfair story, which he took as a slight against his own son. Finally, John told him, "Look Dick, your son just won the Heisman Trophy. What the heck do you care what a guy from Worcester, Massachusetts writes anyway?"

Interestingly, Muldoon, who was from Maryland, was considered one of the top scholastic quarterbacks in the country when he came out of high school. He was 6-foot-1 and a prototype pocket passer. A terrific athlete, he was a big-play, clutch performer, a threat to either pass or run. BC wanted Muldoon badly. His brother Casey Muldoon had played football at BC and Gearan said he wasn't exactly thrilled with the experience, so Peter opted to spurn BC and instead accepted a scholarship offer to play football at Holy Cross. Doug Flutie, who came out of high school at the same time as Muldoon, received the final scholarship Boston College had available in 1981 when Flutie graduated from Natick High School. If Muldoon had accepted BC's scholarship offer, who knows, Doug Flutie could have wound up playing college football at the University of New Hampshire, an Ivy League school or even Holy Cross.

"Muldoon was a fierce competitor," remembered Gearan. "He never backed down from anyone. When he carried the football, he always stuck his nose in there. By the time he graduated, he was pretty banged up, which hurt his chances of catching on in the pros."

In 1986, Gearan amused himself and infuriated his fellow writers in the press box at the final BC-Holy Cross game at Fitton Field. After Holy Cross, sparked by the heroics of the indomitable Gordie Lockbaum, bolted into a quick 14-0 lead, John pulled out a yellow, tattered copy of a 1942 newspaper headlining the shocking 55-12 Holy Cross upset and waved it around for everyone to see.

"I thought Holy Cross was going to win that game," chuckled Gearan. "It was a miserable, rainy day. The field was a muddy mess. Stranger things have happened, but BC was too strong and they pulled away during the second half."

You have got to love it. Imagine the looks on the faces of the other writers once Gearan pulled out that old newspaper and started waving it around. To heck with the stoic, unbiased demeanor writers are suppose to maintain while working, who said there can't be any cheering in the press box?

As a boy, Gearan tuned up for the BC-Holy rivalry with a great schoolboy football match-up, Fitchburg-Leominster, one of the oldest and most hallowed high school football rivalries in the country. Those two central Massachusetts football Goliaths stage black and blue battles every Thanksgiving Day morning. Leominster, incidentally, is the birth place of the great college football Coach Lou Little.

Bonfires, student pep rallies and harmless pranks, over the years have been part of the great college football rivalries such as Army-Navy and Boston College-Holy Cross. At one time or another, the Cadets have been successful in kidnapping the Midshipmen goat, Billy. Conversely, Navy has occasionally stolen the Army mule and then guarded the animal with tight security as part of the hoopla surrounding the Army-Navy game.

Boston College and Holy Cross have participated in similar stunts. One time, Holy Cross students staged a raid on the campus of Boston College and painted the BC Eagle purple. Gearan remembered what happened one year when BC students tried to retaliate. "The BC students hired an airplane to fly over the Holy Cross campus and drop leaflets," Gearan said, laughing as he spoke. "But they missed their mark and the mission failed. Instead of dropping the stuff on the Holy Cross campus, it was dropped on the campus of Worcester Poly Tech, WPI."

Gearan called Johnny Turco, the flashy former Holy Cross back, the "Harry Agganis" of Holy Cross. Agganis, the former Boston University quarterback and Boston Red Sox first baseman, is still considered one of the greatest athletes New England has ever produced. In addition to Turco's racehorse ability as a football halfback, he was a superb baseball player. "As good as he was in football, he might have been even better in baseball," Gearan said.

Who was the greatest all-around football player Dr. Eddie Anderson coached at Holy Cross? "He always said that the best all-around football player he ever coached at Holy Cross was Ronnie Cahill," said Gearan. Cahill was from Leominster and he could throw a football from one ten-yard line on a football field to the other ten-yard line eighty yards away.

Cahill, was a reluctant star, an unlikely football hero. "He was a loner and he never did interviews with the press," said Gearan. "First and foremost, he was an outdoorsman who loved to hunt and fish. He was not the typical Holy Cross student-athlete. Many were surprised when he bothered to show up for practice or a game. Sometimes he even arrived ten minutes after the game started."

Gearan, like everyone else, was not surprised when the Boston College-Holy Cross football series ended in 1986. "You could see it coming," he said. "The series was doomed once Holy Cross decided to eliminate football scholarships."

At the same time, he, like so many others, was saddened to see the great rivalry end. "Along with the Red Sox, the BC-Holy Cross football series was one of the area's top sports attractions," he said. "When the rivalry ended, New England sports fans lost a real treasure."

Finally, Gearan offered an interesting tidbit of information about Doug Flutie, whom he called, "the most exciting football player I've ever seen in all the years I have watched and covered the game."

"Flutie is Lebanese," said Gearan. "There used to be a highly popular restaurant and nightclub in Worcester called the El Morocco. Flutie and actor Danny Thomas were the all-time number one stars at the El Morocco."

Gearan stays in close contact with his former Holy Cross classmates including Attorney John Mee who came out of Brighton to become a solid lineman for the Crusaders in the 1960's.

Thanks for the memories, John!

Addenda

College Hall of Fame

THE NATIONAL FOOTBALL FOUNDATION AND COLLEGE HALL OF FAME was founded in 1947. Grantland Rice, the legendary writer, celebrity and dean of modern sports journalism, and Colonel Earl "Red" Blaik, the scholarly confidant of General Douglas MacArthur and former college coach at Dartmouth and Army, helped put together the founding charter that was aimed at "promoting amateur football."

Today the National Football Foundation has 110 chapters and over one thousand members scattered around the United States. The first annual national dinner and awards ceremony was held in 1958 at the Waldorf Astoria in New York. The principal speaker was President Dwight D. Eisenhower, a former star West Point end, halfback and kicker. Over the years, the event has raised scholarship money for student-athletes. Stone Phillips, NBC television anchor and a former Yale quarterback, is a National Football Foundation scholar-athlete. There are many other NFF scholar-athletes who have gone on to excel in a wide range of fields.

The first induction to the College Hall of Fame was held in 1951. In the original class of inductees there were thirty-five players which included Red Grange (Illinois), Jim Thorpe (Carlisle), Don Hutson (Alabama), George Gipp (Notre Dame), Sammy Baugh (Texas Christian University), Pudge Heffelfinger (Yale), Bronko Nagurski (Minnesota) and Ernie

Nevers (Stanford). Twenty-three coaches were also inducted, including: Knute Rockne (Notre Dame), Walter Camp (Yale), Howard Jones (Tennessee), and Frank Thomas (Alabama).

The original College Hall of Fame opened in 1978 in Kings Mills, Ohio, about twenty miles north of Cincinnati. Since then the College Hall of Fame has relocated to South Bend, Indiana and its spacious, state of the art home was officially dedicated on August 25, 1995.

Fourteen football players and coaches from Boston College and Holy Cross have been inducted into the College Football Hall of Fame. Once his playing career is completed, Doug Flutie almost certainly will join the list of inductees from the two Jesuit colleges. Here are the Boston College and Holy Cross players and coaches who have been enshrined:

Dr. Eddie Anderson - He coached at Loras, DePaul, Holy Cross and Iowa from 1922 to 1964. He learned his football from a Swedish-born chemistry professor and gridiron genius—Knute Rockne. Anderson was a member of Rockne's first team at Notre Dame in 1918, and he played for the Irish teams of the late teens and early twenties that rolled to twenty straight victories. Entering the coaching ranks while continuing studies for his medical degree, Anderson began his career in 1922 at tiny Columbia College (now known as Loras College). His 1922 Columbia team was undefeated. After three years at Columbia, he coached seven years at DePaul. Next came his first term at Holy Cross (1933-'38). His 1935 and 1937 teams were undefeated. In 1939, he moved to Iowa. The Hawkeyes had only won two games in the previous two seasons. Anderson's first Iowa team went 6-1-1, and he was named Coach of the Year. He coached Iowa from 1939 to 1942 and from 1946 to 1949. In between those two terms, he served in the Army Medical Corps during World War II. Anderson returned to Holy Cross from 1950 to 1964. In thirty-nine years as a head coach, his record was 201-128-15. He was a true Renaissance man: a medical doctor, an ear, nose and throat specialist; a natty dresser; he smoked cigarettes using an FDR-like English brass holder; and he went on to become one of the greatest college coaches of all-time. Anderson was known for his cool demeanor. He was head coach of the College All-Stars twice. In 1940, his All-Stars lost to the Green Bay Packers, 45-28, and in 1950, his All-Stars defeated the NFL Champion Philadelphia

Eagles, 17-7. He was inducted into the College Football Hall of Fame in 1971.

Gil Dobie - He coached at North Dakota State, Washington, Navy, Cornell and Boston College from 1906 to 1938. Gilbert Dobie was born on January 21, 1879 in Hastings, Minnesota. He played end and quarterback for the University of Minnesota Golden Gophers from 1900 to 1902, then served as an assistant coach at his alma mater while obtaining a law degree. His first job as a head coach was at North Dakota State (1906-'07). He had a 6-0 record in two seasons. Dobie was the head coach at Washington from 1908 to 1916 and never lost a game. His nine-year record was 58-0-3, which included a 39-game winning streak. Next, he coached at Navy from 1917 to 1919 and compiled a 17-3-0 record. Following his three seasons at the Naval Academy, he moved to Cornell, where he was the head coach from 1920 to 1935. During that span, he led the Big Red to an 82-16-7 record. His 1921, 1922 and 1923 Cornell teams were unbeaten en route to a 26-game unbeaten streak. His star players at Cornell were Eddie Kaw and George Pfann, a pair of flashy All-America halfbacks. Dobie completed his coaching career at Boston College from 1936 to 1938 and led the Eagles to a 16-6-5 record. In all, he coached 33 years and had fourteen undefeated seasons. His career record was 180-45-15, giving him a gaudy .781 winning percentage. He was prone to giving pessimistic predictions about his teams' chances of winning so the press nicknamed him "Gloomy Gil." He was president of the American Football Coaches Association in 1917. He died on December 23, 1948. He is a charter member of the College Football Hall of Fame, elected to the first class of 1951.

Frank Leahy - He was "the bearer of football wisdom at Notre Dame" from 1941 to 1953, a man the writers loved to call "the Master." Indeed, he was all of that! Through thirteen years as a head coach at Boston College and Notre Dame, he compiled a 107-13-9 record. Often compared to his former coach, Knute Rockne, Leahy was far less flamboyant and he stressed efficiency rather than emotion. His Irish teams displayed the precision "which excites the football purists." Leahy used reverse psychology to motivate his teams, often telling the press at the beginning of the season, "The lads don't have it in them this year. I don't see how we can escape losing six games this year." As the record indicates, his clubs rarely lost. He was a perfectionist who regularly slept in his office. His philosophy was clear and he constantly pleaded with his players to "Pay the price! Pay the price!" Leahy coached Boston College in 1939 and 1940 to a 20-2-0 record, two bowl appearances and the only national championship in the school's history. He coached Notre Dame from 1941 to 1943 and from 1946 to 1953 with two years off while he served in the Navy. His Notre Dame teams won national championships in 1943, '46, '47 and '49. He had a streak of 39 games without a loss (1946-'50). When he retired his winning percentage was .864, the second highest in history behind Rockne's .881. He was inducted into the College Football Hall of Fame in 1970.

Frank Cavanaugh - Between 1898 and 1932 he coached at Cincinnati, Holy Cross, Dartmouth, Boston College and Fordham, the only College Hall of Fame coach to lead both Boston College and Holy Cross. He was a legendary leader both in college football and in war. In 1917, at age 41, he enlisted in the Army during World War I and in 1918 he was severely wounded—pieces of shrapnel lodged in his head—while fighting in France. He rose to the rank of major, which led to his colorful nickname, "the Iron Major." A movie, of the same name, starred Pat O'Brien and told the story of Cavanaugh's greatest loves— God, country, family and football. A gifted speaker, he used his considerable oratorical skills to rally the troops or his football players. In twenty-four seasons as a head coach, his record was 145-48-17, good for a sparkling .731 winning percentage. In college, he played end for the Big Green of Dartmouth. His first head coaching job was at Cincinnati in 1898. He led the Bearcats to a 5-1-3 record, including a victory over his alma mater Dartmouth. He coached Holy Cross from 1903 to 1905 and compiled a 16-10-2 record. In between coaching assignments, he practiced law. He coached Dartmouth from 1911 to 1916; Boston College from 1919 to 1926, compiling a 48-14-5 record; and completed his college coaching career at Fordham from 1927 to 1932, going 29-15-8. At Fordham, he ran the T-Formation with a man in motion eleven seasons before Stanford was given credit for unveiling the same formation, which modernized the game and changed it forever. Cavanaugh, who was from Worcester, Massachusetts, died on

August 29, 1933 at age 57. He was inducted into the College Football Hall of Fame in 1954.

Ed Healey - He played tackle for Holy Cross in 1914 and Dartmouth in 1916, '17 and '19. He was a huge man, "thick-necked and full-muscled in the manner of most great linemen." The Holy Cross and Dartmouth star lineman was once described by All-American pollster Walter Camp as "the best tackle I ever saw play." He grew up on a farm outside Springfield, Massachusetts and was the only son in a family of nine children. He first played at Holy Cross and then at Dartmouth for three seasons, interrupted by military service in the Army. He played in the National Football League from 1920 to 1927 with the Rock Island Independents and Chicago Bears, earning All-Pro honors five times. After his pro football career ended, he worked as a salesman, was constantly on the go and moved repeatedly. Wherever he settled, he managed to land side jobs as an assistant football coach. He coached at Creighton University, Notre Dame, Culver Military Academy and at high schools in Ft. Wayne, Indiana and Rock Island, Illinois. Healey was born on December 28, 1894 at Indian Orchard, Massachusetts and he died on December 9, 1978 at Niles, Michigan. He was inducted into the College Football Hall of Fame in 1974. He is also a member of the Pro Football Hall of Fame.

George Connor - He played tackle for Holy Cross in 1942 and '43 and for Notre Dame in 1946 and '47. Connor was "a dream lineman with the toughness to stand firm and break up the power offensive plays of enemy clubs." After beginning his college career at Holy Cross, he transferred to Notre Dame after serving in the military during World War II. At the time, Frank Leahy had returned from a hitch in the Navy for his second term as the head coach at Notre Dame and Connor was one of the finest linemen of the Leahy era. He opened gaping holes for such outstanding backs as Emil Sitko and Terry Brennan, as Notre Dame returned to glory under Coach Leahy. During Connor's two seasons at Notre Dame, the Fighting Irish never lost a game. Notre Dame was 8-0-1 in 1946. Only a 0-0 tie against Army at Yankee Stadium prevented the Irish from posting a perfect season. In 1947, Notre Dame finished the year with a 9-0-0 record. Looking back at those teams, Leahy said, "We never had a defensive tackle superior to George Connor." Connor went on to star for the Chicago Bears in the NFL. In 1962, a panel of 400 sports writers selected Notre Dame's all-time team. Connor and end Leon Hart, the only lineman ever to win the Heisman Trophy, topped the balloting. Each drew 340 votes. In 1946, Connor was the first recipient of the Outland Trophy awarded each year to the nation's best interior lineman. As a senior, he captained the Notre Dame team. He was elected to the College Hall of Fame in 1963.

Bill Osmanski - He played fullback for Holy Cross from 1936 to 1938. Osmanski provided the backfield leadership for the greatest teams in Holy Cross history, "using his bursting speed, instinctive balance and awesome power to bolster one of the most explosive offenses in Eastern football during the 1930s." During Osmanski's career at Holy Cross, the Crusaders posted a 23-3-3 record, losing only three games by scores of 13-12, 7-6 and 3-0. In 1936, his 85-yard run powered Holy Cross over a tough, stubborn Dartmouth team, 7-0. During that same season, he was credited with touchdown runs covering 92, 75, 68, 62 and 45 yards. He was nicknamed "Bullet Bill" and was named an All-America in 1938. In 1939, he was voted the Most Valuable Player of the College All-Star game. He played professional football with the Chicago Bears from 1939 to 1943 and from 1946 to 1947. He served in the Marines during World War II and fought at Okinawa, Guadalcanal and Guam. During his career with the Bears, Coach George Halas' team won four NFL Championships. He earned a dental degree from Northwestern University and he practiced dentistry in the Chicago area. Holy Cross retired his number 25. He was the head coach at his alma mater in 1948 and 1949. *Sports Illustrated* honored him in their Silver Anniversary issue. A YMCA in Evanston, Illinois was named for him and a Chicago Catholic high school league instituted a scholar-athlete award honoring him as a model student-athlete. Osmanski was born on December 29, 1915 and he died on December 25, 1996. He was inducted into the College Hall of Fame in 1973.

Gordie Lockbaum - He played for Holy Cross from 1984 to 1987 and was "Mr. Versatility." Gordie was known as "college football's 60-minute player." He was a halfback on offense, a cornerback on defense and a kick returner on special teams. During the 1987 season, he was selected both Offensive and Defensive Player of the Week for his dual exploits in a single game. He finished fifth in the Heisman Trophy voting in 1986, and third in 1987. He also was second in the Maxwell Trophy vote in 1987. Lockbaum was a two-time All-American, two-time Most Valuable Player of the Patriot League and two-time winner of the Washington Touchdown Club's All-Purpose Back of the Year Award. In 1986, he was Player of the Year in the Eastern Collegiate Athletic Conference, New England Back of the Year and earned a National Scholar-Athlete Award from the National Football Foundation and College Hall of Fame. He scored six touchdowns against Dartmouth in 1986; caught 15 passes for 196 yards against Villanova in 1987; scored 22 touchdowns in 1986; and 22 more in 1987. He recorded 2,173 total yards in 1986, and 2,041 in 1987. In 1987, he caught 78 passes good for 1,152 yards. He holds a host of Holy Cross records, individual game, season and career marks, and he was inducted into the College Football Hall of Fame in 2001.

Chet Gladchuk - He played center for Boston College from 1938 to 1940. He was one of five members of the College Hall of Fame to play for Boston College in 1940, along with Mike Holovak, Gene Goodreault, Msgr. George Kerr and Charlie O'Rourke. The 6-foot-5, 225-pound center was a four-sport standout at Warren Harding High School in Bridgeport, Connecticut. In college, he also played basketball for the Eagles. He was a dominant center during an era of college basketball that produced the likes of big George Mikan of DePaul. At BC, he played for two College Hall of Fame coaches—Gil Dobie, as a sophomore, and Frank Leahy, in his junior and senior seasons. As a sophomore, BC ended up 6-1-2; the only loss was a 29-7 setback against Holy Cross. As a junior, BC powered through a 9-2-0 season, losing two games by a total of ten points: 7-0 to Florida and 6-3 to Clemson in the Cotton Bowl. In 1940, BC capped an 11-0-0 unbeaten and national championship season by beating Tennessee 19-13 in the Sugar Bowl. Gladchuk completed a brilliant college career by being named a first team All-America in 1940. He played for the New York Giants in 1941 and in 1946 and 1947. During World War II, he spent four and one-half years in the military as a Navy officer. Gladchuk was the head football coach at Bridgeport University in 1948 and the Montreal Alouettes in 1949. He also served as the assistant athletic director at the University of Massachusetts. He died in 1967. Gladchuk was inducted into the College Football Hall of Fame in 1975.

Msgr. George Kerr - He played guard for Boston College from 1938 to 1940. Nicknamed the "Righteous Reject," he reported to Coach Gil Dobie "wearing three sweaters and two overcoats" so he would look heavier than 155 pounds after being told he was "too small" to play college football. During his career, he surprised everyone by going from a scrub on the reserve team to All-America mention as a senior during the Eagles' magical unbeaten and national championship run. Coach Frank Leahy called Kerr "the greatest scholar-athlete I ever coached." Ranked near the top of his class academically, he was one of the senior leaders of the great 1940 BC team. During his three-year career, Boston College posted a 26-3-2 record. His fierce play in the Eagles' 19-13 victory over Tennessee in the Sugar Bowl earned him a spot on the all-time Sugar Bowl team. After graduating from college, he entered the seminary and he was ordained a Roman Catholic priest in 1945. He was elevated to Monsignor by Pope Paul VI in 1964. Msgr. Kerr served as chaplain of the Massachusetts House of Representatives. Known for his humanitarian spirit and boundless energy, he championed many causes including mental retardation and educating the inner-city poor. Msgr. Kerr died on January 23, 1983. He was 63. He was inducted posthumously into the College Football Hall of Fame in 1984.

Charlie O'Rourke - He played halfback for Boston College from 1938 to 1940. Charles Christopher O'Rourke was born on May 10, 1917 in Montreal, Canada. He was a triple-threat All-Scholastic tailback at Malden High School. He weighed only 145 pounds and BC almost refused to give him a scholarship because he "was so skinny." Years after he graduated, "Chuckin' Charlie" was considered the greatest football player in Boston College history. It was written that his natural ability was so profuse that "just watching him practice caused a twinkle in the eyes of his head coach," Frank Leahy. In 1939, he led the Eagles to a 9-2-0 record and the school's first bowl invitation, a 6-3 loss to Clemson in the Cotton Bowl. In 1940, O'Rourke was the "cover boy" back who led

Boston College to an 11-0-0 season and the national championship. Charlie was the catalyst who led BC to a come-from-behind 19-13 victory over Tennessee in the Sugar Bowl, a win that sealed the national championship. As a player, he is most remembered for his individual heroics in a game against Georgetown in 1940 at Fenway Park, a contest sports writer Grantland Rice labeled "the greatest college football game ever played." With two minutes remaining and Boston College clinging to a 19-16 lead, O'Rourke ran into his own end zone, eluding one Georgetown tackler after another, before taking a safety. He effectively killed more than a minute off the game clock, and then with under a minute to play, he punted out of his own end zone to preserve the Eagles' 19-18 victory. As a senior, O'Rourke was a unanimous All-America choice. He played five seasons of professional football (1942 and 1946 to 1949) with the Los Angeles Dons, the Chicago Bears and the Baltimore Colts. He was the head football coach at the University of Massachusetts from 1952 to 1959. O'Rourke was also the national commissioner of Pop Warner football. He died on April 14, 2000. O'Rourke was inducted into the College Football Hall of Fame in 1972.

Gene Goodreault - He played end for Boston College from 1938 to 1940 under two Hall of Fame coaches at Boston College, Gil Dobie and Frank Leahy. He was recruited by Dobie, who, like Leahy, had a eye for talent and a penchant "for sealing the deal with recruits." Goodreault, a prototype of what would later be called the "tight end" position, might have been the finest all-around end in the country. Fast, powerful and as smart as a fox, he could catch passes, block and he was a terror on defense, a unit that posted eleven combined shutouts in 1939 and 1940. On offense, he teamed up with backfield game-breakers Charlie O'Rourke, Lou Montgomery and Mike Holovak to make the Eagles an explosive scoring machine. In 1939, BC racked up 216 points, which was a tune-up for 1940 when BC exploded for 320 points while limiting the opposition to 52. In 1940, Goodreault was a consensus All-America selection. He was inducted into the College Football Hall of Fame in 1982.

Mike Holovak - He played fullback for Boston College from 1940 to 1942. As a sophomore, his touchdowns helped power BC to thrilling victories over Georgetown (19-18) and Tennessee (19-13) in the Sugar

Bowl. As a senior, he was co-captain, the second leading rusher in the country (2,011 career yards) and a consensus All-America. In the 1943 Orange Bowl, he set the record for touchdowns (3) and yards-per-carry (15.0). For his career, Holovak, who was a bruising runner, averaged over 5.2 yards per carry. He served in the Navy during World War II and later played pro football with the Los Angeles Rams and Chicago Bears. Holovak was the head coach at Boston College from 1951 to 1959, compiling a 49-29-3 record. He was also the head coach of the Boston Patriots in the old AFL from 1961 to 1968 and general manager of the Houston Oilers of the NFL. Holovak was inducted into the College Football Hall of Fame in 1985.

Bill Swiacki - He played end for Holy Cross in 1942 and end for Columbia from 1946 to 1947. He was a starting end, as a sophomore, in 1942 when Holy Cross shocked top-ranked and heavily favored Boston College 55-12 at Fenway Park on the night of the Cocoanut Grove Fire. After serving in the military during World War II, Swiacki enrolled at Columbia and played for the Lions' great coach Lou Little. He played major roles in not one but two of the biggest upsets in the history of college football. In October 1947, Coach Earl "Red" Blaik's powerhouse Army team, riding a 32-game winning streak, marched into Columbia's Baker Field with so much swagger that women and children were escorted to the exits. In that game against the Cadets, Swiacki caught nine passes, including a miraculous grab that set up Columbia's winning touchdown in a shocking 21-20 victory. On the play, quarterback Gene Rossides fired a low pass that Swiacki dove for and made a sliding, tumbling catch near the right sideline at the three-yard line. On the next play, Lou Kusserow scored, Venton Yablonski kicked the winning conversion point and the roar of the Columbia Lion could be heard from coast-to-coast. Swiacki was known for his marvelous moves and sure, glue-like hands. As a receiver, he was considered an artisan. He was inducted into the College Football Hall of Fame in 1976.

Edward J. O'Melia
Memorial Award

THE O'MELIA TROPHY WAS ESTABLISHED IN 1945 BY THE HOLY CROSS Club of Boston. It was given in memory of World War II veterans who gave their lives for their country after participating in the Boston College-Holy Cross football rivalry.

The award, given to the outstanding player of the annual Boston College-Holy Cross game, is named in honor of Eddie O'Melia, an infantry captain and company commander with the 78th Division of the First Army. Captain O'Melia was killed in March of 1945 while fighting in the European theater of the war. It also honors other fallen war heroes who had played in the Boston College-Holy Cross game. They include: Ernie Ford, Frank Glacken and Nick Opolko from Holy Cross; and John Dodero, Ralph Doe, John Dubzinski, Al Horsfall, Justin McGowan, Bernie Moynahan, Al Ruback and John J. Shea from Boston College.

O'Melia grew up in Lowell, Massachusetts and graduated from Keith Academy, where he was a superb athlete. In 1937, he captained the Holy Cross football team and earned All-American honors as an end. That season, under legendary head coach Dr. Eddie Anderson, the Crusaders posted an 8-0-2 record and crushed Boston College, 20-0. O'Melia also played in the College All-Star game against the New York Giants and he later was an assistant coach at Holy Cross on the staff of head coach Joe Sheeketski (1939-1941). Edward "Moose" Krause, "Mr. Notre Dame," also was an assistant coach on Sheeketski's football staff at Holy Cross. Dr. Anderson, Sheeketski and Krause played college football for Knute Rockne at Notre Dame.

Jim Dieckelman, only a freshman, won the first O'Melia Trophy in 1945, the year that Holy Cross played in the Orange Bowl. Holy Cross won the first three O'Melia Awards. Brilliant quarterback Walter Sheridan, who passed for two touchdowns, won it in 1946 and Bobby Sullivan, who later played for the San Francisco 49ers, took home the award in 1947. In 1948, Ernie Stautner, future pro football legend and an all-time great for the maroon and gold of Boston College, won the award.

In 1950, Johnny Turco, one of the finest backs Holy Cross ever produced, won the award for the Purple by scoring three touchdowns, including a jolting 97-yard kickoff return for a touchdown. In 1952, two awards were presented. One went to Joe Johnson of Boston College and a second was won by Vic Rimkus of Holy Cross. Alan Miller and Vin Hogan, a pair of explosive running backs, won back-to-back O'Melia Awards for Boston College in 1958 and 1959.

In 1964 and 1966, scrambling Holy Cross quarterback Jack Lentz became the first two-time winner of the O'Melia Trophy. Frank "Red" Harris connected on an amazing eighteen out of twenty passes to win the O'Melia Trophy in 1970. In 1971, in a game played at Schaefer Stadium in Foxborough, Joe Wilson of Holy Cross shook off a leg injury and gained 105 yards to win the award. Boston College quarterback Mike Kruczek, the offensive coordinator of the Denver Broncos, won the award in 1974. In 1977, Holy Cross teammates Steve Hunt and Peter Colombo were double O'Melia Trophy winners after leading the Crusaders to a huge upset victory over BC. In 1979, Boston College kicker John Cooper was awarded the O'Melia Trophy after kicking the winning field goal.

In 1984, Doug Flutie won the O'Melia Trophy, narrowly edging out his brother, Darren, for the award. It was his second O'Melia Trophy. He also won it in 1981. In the final game of the series, BC's rifled-armed quarterback Shawn Halloran was awarded the forty-first and last O'Melia Trophy.

Edward J. O'Melia Memorial Trophy Winners

1945: Jim Dieckelman, Holy Cross

1946: Walter Sheridan, Holy Cross

1947: Bobby Sullivan, Holy Cross

1948: Ernie Stautner, Boston College

1949: Al Cannava, Boston College

1950: Johnny Turco, Holy Cross

1951: Jimmy Kane, Boston College

1952: Joe Johnson, Boston College
Vic Rimkus, Holy Cross

1953: John Miller, Boston College

1954: Tom (Magnarelli) Reis,
Boston College

1955: Dick Lucas, Boston College

1956: Billy Smithers, Holy Cross

1957: Tom Greene, Holy Cross

1958: Alan Miller, Boston College

1959: Vin Hogan, Boston College

1960: Pat McCarthy, Holy Cross

1961: Al Snyder, Holy Cross

1962: Jack Concannon, Boston College

1963: Jim Marcellino, Holy Cross

1964: Jack Lentz, Holy Cross

1965: Brendan McCarthy,
Boston College

1966: Jack Lentz, Holy Cross

1967: Joe Devito, Boston College

1968: Dave Bennett, Boston College

1969: no game

1970: Frank Harris, Boston College

1971: Joe Wilson, Holy Cross

1972: Dave Bucci, Boston College

1973: Mike Esposito, Boston College

1974: Mike Kruczek, Boston College

1975: Lou Kobza, Holy Cross

1976: Glen Capriola, Boston College

1977: Steve Hunt, Holy Cross
Peter Colombo, Holy Cross

1978: Glenn Verrette, Holy Cross

1979: John Cooper, Boston College

1980: John Loughery, Boston College

1981: Doug Flutie, Boston College

1982: Tony Thurman, Boston College

1983: Troy Stradford, Boston College

1984: Doug Flutie, Boston College

1985: Kelvin Martin, Boston College

1986: Shawn Halloran, Boston College

Athletic Directors

BILL FLYNN AND RON PERRY WERE THE KEEPERS OF THE ATHLETIC flame at Boston College and Holy Cross respectively during their combined sixty years as athletic directors at the rival Jesuit colleges. Flynn was athletic director at BC from 1957-1991 and Perry was athletic director at Holy Cross from 1972-1998.

Both were highly respected college athletic administrators as well as two of the most recognizable names in the history of intercollegiate sports at the two colleges. They were the heads of the rival athletic departments during the final years of the Boston College-Holy Cross football series, although neither man was ultimately responsible for the series being terminated. The decision to end the series was made by Father John Brooks, S.J., the former president of the College of the Holy Cross, with the approval of the Board of Trustees.

Flynn's association with BC spanned nearly seven decades as a student-athlete, faculty member, coach and finally as athletic director. He was an end and captain of the 1938 BC football team. That team was coached by Gil Dobie and compiled a 6-1-2 record, which included a 33-0 victory over Florida. Holy Cross dealt the Eagles their lone loss, a 29-7 shellacking at Fenway Park. The game's number one star was Holy Cross great Bill Osmanski, who led an attack that chewed up 219 yards on the ground. Following the game, the two coaches, Dobie of BC and Dr.

Eddie Anderson of Holy Cross, both called Osmanski "the best back they had ever seen play college football."

In addition to being a solid, dependable end in football, Flynn was a standout in hockey and the first BC hockey player to score twenty goals in a single season. During his athletic career at the Heights, he played three sports and earned nine varsity letters.

He joined the BC faculty in 1945 as a mathematics teacher and assistant football coach. He also is a former executive secretary of the BC Alumni Association. Dr. Thomas O'Connor, University Historian, prolific author and a friend of Flynn, pointed out that, in addition to his many other talents, Bill Flynn also was ambidextrous. "I first noticed it while he was laying out an alumni publication," said Dr. O'Connor. "Bill would have facing pages in front of him on a table and he would mark the left page with a pen using his left hand and the right page using the same pen with his right hand. As he went from one page to the next, he would switch hands and continue writing as if there were nothing to it at all."

Above all, Bill Flynn was a man known for his integrity, character and warmth. "He had high principles, a man of strong moral fiber," said Father J. Donald Monan, S.J., president emeritus of Boston College. "As a former teacher, he was dedicated to the education of every student-athlete." Reid Oslin, Senior Media Relations Officer at BC and former Sports Information Director, who was hired by Flynn, said that a hand shake from Bill Flynn meant that he had given his word. "If Bill Flynn shook your hand on anything," he said. "You could count on it. It was a done deal and you could forget about it."

During World War II, Flynn served as a special agent with the F.B.I. His specialty was counter espionage. Oslin tells a story about one case in particular during Flynn's career as an agent. "Someone was suspected of spying on the United States," said Oslin. "For two and one-half days, Bill followed that person on trains from Boston to Houston. The suspect would board one train, get off and board another. Bill followed him every step along the journey. If you ever saw the movie 'The French Connection' it was real life drama that must have looked like a scene from that movie."

Flynn was so esteemed along the halls of higher education that in 1979 he became only the second college athletic director to be elected president of the NCAA. He had marvelous people skills and Boston College became the beneficiary of his engaging personality. One time, BC had scheduled a football game against Harvard. However, as the date for the BC-Harvard game approached, Harvard asked if it could get out of the commitment. With a void in the football schedule to fill, Flynn replaced the Crimson on the BC schedule with another Crimson, the University of Alabama Crimson Tide. Bill picked up the telephone and called Paul "Bear" Bryant, the legendary football coach and athletic director at Alabama. Within a short time, Flynn and Bryant had worked out a deal to begin an important intersectional rivalry matching the Eagles against the Crimson Tide.

"How do you think BC got all those big southern schools to play them in football?" asks Dr. O'Connor. "It was because of Bill Flynn. People trusted him. He was known as a man of great integrity. That's how BC was able to upgrade its schedule by adding games against all those big-time colleges with storied football programs."

Bill Flynn was such a gracious individual that it mattered not to him who was on the other end of the telephone. After hanging up following a conversation with an NCAA power broker or an executive of CBS television, the next phone call might be from a student wanting to know if the girls field hockey game against Tufts had been called off because of rain.

"It was amazing," said Oslin. "Bill would tell his secretary to let all the calls that came into the athletic office go directly to him. How many athletic directors at major colleges would allow that to happen?"

As athletic director, Flynn oversaw the construction of every major athletic facility on campus during his thirty-four years as athletic director. He also established the Office of Learning Resources for student-athletes, which helped BC achieve one of the nation's highest student-athlete graduation rates. In all sports, the individual programs prospered and were enriched under Flynn's watch.

Bill Flynn died on June 27, 1997, the same date that Boston sports legend Harry Agganis died forty-two years earlier on June 27, 1955. Flynn was 82. In 1998, the Boston College Athletic Association honored William J. Flynn by renaming the student scholarship fund after him. The William J. Flynn Fund for Student Scholarships replaced Blue Chips as the primary fund through which individuals support Boston College athletics.

When the announcement was made, BC Athletic Director Gene DeFilippo, whose father is a former Holy Cross quarterback, said, "Bill Flynn was known nationally as a symbol of integrity in intercollegiate sports. This is a fitting way to honor a man who was a giant in his field. Bill's name will now be associated with a fund that raises money for scholarships for student-athletes, and that is what he was about."

Ron Perry grew up in Somerville, Massachusetts. He comes from a Portuguese background and the original family name was Pereira. Perry is proud of his roots. Growing up in Somerville, family came first. Both parents worked. His father was a fish cutter and his mother stitched fabric to make sneakers for B.F. Goodrich. One brother, Walter, enjoyed a Hall of Fame career as the head basketball coach at Somerville High and another brother, Al, was captain of the Tufts University basketball team.

At Somerville High, Ron Perry is a legend. As a junior in high school and playing for Coach Vin Cronin, Perry led the Highlanders to the New England Class A Basketball Championship in 1950. He also was a baseball star and he was recruited by a host of big-time colleges. He narrowed his choices to Kentucky, BC, Holy Cross and Columbia before selecting the purple of Holy Cross.

"Holy Cross played a major college basketball schedule and many of their big games were played at Boston Garden," said Perry, explaining the appeal of playing college basketball for the Crusaders. "I had played in the old Tech Tourney at the Boston Garden. There was nothing like that atmosphere so I wanted to be able to play my college games at the Garden. In those days, a big college game would draw 13,909 [which was capacity at the time]."

Perry might be the only major college athlete to play on two national championship teams in different sports. In 1952, as a sophomore, he pitched and won two games in the College World Series, including a complete-game 2-1 victory over the Texas Longhorns, while helping to lead the Crusaders to the Division I NCAA Baseball Championship. As a college pitcher, his career record was a sizzling 23-2.

Then, as a senior, he, Togo Palazzi and sophomore Tom Heinsohn, the future Boston Celtics' great, led Holy Cross to the prestigious NIT

Championship in 1954 at Madison Square Garden. In those days, the NIT was the top post-season college basketball tournament. One of the all-time great announcers, Marty Glickman, a former Olympian of Jewish descent who competed at the 1936 Games in track in Berlin, Germany as Adolph Hitler looked on, was the television and radio voice of Madison Square Garden basketball. In the finals, Holy Cross beat the Dukes of Duquesne and their fabulous guard Sihugo Green, 70-58.

As a junior, Perry and Holy Cross won two games in the NCAA tourney, beating Navy and Wake Forest before losing to LSU and the super smooth Bob Petit, a 6-foot 9 scoring machine who later starred for the old St. Louis Hawks in the NBA.

After graduating from college, Perry spent three years in the Marines. In 1957, he was selected Armed Forces Service Player of the Year. Next, he signed a professional baseball contract with the Milwaukee Braves, went to spring training with the Braves and pitched briefly for the Double A Atlanta Crackers. Perry was a control pitcher who featured two wicked curve balls, one that came straight over-the-top and a second he threw by dropping down to the side.

After briefly playing minor league baseball for $500 a month Perry had had enough. "I had two children and I didn't feel that beating the bushes of the minor leagues was in the best interest of my family," he said. "At the time, I felt I should get on with my life."

Togo Anthony Francis Palazzi, Perry's teammate, arrived at Holy Cross via Union City, New Jersey. He wanted to go to Notre Dame but wound up at Holy Cross. Togo is his real first name. He said his father, for reasons unknown to him, named him after a famous Japanese Admiral whose first name was Togo, which also is slang in Italian for "cool" or "neat." Palazzi said that Perry was the most fundamentally-sound athlete he ever played with or against. "When he passed you the ball, it always arrived at the perfect spot," said Palazzi, who was a sharpshooter for the Boston Celtics and once scored a record of twenty-three points in one quarter against the old Minneapolis Lakers.

Palazzi has followed Holy Cross football for years. He said the BC-Holy Cross football game was special. "Every year you looked forward to it," he said. "It was a great rivalry." He also said that Holy Cross great Johnny Turco, who scored five touchdowns against Brown in 1950, was the best football player he ever saw play for the Crusaders.

Like Flynn at Boston College, Perry is known for his personal warmth and ability to interact smoothly with all types of people. "Ron is a natural with people. Not only does he get along with everybody, but he gets the most out of the people who work for him," said Palazzi, who coached women's basketball at Holy Cross under Perry. "He was president of his college class and he has always been a leader. He is how can I say it— charismatic. As an athlete, he always wanted the ball when the game was on the line; when the band was playing and flags were flying. As athletic director, he was a visionary, a dreamer who always looked for and brought out the best in people around him."

Perry came to Holy Cross as athletic director from Catholic Memorial High School in West Roxbury, Massachusetts, where he had been a teacher, basketball and baseball coach and athletic director. As a basketball coach, his CM teams won 292 games, lost 34, won two state titles, eight New England Catholic crowns and ten straight conference championships. His baseball teams compiled a sparkling 186-53 record. Like Flynn he was a mathematics teacher and he actually had two of Bill Flynn's sons, Mike and Billy, in class at Catholic Memorial. When the Hall of Fame high school coach arrived at Holy Cross, he brought instant name recognition to the position of athletic director.

"Ron Perry brought credibility and respect to the position of athletic director at Holy Cross," said Father Brooks, S.J., president emeritus of the College of the Holy Cross. "He is a good family man and he has many friends and connections in athletics all over the country. All of that experience benefited Holy Cross."

During his twenty-six years as athletic director, Perry oversaw many changes and much growth within the athletic department at Holy Cross, including a phenomenal rise in quality intercollegiate sports programs for women. Women were admitted to Holy Cross for the first time in the fall of 1972, just months after Perry's arrival. He also was behind numerous improvements to the athletic plant and facilities. During his tenure, the football, basketball, hockey and golf teams enjoyed great success. Women's basketball, competing in Division I, averaged more than twenty wins for twelve straight seasons, qualified for the NCAA Tournament a number of times and upset Maryland in the opening round of the 1991 NCAA tournament. Both Boston College and Holy Cross rank among the leaders nationally in student-athlete graduation rates.

Perry and his counterpart at Boston College, Bill Flynn, remained close friends even during difficult times that resulted in Holy Cross ending its 91-year football rivalry with Boston College in 1986. "Bill Flynn was a dear, dear friend," said Perry. Although the end of the rivalry did not dampen their friendship, the strain of seeing the great football rivalry end was felt by the two athletic directors and their schools. Flynn hated to see the series end and spoke openly about it.

As for Perry, who was quick to acknowledge the greatness of the series in the past, he was pragmatic about its ending. "Sure, it had been a great series," he said. "But times change and some things have to end. Sadly, this was one of them. It was the right time. The Boston College football program was playing at another level. We couldn't compete anymore. It was as simple as that."

Venues

IN A RIVALRY THAT SPANNED NINETY-ONE YEARS AND INCLUDED eighty-two games, Boston College and Holy Cross tangled at several sites, including one game at Harvard Stadium.

In 1931, the Jesuit rivals met at venerable Harvard Stadium and the visiting Crusaders eked out a 7-6 win.

Beginning in 1916, BC and Holy Cross played a total of fourteen games at Fenway Park, the home of the Boston Red Sox. Boston College won eight games and Holy Cross won six. BC swept the first four games at Fenway Park, including a 17-14 win in the first game. Holy Cross won the final game at Fenway Park in 1956, 7-0. After that game, Red Sox owner Tom Yawkey gave the Jesuit rivals the boot. He was tired of seeing his precious playing field dug up by the cleats worn by beefy football players.

Beginning in 1920, BC and Holy Cross played eighteen games at Braves Field, the home of the National League Boston Braves. BC won the first game, 14-0. The Eagles held a 10-7-1 advantage in the eighteen games played at Braves Field. The final BC-Holy Cross game at Braves Field was held in 1952 and the Crusaders won, 21-7.

Holy Cross played their first home game on campus in 1903. BC and Holy Cross played a total of eighteen games at Fitton Field with the Eagles holding a 9-8-1 advantage.

Boston College's Alumni Stadium opened in 1957. The rivals played fourteen games at Alumni Stadium and BC dominated with an 11-3 record. BC and Holy Cross also met twice in Foxborough, the home of the New England Patriots of the National Football League. BC won both games, 21-7 in 1971 and 47-7 in 1983. The remaining games in the old rivalry were played at scattered sites in and around Boston and Worcester.

Fight Songs

There are many stirring college fight songs that have become ingrained in our culture. "The Victors" (University of Michigan); "Across the Field" (Ohio State); "On, Wisconsin"; "Minnesota Rouser"; "Washington and Lee Swing"; "Far Above Cayuga's Waters" (Cornell); and the "Notre Dame Victory March" among many others.

Both Boston College and Holy Cross have recognizable fight songs. BC's is called "For Boston" and the Holy Cross fight song has an unforgettable title: "Chu, Chu, Rah, Rah!" In addition to "Chu, Chu, Rah, Rah!", Holy Cross has also adopted a song, whose lyrics were written in 1926 by male students at an all-male college in tribute to "the personification of every college boy's blue-eyed Irish beauty, the college sweetheart of Packachoag," wrote James G. Murray, Class of 1945 in the November 8, 1968 issue of the *Crusader*. They called the song "Mamie Reilly."

"For Boston" was written by Thomas J. Hurley, Class of 1885 at BC. He also wrote "Alma Mater." For decades, both songs have enlivened Boston College social functions and athletic events. During the early years of Boston College, both at James Street and later when the campus was moved from Boston to the Heights in Chestnut Hill, Mr. Hurley's name was "synonymous with music at Boston College."

285

In 1989, the Alumni Board recommended that the language used in two lines of "For Boston" be changed to reflect the fact that BC had progressed from an all-male institution to a university "fully encompassing women and men in every aspect." Father J. Donald Monan, S.J., then president of Boston College, approved the recommended changes.

"For here are men" was changed to "For here all are one" and "Shall thy sons be found" was changed to "Shall thy heirs be found."

For Boston

For Boston, for Boston,
We sing our proud refrain!
For Boston, for Boston,
'Tis Wisdom's earthly fane.
For here all are one
And their hearts are true,
And the towers on the Heights
Reach to the Heav'ns own blue.
For Boston, for Boston,
Till the echoes ring again!

For Boston, for Boston,
Thy glory is our own!
For Boston, for Boston,
'Tis here that Truth is known.
And ever with the Right
Shall thy heirs be found,
Till time shall be no more
And thy work is crown'd.
For Boston, for Boston,
For Thee and Thine alone.

Over the years, at least four songs have been identified with Holy Cross. The first two were written in 1902. Before that, there was no standard college song. One, "On! Holy Cross," was written by J. Leo O'Gorman of New York. A second, "Holy Cross, old Holy Cross!" was written by Augustine P. Conniff of Plains, Pennsylvania. It was adapted to the musical score of "Maryland My Maryland" and became the official College of the Holy Cross Alma Mater. It was revised on January 19, 1976.

In 1903, B.J. Shandley of Southington, Connecticut, a Holy Cross graduate, wrote the "Chu, Chu, Rah, Rah!" song, a rollicking piece, expected to fade and die soon after it was written, lives on today as spirited as ever.

Chu, Chu, Rah, Rah!

Ring out then your Hoiah! with
A Chu, Chu, Rah, Rah!
A Chu, Chu, Rah, Rah!
A Chu, Chu, Rah, Rah!
Give another Hoiah and A Chu, Chu, Rah, Rah!
A Chu, Chu, Rah, Rah! for Holy Cross!
March on as knights of old
(With hearts as) loyal and true and bold,
And wage the bitter fight with all your might,
Fight hard for Holy Cross!
You'll know when battle's done,
(It was for) her that the fight was won,
Oh, may it never die, that battle cry,
On, on for Holy Cross!

"Mamie Reilly" was born from an era when moustached college boys entertained themselves by forming quartets, usually after the evening meal outside under a sloping tree on a hill, and sang barbershop harmony and corridor quartet favorites.

The grande dame of song herself, Miss Mamie Reilly, was adapted from old time classics such as "Old Black Joe," "Casey at the Bat" and

"Old Virginny." In the 1960s, the song was revised, eliminating the offensive phrase "Old Black Joe," which, as was reported at the time, "has no place on a Catholic campus—any campus today." Over the years, that spirited gal, Mamie Reilly, remains the stuff of legends at Holy Cross.

Mamie Reilly

Oh, Mamie Reilly, goin far away
Oh, Mamie Reilly, won't be back today!
Come kiss your daddy now before we part.
Oh, Mamie, Mamie, Mamie Reilly!
Slide Kelly, Slide
Casey's at the bat.
Oh, Mamie Reilly, where'd you get that hat?
Down in Old Kentucky. Go, Cross, Go!
Oh, Mamie, Mamie, Mamie Reilly!

A Family Affair

OVER THE YEARS, MEMBERS OF THE SAME FAMILY HAVE BOLSTERED THE Boston College-Holy Cross football rivalry and contributed to the lore of the grand old series. Take the Harringtons, for instance. Beginning with Joe Harrington, Sr., three generations of Harrington men played football for Holy Cross.

Joe Harrington, Sr. graduated from Holy Cross in 1930 and briefly played football for the Crusaders until an injury ended his college football career.

His son, Joe, Jr., graduated from Holy Cross in 1954. At 6-foot-2, 205 pounds, he played end, linebacker and fullback for the Crusaders during the 1950-1953 era under Dr. Eddie Anderson. During those years, Holy Cross won 25 games and produced back-to-back 8-2-0 clubs, in 1951 and 1952. In his senior year, 1953, a season during which the Crusaders were led by end and Captain Henry Lemire, the Purple ended up 5-5-0 and lost to Boston College 6-0 at Fenway Park.

Joe Harrington, Jr. fathered nine children. One of his sons, Kevin, despite a series of knee injuries, was an excellent football player for the Crusaders. Kevin played linebacker and he was a bone-rattling hitter for Holy Cross, graduating in 1980.

The Harrington children excelled in athletics at Acton-Boxborough High School. In recent years, the blue and gold clad A-B Colonials have produced a powerhouse football program, a legitimate dynasty and one of the top programs in the state—along with Everett, St. John's Prep and Xaverian.

In addition to Kevin, two more of Joe Harrington's children were outstanding college athletes. Joe III, played quarterback and safety for the UMass Minutemen and daughter Cathy was a college basketball sensation at Bentley College, where she is enshrined in the school's athletic Hall of Fame.

Like many from his era, Harrington remembers the sting of the 20-14 loss to Tulane, one of only two defeats Holy Cross was dealt during the 1951 season. A long touchdown run in the fourth quarter—a play on which practically the entire Holy Cross defense had a shot at tackling the runner but failed to bring the Tulane back down—spelled defeat for the Crusaders.

Looking back, Harrington also recalled that "two costly penalties in that game hurt us badly."

He also pointed out that Charlie O'Rourke, the great BC quarterback who led the Eagles to the national championship in 1940, was an assistant coach at Holy Cross for one year. What he remembers most about his college football career is the quality of athletes who were recruited to play football for the Cross. "The college really recruited well," he said. "You were surrounded by great football players. As a result, our teams had balance and were well-rounded."

Interestingly, the head coach, Dr. Anderson, an ear, nose and throat specialist, was too busy so he delegated much of the recruiting duties to his assistant coaches, although his reputation as one of the finest college coaches in the country certainly enhanced the recruiting effort.

Joe Harrington, Jr. also comes from a family of nine children. He and four of his brothers played high school football for St. Mary's in Waltham, Massachusetts, which has long since closed.

Another one of the Harrington boys who played football for St. Mary's is Richard Harrington. He was a quarterback. Later, he graduated from Boston College and then entered the seminary. Today, he is Father Richard Harrington, pastor of St. Mary's parish in Randolph, Massachusetts.

The priest-football connection at St. Mary's extends to another cleric, Father Charles McCoy, out of South Boston, BC High and Boston

College. Today, Father McCoy is the pastor of St. Philip Neri parish in Newton.

Back in 1943, he played one season of varsity football for the Eagles. He was the back-up quarterback behind Eddie Doherty, the only former Boston College football player to become head coach at Holy Cross (1971-1975). Because of World War II, BC played a truncated six-game schedule, completing the season with a 6-6 tie against Harvard. Despite an injury sustained during the 1943 season, Doherty was selected to play in the East-West game that year.

There was no BC-Holy Cross game scheduled in 1943 and Father McCoy remembers "how disappointed everyone on the team was not to have a chance to play Holy Cross."

Father McCoy, who was only sixteen when he enrolled at BC, joined the Marines after his sophomore year. After the war, he returned to school and graduated from BC in 1949. He entered the seminary in 1956 and was ordained a priest in 1961.

Along the way, he played semipro football for the Portland Sagamores, picking up 80 dollars a game, and coached high school football at several schools including St. Mary's in Waltham.

Father McCoy spent 28 years in the military, three years in the Marines as an enlisted man and 25 years in the Navy as a chaplain. He was wounded in Vietnam and in 1995, at age 71, Captain McCoy was recalled into the Navy to serve as a chaplain at the Merchant Marine Academy at Kings Point.

As a boy growing up in South Boston, Father McCoy said that he was a big BC fan. His favorite player was Gil Bouley, the Eagles' All-American tackle. He said that Bouley let him carry his helmet onto the field before games and young McCoy sat on the BC bench during the startling 1942 game, when heavily underdog Holy Cross battered unbeaten and top-ranked BC, 55-12.

Over the years, Father McCoy and Bouley have remained good friends. "I taught him to play handball," said the Newton pastor.

The Harringtons and Father McCoy are examples of the big picture of the Boston College-Holy Cross football rivalry. Two Jesuit institutions, 40 miles apart, competed on the gridiron for 91 years, which guarantees, at least in this "family feud," that the lives of the participants, the stories and the memories will overlap.

If you had reached the age of reason by 1942, you knew exactly where you were and what you were doing when you first heard about the devastation of the Cocoanut Grove fire, which erupted only hours after Holy Cross' stunning 55-12 victory over Boston College earlier in the day.

"I was ten years old," remembered Joe Harrington. " I was walking on Waverly Oaks Road, heading to Mass at St. Luke's Church, when I first heard about the dreadful fire."

More often than not, the storied Boston College-Holy Cross football rivalry impacted entire families. Take the Sullivans of North Andover, Massachusetts, for instance. Tommy, Bobby and Ray Sullivan, three brothers, all played football for the Crusaders. All three were star athletes at Johnson High School, later renamed North Andover High School.

Tommy Sullivan, the oldest, graduated from Holy Cross in 1942. He was an outstanding back for the Crusaders. One of the most vivid memories of his college football career at the Cross was a hard-fought 13-7 victory his junior year over the Violets of NYU played at Yankee Stadium. In that game, he pitched a pair of touchdown passes, one to Varsity Club Hall of Famer Eddie Murphy and a second to Frank Calabrese.

Ron Cahill, a triple-threat Varsity Club Hall of Famer, was one of the stars of Holy Cross teams during that era. He got hurt, bruised and cracked ribs, playing against Carnegie Tech. As a result, Sullivan replaced him and then started the next game against NYU. The 1940 Holy Cross team, coached by Joseph L. Sheeketski, who played halfback for Knute Rockne at Notre Dame, completed the season with a 4-5-1 record. In addition to beating NYU, the Crusaders also defeated Providence College, 34-6; Carnegie Tech, 18-0; and Manhattan, 33-25. Holy Cross lost that season to LSU, 25-0; Brown, 9-6; Colgate, 6-0; Mississippi, 34-6; and Boston College, 7-0, a game during which the fired-up Crusaders, with a break or two, could have derailed the Eagles on their way to a 19-13 victory over Tennessee and the national championship. The only tie in 1940 was a hard-fought 6-6 battle against Temple.

Tommy Sullivan missed the BC game. He was in a hospital recovering from pneumonia. "It was a big disappointment, not being able to play in that game," he said.

The next season, 1941, when Holy Cross finished with a 4-4-2 record, including a bitter 14-13 loss to Boston College at Fenway Park, Sullivan tore up a knee in the opening game of the season, a 19-13 victory over the Tigers of LSU, which ended his college football career. In addition to beating LSU, Holy Cross claimed victories over Providence College, 13-0; NYU, 13-0; and Brown, 13-0. The Crusaders lost to Syracuse, 6-0; Mississippi, 21-0; and Temple, 31-13, in addition to their loss against BC. They also had a pair of ties, 13-13 against Manhattan and 6-6 against Colgate.

Tommy Sullivan remembers watching the classic 1942 Holy Cross-BC game. What did Sullivan do after the game? "I was fortunate," he said. "Along with the people I was with, we had made arrangements to stay overnight with friends in Cambridge."

Bobby Sullivan was a fabulous college football player. In 1942, as a sophomore, he was one of the many stars of the Crusaders' mind-boggling 55-12 victory over the Eagles.

He spent three years in the Army following his sophomore season and returned to Holy Cross after the war, graduating in 1948. In 1947, he and Ray Ball were co-captains of a Holy Cross team that wound up with a 4-4-2 record, which included victories over Temple, 19-13; Syracuse, 26-0; Fordham, 48-0; and a convincing 20-6 win over a Boston College squad that completed the season with a 5-4-0 record. In 1947, Holy Cross dropped games to Villanova, 13-6; Harvard, 7-0; Brown, 20-19; and Columbia, 10-0. That season the Crusaders also fought to a 0-0 tie against Dartmouth and a 6-6 tie against Colgate.

Nevertheless, Bobby Sullivan enjoyed a blockbuster season. He was awarded the O'Melia Trophy as the outstanding player in the Boston College-Holy Cross game. In addition, he was awarded the George H. "Bulger" Lowe Award, presented for the first time in 1939 and annually awarded to the outstanding college football player in New England. Sullivan also was selected to play in the East-West game. The starting quarterback for the East squad was Johnny Lujack of Notre Dame. Bobby also played two seasons in the National Football League with the San Francisco 49ers.

All three Sullivan brothers—Tom, Bob and Ray—could run. Which of the three was the fastest? Tom Sullivan was asked.

"Oh, Bobby was the fastest," answered Tom. "Not many could catch him."

Like his older brothers, Ray Sullivan was a solid football player for Holy Cross. In one game, against one of the many service teams that regularly competed against college squads, Ray intercepted a pass in the end zone and ran it back 100 yards for a touchdown. He graduated in 1949. For years, he worked as a supervisor for Western Electric. Tom and Bobby both were F.B.I. agents. Bobby also coached high school football at Hudson High School, Amesbury High School and at North Andover High School, his alma mater. All three brothers served in the military during the war.

Incidentally, the three Sullivan brothers played high school football for Jim Cavalieri at Johnson (North Andover) High School. Cavalieri (Class of '32) was a great end for the Crusaders whose head coach was Captain John McEwen, a former All-American center for the Army Cadets in 1914. He also coached the University of Oregon Ducks before moving to Holy Cross. He coached at Holy Cross from 1930-'32 and compiled an outstanding 21-5-1 record, although he was fired with three games remaining in his final season because of a fight along the sidelines in which he was involved. Later, Colonel McEwen served as Chairman of the New York Touchdown Club, coached the Brooklyn (football) Dodgers and was voted into the National Football Foundation Hall of Fame.

Cavalieri played one end for the Crusaders. The other end was another terrific football player named Tony Colucci. Because of their collective abilities and Italian heritage, the two ends were nicknamed "The Opera Twins," although neither sang with particular gusto, except possibly in the shower.

Acknowledgements

Many contributed greatly to the writing of this book. At the top of the list are two very special women, my wife, Mary, and Joanne Carr, the assistant archivist at the College of the Holy Cross.

My wife, who was the first to read every chapter, provided marvelous insights and often recommended subtle changes that, more often than not, were right on the money. Equally important, her belief in me and the project of writing about the BC-Holy Cross football rivalry never wavered. Plus, she patiently and lovingly tolerated my obsession with the book, once I got into it. My wife is the greatest.

Joanne, out of kindness to me, went way beyond what any writer could possibly expect from an assistant archivist at a major college. She copied hundreds of pages of clippings and documents. She often provided material, using her keen judgment and news sense, that I hadn't even asked for. Always cheerful, always helpful, I never could have written this book without her assistance.

I owe a deep debt of gratitude to Dr. Tom O'Connor, Reid Oslin and Ed Copenhagen of Boston College. All three went out of their way to assist me. Their constant encouragement pushed me along and kept me going which allowed me to remain focused, even when I became discouraged. Dr. O'Connor, the university historian at Boston College, is the prolific author of many best-selling books. Oslin, the former sports information director at BC, is a senior media relations officer at Boston College. Copenhagen is the assistant archivist at the Burns Library at Boston College.

I also want to thank Pat McCarthy, the director of the alumni office at Holy Cross, and Jack Moynihan, the director of the alumni office at Boston College, for their assistance.

In addition, I am grateful for the assistance I received from the staff at the National Football Foundation and College Hall of Fame as well as the contributions of John Ziemann, the community outreach coordinator of the Babe Ruth Museum in Baltimore, which also showcases a treasury of old Baltimore Colts memorabilia.

Eric Holmes, the communications coordinator of the Canadian Football League, is another person who was a huge help to me in the writing of this book.

I also want to thank Frank Mastrandrea, the assistant athletic director at Holy Cross for marketing and media relations, and Larry Napolitano, the director of media relations at Holy Cross, as well as, Joseph DeBari, the sports information director at Fordham University, Margaret Morrissey, adult services librarian at the Jacob Edwards Library in Southbridge, Massachusetts, and Laura Drazdowski, communications intern at Columbia University.

Father John Brooks, S.J., president emeritus of the College of the Holy Cross, and Father J. Donald Monan, S.J., president emeritus of Boston College, were especially kind and patiently put up with my numerous phone calls.

Finally, I am deeply grateful to the staff of Ambassador Books, Inc. The idea of writing this book came to me in a dream that-would-not-go-away. From day one, they believed in the project and ran with it, letting no obstacle stand in the way. For that, I am forever grateful.

Selected Bibliography

Listed here are only the works that have been of use in writing this book. This bibliography is by no means a complete record of all the works and sources that were consulted. It indicates the substance and range of reading upon which I have formed my ideas and is intended to serve as a convenience for those who wish to read further on the history of the Boston College-Holy Cross series.

— W.C.

Books

Donovan, Jr., Arthur, Arthur Donovan, Bob Drury. *Fatso: Football When Men Were Really Men.* New York: Avon, 1988.

Donovan, S.J., Charles F., et al. *History of Boston College.* Chestnut Hill: The University Press of Boston College, 1990.

Falla, Jack. *'Til The Echoes Ring Again: A Pictorial History of Boston College Sports.* Brattleboro, Vermont: Stephen Greene Press, 1982.

Hasenfus, Nathaniel J. *Athletics At Boston College*, Volume I. Worcester, Massachusetts: Heffernan Press, 1943.

Keyes, Edward. *Cocoanut Grove.* New York: Scribner, 1984.

Leckie, Robert. *The Story of Football.* New York: Random House, Inc. 1965.

Articles

"BC 27, Holy Cross 26; Cancel Series?" *Worcester Sunday Telegram* (November 30, 1980).

"400 Dead In Night Club Fire." *Boston Sunday Globe* (November 29, 1942).

"Anderson Aims to Rejuvenate H.C." *Boston Herald* (February 9, 1950).

"Can He Repeat?" *Wocester Sunday Telegram* (April 23, 1950).

"Carter Always the Gentleman." *Worcester Telegram* (February 3, 1986).

"Dean of College Coaches." *Wocester Sunday Telegram* (October 13, 1957).

"He Should Have Been the Greatest Player of All Times." *Worcester Magazine* by Paul Della Valle, (June 9, 1993).

"Holy Cross Grid Season Ended Early by Illness." *Wocester Telegram* (October 6, 1969).

"Holy Cross Stuns B.C., 55-12." *Boston Sunday Herald* (November 29, 1942).

"Holy Cross, 76-0." *Wocester Telegram* (November 26, 1949).

"Last Game, Loss Takes Toll on Holy Cross Seniors." *Wocester Telegram* (November 23, 1986).

"Looking for an Answer." *Boston Globe* by Jackie MacMullen, (February 6, 1986).

"Remembering Bill Swiacki, All-American Hometown Hero." *Southbridge News* (September 3, 1988).

"The Strange Case of the Holy Cross Football Team." *Wocester Sunday Telegram* (October 19, 1969).

"Water Pipe May Be Viris Source." *Worcester Telegram* (October 7, 1969).

"Woe, Tragedy, Heroism Mark Club Holocaust." *Boston Sunday Globe* (November 29, 1942).

Index